Graph-Driven Language

Mastering Intelligent Workflows with LangGraph Python

©

Written By

Maxime Lane

Graph-Driven Language: Mastering Intelligent Workflows with LangGraph Python
Copyright © 2025 by Maxime Lane

Printed in United States

First Edition 2025

This book is intended for educational purposes only. The publisher and author disclaim any liability in connection with the use of the information provided herein.

Table of Content

Table of Content

Preface

A: About This Book

Welcome to **"Graph-Driven Language: Mastering Intelligent Workflows with LangGraph Python."** This book is designed to guide you through the innovative world of graph-based workflows and their powerful applications in natural language processing (NLP) using LangGraph Python. Whether you are a developer looking to expand your skill set, a data scientist interested in new approaches to data analysis, or an AI enthusiast eager to explore cutting-edge technologies, this book will serve as a comprehensive resource for mastering these concepts.

What You Can Expect

Comprehensive Coverage:
This book takes you on a step-by-step journey from foundational concepts in graph theory and basic Python programming to advanced applications in NLP and workflow design. We start by explaining the essential building blocks, such as nodes, edges, and graph structures, then move on to explore how these elements integrate with language models and modern AI techniques.

Practical Examples and Hands-On Exercises:
Each chapter is enriched with detailed code examples, complete tables, and clear diagrams to illustrate key points. For instance, when introducing a new graph algorithm, we provide a fully explained Python code snippet that you can run and experiment with. Here's a brief example to illustrate how a simple graph might be constructed in Python:

```python
# Example: Creating a basic graph structure using a
dictionary
graph = {
    'A': ['B', 'C'],
    'B': ['A', 'D'],
    'C': ['A', 'D'],
    'D': ['B', 'C']
}

def display_graph(g):
    for node, edges in g.items():
```

```
    print(f"{node}: {', '.join(edges)}")

display_graph(graph)
```

In this snippet, the graph is represented using a dictionary where each key is a node, and the associated list contains its connected nodes. We provide thorough explanations of each line of code, ensuring that you understand not only how it works but also why it is structured in that way.

Step-by-Step Guidance:
Our goal is to demystify complex topics. Therefore, each chapter is structured to build on the previous one, ensuring that you have the necessary background before moving into more advanced material. Detailed explanations accompany each new concept, and tables summarizing key ideas are provided to reinforce your understanding.

Professional yet Accessible Language:
We have written this book in a clear, simple, and professional style. Our language is designed to be accessible, ensuring that readers with basic programming knowledge can follow along without feeling overwhelmed by technical jargon. However, as you progress, you'll discover that the content is equally valuable for advanced practitioners looking for in-depth analysis and practical insights.

Interactive and Real-World Focus:
In addition to theoretical discussions, this book emphasizes practical applications. Throughout the chapters, you will find real-world case studies and interactive exercises that challenge you to apply what you have learned. These activities are intended to cement your understanding and inspire you to implement your own graph-driven language workflows.

How to Use This Book

- **Begin at the Beginning:** Start with the foundational chapters if you are new to graph theory or LangGraph Python. These chapters are structured to provide you with the necessary background and a smooth learning curve.
- **Practice Actively:** Make sure to run the provided code examples on your own machine. Experiment with modifications and explore the suggested exercises to deepen your understanding.

- **Refer Back:** Use the tables, diagrams, and summaries as quick reference guides. They are designed to help you recall critical information and clarify complex topics.
- **Supplement Your Learning:** While this book aims to be comprehensive, we also encourage you to explore additional resources and stay updated with the latest trends in NLP and graph-based technologies.

"Graph-Driven Language: Mastering Intelligent Workflows with LangGraph Python" is more than just a technical manual; it is an invitation to explore a transformative approach to building intelligent systems. We are confident that by the end of this book, you will have gained the skills and insights needed to harness the power of graph-based language workflows in your own projects.

B: Who Should Read This Book

"Graph-Driven Language: Mastering Intelligent Workflows with LangGraph Python" is written for a wide range of readers who are interested in exploring the intersection of graph theory, natural language processing (NLP), and Python programming. Whether you're just starting out or you're looking to deepen your expertise, this book is structured to meet your needs. Below is a detailed overview of who will benefit from this book and why.

Target Audiences

1. **Python Developers**
   If you are a Python developer looking to expand your skill set, this book will help you learn how to integrate graph-based thinking into your programming. You'll discover how to structure your code using nodes and edges, and how to create dynamic workflows that can adapt to complex data and processing requirements.
   Example Table for Python Developers:

Focus Area	Benefit	Experience Level
Graph Theory Integration	Learn to implement graph data structures in Python	Intermediate to Advanced

Focus Area	Benefit	Experience Level
Workflow Automation	Design, implement, and optimize intelligent workflows	Intermediate to Advanced
Code Optimization and Debugging	Use practical examples to troubleshoot and refine your code	All levels (with a focus on practice)

2. **Data Scientists and Analysts**
   Data scientists often work with complex data relationships and need effective tools to model and analyze these connections. This book shows you how to leverage graph-based models to represent data relationships in a clear, visual, and intuitive manner. The hands-on projects and real-world case studies provide practical examples of how graphs can enhance data analysis and decision-making.

3. **NLP Enthusiasts and Practitioners**
   Natural language processing is a rapidly evolving field. For those focused on NLP, this book offers insights into integrating language models with graph-based workflows. Learn how to build systems that process and understand language in context, using graphs to manage complex data flows and relationships.
   Practical Example:

```python
# Simple example of using a graph to model language
dependencies:
language_graph = {
    'Subject': ['Verb'],
    'Verb': ['Object'],
    'Object': []
}

def print_sentence_structure(graph):
    for part, connections in graph.items():
        print(f"{part} -> {', '.join(connections) if
connections else 'None'}")

print_sentence_structure(language_graph)
```

This code snippet demonstrates a basic graph representing sentence structure. It's a starting point that you will expand upon to build more sophisticated NLP workflows.

4. **AI and Machine Learning Researchers**
    Researchers in AI and machine learning will find this book a valuable resource as it bridges theory with practical implementation. The book not only covers traditional graph theory but also explores advanced topics such as graph neural networks and dynamic workflow adaptations. It's an excellent guide for those who want to push the boundaries of current AI applications by incorporating graph-driven techniques.
5. **Technology Enthusiasts and Hobbyists**
    Even if you are an independent learner or a technology hobbyist with a basic understanding of Python, this book is designed to be accessible and informative. Starting with foundational concepts, the book gradually introduces you to more advanced topics, ensuring a smooth learning curve. Hands-on exercises and real-world projects make it easy to see immediate applications of the concepts discussed.

Why This Book is Essential for These Audiences

- **Comprehensive Coverage:**
  The book starts from the basics of graph theory and Python programming and builds up to complex integrations with NLP and AI systems. This step-by-step approach ensures that you don't miss any critical concepts.
- **Practical Examples and Hands-On Exercises:**
  Detailed code snippets, tables, and diagrams are provided throughout the book. These examples are carefully explained to ensure clarity and to help you apply the concepts directly to your projects.
- **Clear and Professional Language:**
  The language used throughout is clear, simple, and professional. This ensures that readers from various backgrounds, regardless of their technical expertise, can follow along without being overwhelmed by jargon.
- **Real-World Applications:**
  The book includes case studies and projects that mirror real-world scenarios, helping you understand how to apply what you've learned in practical settings.

In summary, this book is ideal for Python developers, data scientists, NLP practitioners, AI researchers, and technology enthusiasts alike. Each section is designed to provide you with the knowledge and tools you need to create and manage intelligent, graph-driven language workflows effectively.

C. How to Use This Book

"Graph-Driven Language: Mastering Intelligent Workflows with LangGraph Python" is designed to be both a comprehensive reference and a practical guide. Here are some detailed guidelines to help you get the most out of this book.

1. Start at the Beginning

- **Sequential Learning:**
  If you are new to graph theory, NLP, or even LangGraph Python, it is best to start with the foundational chapters. These sections introduce the core concepts and gradually build your understanding.
  Tip: Read each chapter in order to establish a strong base before tackling more advanced topics.
- **Familiarize Yourself with the Basics:**
  Even if you are experienced, a quick review of the basics can be beneficial. The introductory chapters are designed to refresh your memory and ensure everyone is on the same page.

2. Engage with the Code Examples

- **Hands-On Practice:**
  Each chapter includes code examples that illustrate key concepts. We encourage you to type out the code, run it on your own system, and experiment with modifications. This practical approach will deepen your understanding.
- **Example Walkthrough:**
  Consider this simple example, which demonstrates how to create and display a basic graph:

```python
# Example: Creating a basic graph structure using a
dictionary
graph = {
    'A': ['B', 'C'],
    'B': ['A', 'D'],
    'C': ['A', 'D'],
    'D': ['B', 'C']
}

def display_graph(g):
    """
```

```
    This function prints the graph in a readable
format.
    Each node and its connected nodes are displayed.
    """
    for node, edges in g.items():
        print(f"{node}: {', '.join(edges)}")

# Display the graph
display_graph(graph)
```

Explanation:

- o **Dictionary Structure:** The graph is represented as a dictionary where keys are nodes and the values are lists of connected nodes.
- o **Display Function:** The `display_graph` function iterates through the dictionary and prints each node with its adjacent nodes.

By understanding and running such examples, you will gain a solid grasp of how graph structures work in Python.

3. Utilize the Diagrams and Tables

- **Visual Aids:**
  Throughout the book, diagrams and tables are provided to summarize complex ideas. These visual aids serve as quick reference points.
  Example Table: Graph Components

Component	Description	Example
Node	A point or vertex in the graph	'A', 'B', 'C'
Edge	A connection between two nodes	Connection between A and B
Graph	A collection of nodes and edges	{'A': ['B', 'C'], ...}

- Use these tables to review the essential components and revisit them whenever needed.

4. Work Through the Exercises and Projects

- **Interactive Learning:**
  At the end of each chapter, you will find exercises and mini-projects designed to test your understanding. Do not skip these sections; they are integral to reinforcing what you've learned.
- **Project Ideas:**
  - **Graph Traversal:** Implement and experiment with different graph traversal algorithms.
  - **NLP Pipeline:** Create a simple natural language processing pipeline using LangGraph Python and popular NLP libraries.
- **Step-by-Step Projects:**
  Detailed project instructions guide you through each step, from setting up your environment to deploying a final application. These projects are designed to simulate real-world scenarios and provide you with a tangible skill set.

5. Refer Back as Needed

- **Bookmark Key Sections:**
  As you progress, you may find certain topics or examples particularly useful. Bookmark these pages or create a personal index for quick reference.
- **Revisit Appendices:**
  The appendices include additional resources, troubleshooting tips, and a glossary of terms. Use them to clarify doubts or refresh your memory on key concepts.

6. Supplement Your Learning

- **Online Resources:**
  We provide downloadable resources, such as code repositories and additional reading materials, to enhance your learning experience. Make sure to visit the companion website or repository mentioned in the book.
- **Community and Support:**
  Engage with online communities, forums, or study groups. Sharing insights and discussing challenges with peers can offer new perspectives and accelerate your learning.

7. Adopt an Iterative Approach

- **Review and Reflect:**
  After completing each chapter, take time to review the key points and ensure you fully understand the material. Try explaining the concepts in your own words or teaching them to someone else.
- **Incremental Progress:**
  Learning complex topics such as graph-driven workflows and NLP takes time. Don't rush through the material; allow yourself to absorb and practice each concept before moving forward.

By following these guidelines, you'll be well-equipped to navigate through **"Graph-Driven Language: Mastering Intelligent Workflows with LangGraph Python"** and make the most of the rich, hands-on content provided. This structured approach is designed to transform your learning experience from passive reading to active engagement, ultimately leading to a deeper and more practical understanding of the material.

D Acknowledgments

Creating a comprehensive guide such as **"Graph-Driven Language: Mastering Intelligent Workflows with LangGraph Python"** is never a solo endeavor. It is the result of collaborative effort, insightful feedback, and unwavering support from many individuals and organizations. In this section, I express my heartfelt thanks to everyone who played a part in bringing this book to life.

Support from Our Institutions

I would also like to acknowledge the institutions and organizations that provided the resources and platforms necessary for this project:

- **The Open Source Community:** Your collective wisdom and the freely available libraries and tools have been an endless source of inspiration and support.
- **Educational Institutions:** Universities and training centers that encourage the exploration of emerging technologies have indirectly contributed to our work by nurturing the next generation of developers and researchers.
- **Professional Organizations:** Groups like the Python Software Foundation and various AI research communities have provided not

only technical guidance but also the frameworks within which innovation thrives.

Personal Thanks

On a personal note, I would like to extend my thanks to my family and friends. Your patience, understanding, and constant encouragement have been our foundation during the challenging times of writing and research.

Thank you all for your support and collaboration. It is my hope that this book not only imparts knowledge but also fosters a spirit of innovation and community in every reader who embarks on this journey.

Part I: Foundations

Chapter 1: Introduction to Graph-Driven Language

1.1 The Evolution of Graph-Based Thinking in AI

Graph-based thinking has been a foundational concept in many areas of computer science and artificial intelligence (AI). Over time, the use of graphs has evolved from simple data representation to a sophisticated tool for modeling complex relationships and reasoning within AI systems. In this section, we will explore the historical development of graph-based methods in AI, highlighting key milestones, innovations, and applications that have shaped the field.

Early Beginnings: Graph Theory Fundamentals

Graph theory, a branch of mathematics focused on the study of nodes (or vertices) and edges (or links), has been around for centuries. Early work in this area can be traced back to the 18th century with the study of the Seven Bridges of Königsberg problem by Leonhard Euler. This problem, which asked whether it was possible to walk through the city of Königsberg crossing each of its seven bridges only once, laid the groundwork for modern graph theory.

Key Concepts Introduced:

- **Nodes and Edges:** The basic units of a graph where nodes represent entities and edges represent relationships.
- **Connectivity:** How nodes are connected, leading to the development of concepts like paths and cycles.
- **Graph Traversal:** Methods for exploring graphs, such as depth-first search (DFS) and breadth-first search (BFS).

These foundational ideas became critical as researchers began to apply them to computer science and, later, AI.

Graphs in Early AI Research

In the early days of AI research (the 1950s and 1960s), graphs were primarily used to model simple problems such as puzzles, games, and decision trees. During this period, AI systems were rule-based, and graphs helped represent state spaces and decision paths. A classic example is the use of decision trees, where each node represents a decision point and edges represent possible outcomes.

Example: Representing a Decision Tree

Consider a simple decision tree for a game where a player can choose to "Attack" or "Defend." The tree might look like this in a basic Python representation:

```python
# Example: Representing a simple decision tree for a game
decision_tree = {
    'Start': ['Attack', 'Defend'],
    'Attack': ['Win', 'Lose'],
    'Defend': ['Stalemate', 'Counterattack']
}

def print_decision_tree(tree, node, depth=0):
    """
    Recursively prints the decision tree starting from the
given node.
    """
    indent = "   " * depth
    print(f"{indent}{node}")
    if node in tree:
        for child in tree[node]:
            print_decision_tree(tree, child, depth + 1)

# Display the decision tree starting from 'Start'
print_decision_tree(decision_tree, 'Start')
```

Explanation:

- **Dictionary Structure:** We represent the decision tree using a dictionary where each key is a node, and the corresponding value is a list of child nodes (possible decisions or outcomes).
- **Recursive Function:** The `print_decision_tree` function recursively traverses the tree and prints each node with indentation corresponding to its depth in the tree.

This simple example demonstrates how graphs (in this case, trees) provided an effective way to model decision-making processes in early AI.

The Rise of Knowledge Graphs and Semantic Networks

As AI evolved, so did the complexity of the problems it sought to solve. In the 1980s and 1990s, researchers began developing knowledge graphs and semantic networks. These structures allowed AI systems to represent and reason about the relationships between a vast array of entities and concepts. Knowledge graphs became central to tasks such as natural language understanding, information retrieval, and expert systems.

Key Innovations:

- **Semantic Relationships:** Knowledge graphs incorporate not just connectivity but also the types of relationships between nodes (e.g., "is a," "part of," "related to").
- **Scalability:** They enabled the representation of large-scale, interconnected data, which is crucial for understanding complex domains.

Table: Comparison of Graph Types

Graph Type	Primary Use	Characteristics
Simple Graphs	Basic data structure representation	Nodes and edges without additional semantics
Decision Trees	Modeling sequential decision processes	Hierarchical, branching structure
Semantic Networks	Representing relationships between concepts	Labeled edges that denote specific types of relationships
Knowledge Graphs	Large-scale representation of interconnected data	Scalable, rich with semantic meaning, used in real-world AI

These advancements laid the foundation for modern AI systems that rely on complex, interrelated data to make informed decisions.

Modern Applications: Graph Neural Networks and Beyond

In recent years, graph-based methods have experienced a renaissance with the advent of graph neural networks (GNNs). GNNs combine the power of traditional neural networks with the structural insights of graph theory, enabling AI systems to process data that is inherently relational.

Highlights of Modern Graph-Based AI:

- **Graph Neural Networks (GNNs):**
  GNNs are designed to learn from graph-structured data. They are particularly useful in applications like social network analysis, recommendation systems, and molecular chemistry.
- **Dynamic Graphs:**
  Modern systems can handle graphs that change over time, capturing dynamic relationships in real-world data (e.g., evolving social interactions or real-time data streams).
- **Integration with NLP:**
  Graph-based methods are now integral to many natural language processing (NLP) tasks. For example, knowledge graphs enhance language models by providing structured context, improving tasks like question-answering and semantic search.

Code Example: A Simple Graph Neural Network Setup

While building a full GNN is beyond the scope of this section, here is a simplified code snippet to illustrate how one might begin to set up a GNN using a popular library like PyTorch Geometric:

```python
import torch
import torch.nn.functional as F
from torch_geometric.nn import GCNConv

# Define a simple Graph Convolutional Network (GCN)
class SimpleGCN(torch.nn.Module):
    def __init__(self, num_features, hidden_channels,
num_classes):
        super(SimpleGCN, self).__init__()
        self.conv1 = GCNConv(num_features, hidden_channels)
        self.conv2 = GCNConv(hidden_channels, num_classes)

    def forward(self, data):
        x, edge_index = data.x, data.edge_index
```

```
# First graph convolution layer with ReLU activation
x = self.conv1(x, edge_index)
x = F.relu(x)
# Second graph convolution layer
x = self.conv2(x, edge_index)
return F.log_softmax(x, dim=1)

# Note: This is a simplified example. In a full
implementation, you would need to:
# - Load a graph dataset (e.g., from PyTorch Geometric's
dataset module)
# - Preprocess the data to create the 'data' object with
attributes like 'x' and 'edge_index'
# - Train the model with an appropriate loss function and
optimizer
```

Explanation:

- **Graph Convolutional Layers:** The `SimpleGCN` class defines two graph convolutional layers using `GCNConv`, which perform convolution operations on the graph.
- **Activation and Output:** After the first convolution, a ReLU activation function is applied, and the final output is computed with a softmax activation for classification tasks.

This snippet serves as an introduction to how modern AI models can leverage graph structures to learn from complex, interconnected data.

Summary

The evolution of graph-based thinking in AI is a testament to the power of visual and relational models in understanding and solving complex problems. From the early days of simple graph theory to the sophisticated models of knowledge graphs and graph neural networks, each stage of development has contributed to the rich tapestry of modern AI. By understanding this evolution, you gain valuable insight into how contemporary AI systems are built and how graph-based approaches continue to drive innovation in the field.

1.2 Overview of LangGraph Python

LangGraph Python is an innovative framework that brings together the power of graph theory and modern language processing to create dynamic, intelligent workflows. Designed with both beginners and experienced developers in mind, LangGraph Python simplifies the process of building, visualizing, and managing complex systems that leverage natural language processing (NLP) techniques alongside graph-based data structures.

What is LangGraph Python?

At its core, LangGraph Python is a library that allows you to construct workflows using graph-based concepts. In this context, a workflow is represented as a network of nodes (which perform specific functions or operations) connected by edges (which define the flow of data or control between these operations). This design philosophy makes it easier to conceptualize and manage the interactions within complex systems, whether you're building a chatbot, an information retrieval system, or a data analysis pipeline.

Key Features:

- **Modularity:**
  Build and reuse components (nodes) to create scalable and maintainable workflows.
- **Visualization:**
  Easily visualize the graph structure of your workflow, helping you understand data flow and dependencies.
- **Integration with NLP:**
  Seamlessly integrate with popular NLP libraries and frameworks, such as Hugging Face and LangChain, to enhance the capabilities of your application.
- **Flexibility:**
  Customize and extend nodes to meet specific project requirements, adapting to different data types and processing needs.

The Architecture of LangGraph Python

LangGraph Python is built on a simple yet powerful architecture that emphasizes clarity and ease of use. Here's a breakdown of its main components:

1. **Nodes:**
   These are the fundamental units of the workflow. Each node represents an individual operation, such as data input, processing, transformation, or output.
2. **Edges:**
   Edges define the connections between nodes, specifying how data moves from one operation to the next. They ensure that the workflow flows logically and that dependencies are maintained.
3. **Graph Manager:**
   This component orchestrates the entire workflow, handling the creation, modification, and execution of the graph. It serves as the control center, allowing you to start, pause, or stop the workflow as needed.
4. **Visualization Tools:**
   Integrated tools help in visualizing the graph structure, making debugging and optimization more intuitive. This visual feedback is essential for understanding how individual components interact within the workflow.

Table: Core Components of LangGraph Python

Component	Description	Role in Workflow
Nodes	Units that perform specific operations (e.g., data processing)	Execute discrete tasks in the workflow
Edges	Connections that define data flow between nodes	Manage dependencies and control flow
Graph Manager	Oversees the creation, execution, and modification of the workflow	Orchestrates and manages overall process
Visualization Tools	Tools for creating graphical representations of the workflow	Aid in debugging and optimizing the design

How LangGraph Python Works

LangGraph Python is designed to be intuitive and straightforward. Developers define nodes and edges using Python code, then use the graph manager to execute the workflow. The framework handles the underlying complexity, such as managing state and ensuring that data flows correctly between components.

Example: Creating a Simple Workflow

Below is a complete and well-explained code example that demonstrates how to set up a basic workflow using LangGraph Python. This example illustrates creating nodes, linking them with edges, and executing the workflow.

```python
python

# Import the LangGraph Python module (assumed to be
installed)
from langgraph import Node, GraphManager

# Define a simple node that prints a message
class PrintNode(Node):
    def __init__(self, message):
        super().__init__()
        self.message = message

    def run(self, data=None):
        # This method is called when the node is executed.
        print(self.message)
        # Pass data to the next node if required
        return data

# Create instances of PrintNode
node1 = PrintNode("Starting the workflow...")
node2 = PrintNode("Processing data...")
node3 = PrintNode("Workflow completed!")

# Instantiate the GraphManager
graph_manager = GraphManager()

# Add nodes to the graph
graph_manager.add_node("start", node1)
graph_manager.add_node("process", node2)
graph_manager.add_node("end", node3)

# Connect the nodes (defining the workflow path)
graph_manager.connect("start", "process")
```

```
graph_manager.connect("process", "end")

# Execute the workflow starting from the 'start' node
graph_manager.run("start")
```

Explanation:

- **Node Definition:**
  We define a custom node class, `PrintNode`, that inherits from the
  base `Node` class provided by LangGraph Python. The `run` method is
  overridden to print a message and optionally process or forward data.
- **Graph Construction:**
  We create instances of `PrintNode` with different messages to
  represent different stages of the workflow. These nodes are then
  added to the graph via the `GraphManager`.
- **Connecting Nodes:**
  The `connect` method establishes directed edges between nodes. In
  this example, the output of the "start" node is directed to the
  "process" node, and so on.
- **Execution:**
  Finally, calling `graph_manager.run("start")` begins the execution
  of the workflow from the specified starting node.

This simple workflow demonstrates the modularity and ease-of-use that
LangGraph Python offers, allowing developers to build, visualize, and
manage complex processes with minimal code.

Integration with NLP and Other Libraries

LangGraph Python is built with extensibility in mind. You can integrate it
with various NLP frameworks to enhance your applications. For instance,
you might incorporate a node that processes text using a pre-trained language
model from Hugging Face. This flexibility means you can create
sophisticated pipelines that combine multiple technologies seamlessly.

Example: Integrating an NLP Node

Below is a conceptual example showing how you might integrate an NLP
processing node into your LangGraph workflow:

```python
from langgraph import Node
from transformers import pipeline

# Define a node that performs sentiment analysis using
Hugging Face's pipeline
class SentimentAnalysisNode(Node):
    def __init__(self):
        super().__init__()
        # Initialize the sentiment analysis pipeline
        self.analyzer = pipeline("sentiment-analysis")

    def run(self, text):
        # Perform sentiment analysis on the provided text
        results = self.analyzer(text)
        # Print the results for demonstration purposes
        print("Sentiment Analysis Results:", results)
        return results

# Create an instance of SentimentAnalysisNode
sentiment_node = SentimentAnalysisNode()

# Add this node to the graph and connect it as needed
(similar to the previous example)
# This integration shows how LangGraph Python can work with
external libraries to process and analyze data.
```

Explanation:

- **Node Inheritance:**
  The `SentimentAnalysisNode` inherits from the base `Node` class.
- **Integration:**
  Inside the node, we initialize a sentiment analysis pipeline from the Hugging Face library. The node's `run` method processes incoming text and outputs the sentiment analysis results.

This integration illustrates the versatility of LangGraph Python and its ability to serve as a backbone for complex, multi-functional workflows.

Summary

LangGraph Python is a robust framework that leverages graph theory to simplify the creation and management of intelligent workflows. Its modular design, ease of visualization, and seamless integration with NLP libraries make it a powerful tool for developers, data scientists, and AI enthusiasts alike. Through its intuitive architecture, LangGraph Python empowers you to break down complex processes into manageable, interconnected components, facilitating a clear and organized approach to building modern AI applications.

By understanding and utilizing the principles covered in this overview, you are now ready to explore the deeper functionalities of LangGraph Python throughout the rest of this book. Whether you are creating simple decision trees or intricate, multi-stage workflows, LangGraph Python provides a flexible and scalable solution that grows with your ambitions.

1.3 The Intersection of Graph Theory and NLP

The fields of Graph Theory and Natural Language Processing (NLP) may seem distinct at first glance—one rooted in mathematical structures and the other in language and text—but they intersect in many exciting and practical ways. In this section, we explore how graph theory principles can be applied to solve NLP problems, the benefits of such an approach, and provide clear, practical examples to illustrate these ideas.

How Graph Theory Enhances NLP

Graph theory provides a natural way to model complex relationships and structures. In NLP, language data—whether it's a sentence, a document, or a collection of texts—often contains relationships that can be effectively represented as graphs. Here are some key ways that graph theory intersects with NLP:

1. **Dependency Parsing:**
   Dependency parsing involves analyzing the grammatical structure of a sentence and establishing relationships between "head" words and words which modify those heads. These relationships form a directed graph, where each word is a node and the grammatical relationships are edges.
2. **Semantic Networks and Knowledge Graphs:**
   Semantic networks represent concepts as nodes and semantic relationships as edges. Knowledge graphs, a more advanced form, integrate vast amounts of structured information, providing context

and enhancing understanding in NLP tasks such as question answering and recommendation systems.

3. **Word Co-occurrence Networks:**
   By representing words as nodes and their co-occurrence in text as edges, we can uncover semantic relationships and identify clusters or communities within large corpora. This network can aid in tasks like topic modeling and sentiment analysis.

4. **Graph-Based Ranking Algorithms:**
   Algorithms like PageRank, originally developed for ranking web pages, have been adapted to rank sentences in a document (e.g., for summarization) or to determine the importance of words in a text (e.g., TextRank for keyword extraction).

Practical Applications and Benefits

Using graph-based methods in NLP provides several advantages:

- **Improved Contextual Understanding:**
  Graphs naturally capture relationships between words or concepts, which can lead to a better understanding of context and meaning.
- **Enhanced Data Representation:**
  Representing language data as graphs allows for more intuitive visualizations and analysis, which can be especially useful in understanding complex text structures.
- **Scalability:**
  Graphs can efficiently represent large datasets with complex interconnections, enabling the processing and analysis of big data in NLP.
- **Versatility:**
  Graph-based methods are applicable to a variety of NLP tasks, from parsing and entity recognition to text summarization and sentiment analysis.

Table: Graph Theory Applications in NLP

Application Area	Graph Representation	Benefits
Dependency Parsing	Nodes represent words; directed edges represent grammatical dependencies	Enhanced syntactic analysis and language understanding

Application Area	Graph Representation	Benefits
Semantic Networks	Nodes represent concepts; edges represent semantic relationships	Rich contextual insights and improved information retrieval
Word Co-occurrence Networks	Nodes represent words; edges represent co-occurrence frequency	Identifies clusters, topics, and semantic communities
Text Summarization	Nodes represent sentences; edges represent similarity or relevance	Efficiently ranks and extracts key sentences from text
Keyword Extraction (TextRank)	Nodes represent words; edges represent co-occurrence in text	Automatically identifies important keywords

Code Example: Dependency Parsing Visualization

Below is an example demonstrating how to use graph theory for dependency parsing in NLP. We will use the Python library spaCy to perform dependency parsing on a sentence and then represent the parse as a graph using the networkx library.

1. **Setup and Installation**

   First, ensure you have the required libraries installed:

   ```bash
   pip install spacy networkx matplotlib
   python -m spacy download en_core_web_sm
   ```

2. **Code Implementation**

   ```python
   import spacy
   import networkx as nx
   import matplotlib.pyplot as plt

   # Load the spaCy English model
   nlp = spacy.load("en_core_web_sm")

   # Define a sentence to parse
   ```

```
sentence = "The quick brown fox jumps over the lazy
dog."
doc = nlp(sentence)

# Create a directed graph
G = nx.DiGraph()

# Add nodes and edges based on dependency parsing
for token in doc:
    # Add each token as a node
    G.add_node(token.text, label=token.dep_)
    # Add an edge from the head to the token, except if
the token is the root
    if token.dep_ != "ROOT":
        G.add_edge(token.head.text, token.text,
label=token.dep_)

# Draw the graph
pos = nx.spring_layout(G)
plt.figure(figsize=(10, 7))
nx.draw(G, pos, with_labels=True, node_color='skyblue',
node_size=1500, edge_color='gray', arrows=True)

# Draw edge labels (dependency labels)
edge_labels = nx.get_edge_attributes(G, 'label')
nx.draw_networkx_edge_labels(G, pos,
edge_labels=edge_labels)
plt.title("Dependency Parsing Graph")
plt.show()
```

Explanation:

- **Loading Libraries:**
  We import `spaCy` for NLP processing, `networkx` for graph
  creation, and `matplotlib` for visualization.
- **Processing the Sentence:**
  The sentence is processed using spaCy's NLP model, which
  performs dependency parsing.
- **Graph Construction:**
  Each word in the sentence is added as a node in the graph. For
  every token (except the root), an edge is added from its head
  (the word it depends on) to the token, with the dependency
  label as the edge attribute.
- **Visualization:**
  The graph is drawn using `networkx` and `matplotlib`,
  showing nodes (words) and directed edges (dependency
  relations) with labels.

Summary

The intersection of graph theory and NLP provides powerful tools to model, analyze, and extract meaning from language data. By representing linguistic structures as graphs, we can gain a deeper understanding of syntax, semantics, and the intricate relationships between words and concepts. This approach not only enhances traditional NLP tasks such as parsing and summarization but also opens new avenues for research and application in AI.

As you continue reading this book, you will discover more practical examples and detailed projects that further illustrate how graph-driven techniques can transform NLP workflows. Whether you are visualizing sentence structures or building complex knowledge graphs, the principles discussed here will serve as a foundation for your journey into the world of graph-based language processing.

1.4 Key Use Cases and Real-World Applications

Graph-Driven Language techniques, powered by LangGraph Python, have a wide range of practical applications in today's data-driven world. By combining graph theory with natural language processing (NLP), developers and data scientists can build powerful systems that are efficient, scalable, and capable of solving complex real-world problems. In this section, we explore several key use cases and real-world applications, providing clear explanations, detailed examples, and practical code snippets.

1. Customer Support Chatbots and Conversational Agents

Overview:
Modern customer support systems often rely on conversational agents to answer frequently asked questions, troubleshoot issues, and provide product recommendations. Using graph-based workflows, these chatbots can manage conversation flow, track user context, and seamlessly integrate NLP modules for language understanding.

How It Works:

- **Nodes:** Each node represents a conversational turn or an action (e.g., greeting, query handling, escalation).
- **Edges:** Edges define the transition between conversation states based on user input and system responses.
- **NLP Integration:** NLP nodes process and classify user input, enabling dynamic responses.

Example Workflow:

python

```python
from langgraph import Node, GraphManager
from transformers import pipeline

# Define a node that greets the user
class GreetingNode(Node):
    def run(self, data=None):
        print("Hello! How can I assist you today?")
        return data

# Define a node that processes user input using an NLP model
class IntentAnalysisNode(Node):
    def __init__(self):
        super().__init__()
        # Initialize a sentiment analysis or intent
classification pipeline
        self.classifier = pipeline("sentiment-analysis")

    def run(self, data):
        # For demonstration, assume 'data' is a user message
        result = self.classifier(data)
        print("Intent Analysis Results:", result)
        return result

# Define a node for closing the conversation
class GoodbyeNode(Node):
    def run(self, data=None):
        print("Thank you for reaching out. Have a great
day!")
        return data

# Build the workflow graph
graph_manager = GraphManager()
graph_manager.add_node("greeting", GreetingNode())
graph_manager.add_node("intent", IntentAnalysisNode())
graph_manager.add_node("goodbye", GoodbyeNode())
```

```
graph_manager.connect("greeting", "intent")
graph_manager.connect("intent", "goodbye")

# Simulate a conversation by running the workflow
graph_manager.run("greeting")
user_input = "I love the new update on your app!"  #
Simulated user input
graph_manager.run("intent", user_input)
```

Explanation:

- **GreetingNode:** Initiates the conversation.
- **IntentAnalysisNode:** Uses an NLP model (via Hugging Face's pipeline) to analyze the sentiment or intent behind the user's input.
- **GoodbyeNode:** Concludes the interaction.
- **Workflow Execution:** The graph manager executes the nodes in sequence, demonstrating a basic conversational flow.

---

2. Knowledge Graphs for Enhanced Information Retrieval

Overview:
Knowledge graphs represent real-world entities and their interrelationships. They are widely used in search engines, recommendation systems, and enterprise data management. By integrating NLP, these graphs help in contextualizing search queries and retrieving relevant information more effectively.

Key Components:

- **Entities:** Represented as nodes (e.g., people, places, concepts).
- **Relationships:** Represented as edges (e.g., "is a part of", "related to").
- **Query Processing:** NLP nodes interpret user queries and map them to graph entities.

Table: Knowledge Graph Use Cases

Use Case	Entities	Relationships	Benefit
Enterprise Search	Documents, Departments, People	"authored by", "belongs to"	Improved relevance and context-based search results
Recommendation Systems	Products, Users, Categories	"purchased by", "related to"	Personalized recommendations based on user history
Healthcare Information	Symptoms, Diseases, Treatments	"indicates", "treated by"	Enhanced diagnostics and treatment suggestions

Example Implementation:

Imagine building a small knowledge graph to connect research papers, authors, and research topics. The graph can be queried to retrieve all papers by a particular author or on a specific topic.

```python
import networkx as nx

# Create a knowledge graph using NetworkX
KG = nx.DiGraph()

# Add entities (nodes)
KG.add_node("Alice", type="Author")
KG.add_node("Bob", type="Author")
KG.add_node("Graph Theory", type="Research Topic")
KG.add_node("NLP", type="Research Topic")
KG.add_node("Paper1", type="Paper")
KG.add_node("Paper2", type="Paper")

# Add relationships (edges)
KG.add_edge("Alice", "Paper1", relation="authored")
KG.add_edge("Bob", "Paper2", relation="authored")
KG.add_edge("Paper1", "Graph Theory", relation="about")
KG.add_edge("Paper2", "NLP", relation="about")

# Function to query papers by an author
def get_papers_by_author(graph, author):
    papers = []
    for neighbor in graph.neighbors(author):
        if graph.nodes[neighbor].get("type") == "Paper":
            papers.append(neighbor)
```

```
    return papers

# Retrieve papers authored by Alice
alice_papers = get_papers_by_author(KG, "Alice")
print("Papers by Alice:", alice_papers)
```

Explanation:

- **Graph Creation:** A directed graph is created using NetworkX.
- **Nodes and Edges:** Nodes represent authors, papers, and topics, while edges represent relationships like "authored" and "about."
- **Query Function:** The `get_papers_by_author` function searches for papers linked to an author node.
- **Output:** The function prints the papers authored by "Alice."

---

3. Social Network Analysis and Community Detection

Overview:
Graph theory is naturally suited for analyzing social networks, where individuals are nodes and their relationships (friendships, communications, etc.) are edges. By incorporating NLP, these analyses can extend to understanding user sentiments, identifying influential figures, and tracking trends within communities.

Benefits:

- **Community Detection:** Identify clusters or groups within large social networks.
- **Influence Analysis:** Determine which individuals are most influential based on their connectivity and interactions.
- **Sentiment Analysis:** Integrate NLP to gauge the overall sentiment within a community or network.

Example Workflow:

```python
import networkx as nx
import matplotlib.pyplot as plt

# Create a simple social network graph
social_graph = nx.Graph()
```

```
social_graph.add_edges_from([
    ("Alice", "Bob"),
    ("Alice", "Charlie"),
    ("Bob", "Diana"),
    ("Charlie", "Diana"),
    ("Diana", "Eve"),
    ("Eve", "Frank")
])

# Function to visualize the social network
def visualize_social_network(graph):
    pos = nx.spring_layout(graph)
    plt.figure(figsize=(8, 6))
    nx.draw(graph, pos, with_labels=True,
node_color='lightgreen', node_size=2000, edge_color='gray')
    plt.title("Social Network Graph")
    plt.show()

# Visualize the network
visualize_social_network(social_graph)
```

Explanation:

- **Graph Construction:** A simple undirected graph is built to represent a social network.
- **Visualization:** The network is visualized using NetworkX and Matplotlib to understand the community structure.
- **Further Analysis:** NLP techniques can be applied to social media posts or messages associated with these nodes to analyze sentiment or topic trends, providing deeper insights into the community dynamics.

---

4. Document and Text Summarization

Overview:
Summarization is a critical application in managing large volumes of text. Graph-based approaches, such as TextRank, leverage the structure of text to identify and rank important sentences or keywords, creating concise summaries of long documents.

How It Works:

- **Graph Construction:** Sentences are nodes, and edges represent similarities between sentences.
- **Ranking:** Graph-based ranking algorithms (e.g., PageRank) score each sentence.
- **Summary Generation:** Top-ranked sentences are selected to form the summary.

Example: Text Summarization Using TextRank

python

```
import networkx as nx
import numpy as np
from sklearn.metrics.pairwise import cosine_similarity
from sklearn.feature_extraction.text import CountVectorizer

# Sample document: list of sentences
sentences = [
    "Graph theory provides a robust framework for modeling
relationships.",
    "NLP techniques can extract meaning from complex text
data.",
    "Combining graph theory and NLP leads to powerful data
analysis tools.",
    "Real-world applications include chatbots, knowledge
graphs, and social network analysis."
]

# Create a sentence similarity matrix
vectorizer = CountVectorizer().fit_transform(sentences)
vectors = vectorizer.toarray()
similarity_matrix = cosine_similarity(vectors)

# Build a graph from the similarity matrix
nx_graph = nx.from_numpy_array(similarity_matrix)
scores = nx.pagerank(nx_graph)

# Rank sentences based on the scores
ranked_sentences = sorted(((scores[i], s) for i, s in
enumerate(sentences)), reverse=True)
summary = " ".join([s for score, s in ranked_sentences[:2]])

print("Document Summary:")
print(summary)
```

Explanation:

- **Sentence Representation:** Sentences are vectorized using a CountVectorizer.
- **Similarity Matrix:** Cosine similarity is computed between sentence vectors.
- **Graph and Ranking:** A graph is constructed from the similarity matrix, and PageRank is applied to rank the sentences.
- **Summary Generation:** The top-ranked sentences are selected to form a summary.

Summary

Graph-driven approaches provide a versatile and robust framework for a wide range of real-world applications. By representing data and relationships in a graph format, systems become more intuitive, scalable, and efficient in handling complex tasks. Whether it is powering customer support chatbots, enhancing information retrieval with knowledge graphs, analyzing social networks, or summarizing documents, the fusion of graph theory and NLP opens new horizons for innovation.

As you progress through this book, you will encounter more detailed projects and exercises that will further illustrate these concepts, enabling you to apply graph-driven language techniques in your own work. With LangGraph Python as your toolkit, you are well-equipped to explore and implement these cutting-edge applications.

Chapter 2: Fundamentals of Graph Theory

2.1 Basic Concepts: Nodes, Edges, and Graph Types

Graph theory is a branch of mathematics that provides a framework to model pairwise relationships between objects. In computer science and various applications like network analysis, natural language processing, and even bioinformatics, graphs are indispensable. In this section, we will introduce the foundational concepts of graph theory, including nodes, edges, and different types of graphs. Our goal is to explain these ideas in a clear and straightforward manner, using practical examples, tables, and code snippets to illustrate each point.

Nodes (Vertices)

Definition:
Nodes, also known as vertices, represent the individual entities in a graph. They are the basic building blocks that can represent a variety of objects, such as people in a social network, cities on a map, or words in a sentence.

Key Points:

- **Unique Identity:** Each node typically has a unique identifier.
- **Attributes:** Nodes can store additional information (attributes) such as names, labels, or numerical values.

Example:
Imagine a social network where each person is represented as a node. The node may contain attributes like the person's name, age, or interests.

Edges (Links)

Definition:
Edges are the connections between nodes. They represent relationships or

interactions between the entities. An edge can be directed (having a clear source and destination) or undirected (bidirectional).

Key Points:

- **Directionality:**
    - **Directed Edge:** Indicates a one-way relationship (e.g., Twitter follows).
    - **Undirected Edge:** Represents a mutual or bidirectional relationship (e.g., Facebook friends).
- **Attributes:** Like nodes, edges can also store information such as weight (indicating the strength or capacity of the connection), type, or label.

Example:
In a transportation network, nodes might represent cities, and edges could represent roads connecting these cities. A weight on an edge might indicate the distance or travel time between the cities.

Graph Types

Graphs can be classified into several types based on their characteristics. Understanding these classifications is important as each type has its own properties and suitable use cases.

Common Graph Types:

Graph Type	Description	Examples
Undirected Graph	Edges have no direction. The connection between two nodes is bidirectional.	Social networks (mutual friendships)
Directed Graph	Edges have a specific direction, indicating a one-way relationship.	Web page links, Twitter following
Weighted Graph	Each edge has an associated weight, representing the cost, distance, or capacity of the connection.	Road networks (distance between cities)

Graph Type	Description	Examples
Unweighted Graph	Edges do not carry any weight; the relationship is binary (either there is a connection or there is not).	Basic network diagrams, simple organizational charts
Simple Graph	A graph without loops (edges connecting a node to itself) or multiple edges between the same set of nodes.	Many real-world network models
Multigraph	A graph that can have multiple edges (parallel edges) between the same set of nodes, allowing for more complex relationships.	Transportation networks (multiple routes)

Code Examples

To bring these concepts to life, we will use Python with the `networkx` library, a popular tool for creating and manipulating graphs. Below are a few examples that demonstrate how to create nodes, add edges, and work with different types of graphs.

1. Creating a Simple Graph with Nodes and Edges

python

```
import networkx as nx
import matplotlib.pyplot as plt

# Create an undirected graph
G = nx.Graph()

# Add nodes to the graph
G.add_node("A")   # Node representing an entity, e.g., a
person or a city
G.add_node("B")
G.add_node("C")

# Add edges between nodes
G.add_edge("A", "B")   # An undirected edge between A and B
G.add_edge("B", "C")
G.add_edge("A", "C")

# Draw the graph
pos = nx.spring_layout(G)   # Compute layout for visualization
```

```
plt.figure(figsize=(6, 4))
nx.draw(G, pos, with_labels=True, node_color='lightblue',
edge_color='gray', node_size=1500)
plt.title("Simple Undirected Graph")
plt.show()
```

Explanation:

- **Graph Creation:**
  We create an undirected graph `G` using `nx.Graph()`.
- **Adding Nodes and Edges:**
  Nodes "A", "B", and "C" are added to the graph, followed by undirected edges connecting them.
- **Visualization:**
  We use `nx.spring_layout` to position the nodes for visualization and then draw the graph with labels.

2. Creating a Directed, Weighted Graph

python

```
# Create a directed graph
DG = nx.DiGraph()

# Add nodes (entities)
DG.add_node("City1")
DG.add_node("City2")
DG.add_node("City3")

# Add weighted, directed edges (routes with distances)
DG.add_edge("City1", "City2", weight=50)  # Directed edge
with a weight
DG.add_edge("City2", "City3", weight=70)
DG.add_edge("City1", "City3", weight=120)

# Draw the directed graph with edge labels for weights
pos = nx.spring_layout(DG)
plt.figure(figsize=(6, 4))
nx.draw(DG, pos, with_labels=True, node_color='lightgreen',
edge_color='blue', node_size=1500, arrows=True)
edge_labels = nx.get_edge_attributes(DG, 'weight')
nx.draw_networkx_edge_labels(DG, pos,
edge_labels=edge_labels)
plt.title("Directed, Weighted Graph")
plt.show()
```

Explanation:

- **Directed Graph Creation:**
  A directed graph `DG` is created using `nx.DiGraph()`.
- **Adding Weighted Edges:**
  Edges are added with a `weight` attribute representing, for instance, the distance between cities.
- **Visualization:**
  The graph is drawn with arrows to denote direction, and edge labels are added to display the weights.

Summary

Understanding the basic concepts of graph theory—nodes, edges, and graph types—is essential for building and analyzing complex systems. These concepts form the foundation upon which more advanced topics, such as graph algorithms and graph-based workflows, are built. Through the definitions, tables, and code examples provided in this section, you now have a solid grasp of how graphs are structured and how they can be used to represent and analyze relationships in various domains.

As you progress in this book, you will see these fundamentals applied in more sophisticated scenarios, including the integration of graph theory with natural language processing and the construction of dynamic workflows using LangGraph Python.

2.2 Graph Representations: Adjacency Matrices and Lists

Graph representations are essential for implementing and working with graphs in computer science. Two common representations are **adjacency matrices** and **adjacency lists**. Each representation has its advantages and trade-offs, and the choice between them depends on the type and density of the graph, as well as the operations that need to be performed.

In this section, we will explore these two representations in detail, including their definitions, pros and cons, and complete code examples to demonstrate how they work.

Adjacency Matrix

Definition:
An adjacency matrix is a 2-dimensional array (or matrix) used to represent a graph. Each cell in the matrix indicates whether a pair of vertices is connected by an edge. For a graph with nnn vertices, the adjacency matrix is an n×nn \times nn×n matrix where:

- **For an Unweighted Graph:**
  - A value of 1 (or True) indicates an edge between the corresponding vertices.
  - A value of 0 (or False) indicates no edge.
- **For a Weighted Graph:**
  - The matrix stores the weight of the edge between vertices.
  - A special value (like 0 or ∞) is used to denote the absence of an edge.

Advantages:

- **Simplicity:** Easy to implement and understand.
- **Constant-Time Edge Check:** Determining if there is an edge between two vertices takes $O(1)O(1)O(1)$ time.
- **Suitable for Dense Graphs:** Works well when the graph has many edges.

Disadvantages:

- **Space Inefficiency:** Requires $O(n2)O(n^2)O(n2)$ space, which can be wasteful for sparse graphs.
- **Inefficient for Iterating Neighbors:** Iterating through all neighbors of a vertex takes $O(n)O(n)O(n)$ time.

Example Code:

Below is an example of how to create and use an adjacency matrix in Python for an unweighted, undirected graph.

```python
python

def create_adjacency_matrix(num_vertices):
```

```
    """
    Create an adjacency matrix for a graph with num_vertices.

    Parameters:
    - num_vertices: Number of vertices in the graph.

    Returns:
    - A 2D list initialized to 0.
    """
    return [[0 for _ in range(num_vertices)] for _ in
range(num_vertices)]

def add_edge(matrix, src, dest, weight=1):
    """
    Add an edge to the graph represented by an adjacency
matrix.

    Parameters:
    - matrix: The adjacency matrix.
    - src: The source vertex index.
    - dest: The destination vertex index.
    - weight: The weight of the edge (default is 1 for
unweighted graphs).
    """
    matrix[src][dest] = weight
    matrix[dest][src] = weight  # For undirected graphs

# Example usage:
num_vertices = 4  # For vertices labeled 0, 1, 2, 3
adj_matrix = create_adjacency_matrix(num_vertices)

# Add some edges: 0-1, 0-2, 1-2, and 2-3
add_edge(adj_matrix, 0, 1)
add_edge(adj_matrix, 0, 2)
add_edge(adj_matrix, 1, 2)
add_edge(adj_matrix, 2, 3)

# Display the adjacency matrix
print("Adjacency Matrix:")
for row in adj_matrix:
    print(row)
```

Explanation:

- **Matrix Initialization:**
  create_adjacency_matrix initializes a 2D list filled with zeros.
- **Adding Edges:**
  The add_edge function sets the corresponding cells in the matrix to 1

(or a specified weight). Since the graph is undirected, the matrix is symmetric.

- **Output:**
  The matrix is printed row by row, clearly showing the connections between vertices.

Adjacency List

Definition:
An adjacency list represents a graph as a collection of lists (or dictionaries) where each vertex has a list of its adjacent vertices (neighbors). In weighted graphs, each neighbor can be stored along with the weight of the edge connecting them.

Advantages:

- **Space Efficiency:** Requires $O(V+E)O(V + E)O(V+E)$ space, where VVV is the number of vertices and EEE is the number of edges, making it ideal for sparse graphs.
- **Efficient Neighbor Iteration:** Quickly iterates through the neighbors of a given vertex.

Disadvantages:

- **Edge Check Time:** Determining if an edge exists between two vertices can take $O(d)O(d)O(d)$ time, where ddd is the degree of the vertex.
- **Less Intuitive for Dense Graphs:** For graphs with a high density of edges, the adjacency matrix might be simpler to manage.

Example Code:

Below is an example of how to create and use an adjacency list in Python for an unweighted, undirected graph.

```python
def create_adjacency_list(num_vertices):
    """
    Create an adjacency list for a graph with num_vertices.
```

```
    Parameters:
    - num_vertices: Number of vertices in the graph.

    Returns:
    - A dictionary where keys are vertex indices and values
are lists of adjacent vertices.
    """
    return {i: [] for i in range(num_vertices)}

def add_edge_adj_list(adj_list, src, dest):
    """
    Add an edge to the graph represented by an adjacency
list.

    Parameters:
    - adj_list: The adjacency list.
    - src: The source vertex index.
    - dest: The destination vertex index.
    """
    adj_list[src].append(dest)
    adj_list[dest].append(src)   # For undirected graphs

# Example usage:
num_vertices = 4   # For vertices labeled 0, 1, 2, 3
adj_list = create_adjacency_list(num_vertices)

# Add some edges: 0-1, 0-2, 1-2, and 2-3
add_edge_adj_list(adj_list, 0, 1)
add_edge_adj_list(adj_list, 0, 2)
add_edge_adj_list(adj_list, 1, 2)
add_edge_adj_list(adj_list, 2, 3)

# Display the adjacency list
print("\nAdjacency List:")
for vertex, neighbors in adj_list.items():
    print(f"{vertex}: {neighbors}")
```

Explanation:

- **List Initialization:**
  `create_adjacency_list` creates a dictionary with keys for each vertex and empty lists as values.
- **Adding Edges:**
  The `add_edge_adj_list` function appends the destination vertex to the source's list and vice versa for an undirected graph.
- **Output:**
  The adjacency list is printed, showing each vertex and its corresponding list of neighbors.

Comparison Table: Adjacency Matrix vs. Adjacency List

Aspect	Adjacency Matrix	Adjacency List
Space Complexity	O(n2)O(n^2)O(n2)	O(V+E)O(V + E)O(V+E)
Edge Existence Check	O(1)O(1)O(1) (direct index lookup)	O(d)O(d)O(d) (where ddd is the degree of the vertex)
Neighbor Iteration	O(n)O(n)O(n) (iterate over entire row)	O(d)O(d)O(d) (iterate over actual neighbors)
Best Suited For	Dense graphs with many edges	Sparse graphs with fewer edges
Ease of Implementation	Simple and intuitive, especially for small graphs	More efficient for large, sparse graphs

Summary

Understanding how to represent graphs efficiently is fundamental to solving problems in graph theory and its applications. An **adjacency matrix** offers simplicity and constant-time edge checking, making it suitable for dense graphs, while an **adjacency list** is more space-efficient and better for sparse graphs.

The provided examples demonstrate how to implement both representations in Python, ensuring that you can choose the most appropriate method based on your specific needs. These basic structures serve as the foundation for more advanced graph algorithms and workflows, which you will explore in subsequent chapters.

2.3 Graph Traversal and Search Algorithms

Graph traversal is the process of visiting, checking, or updating each node in a graph in a systematic way. Search algorithms built on these traversals are essential for solving many practical problems such as finding the shortest path, checking connectivity, and exploring network structures. In this section, we will discuss two of the most common graph traversal techniques: Depth-First Search (DFS) and Breadth-First Search (BFS). We will also provide detailed code examples, comparisons, and tables to help you understand these algorithms thoroughly.

Depth-First Search (DFS)

Overview:
Depth-First Search is a traversal technique that explores as far as possible along each branch before backtracking. It uses a stack data structure (either implicitly through recursion or explicitly with a stack) to keep track of the nodes to visit.

Key Characteristics:

- **Recursive or Iterative:** DFS can be implemented using recursion, where the call stack manages the traversal, or iteratively using an explicit stack.
- **Path Exploration:** It goes deep into the graph first, which makes it useful for scenarios such as finding a path or exploring all possible configurations.
- **Space Complexity:** In the worst case, DFS can use space proportional to the depth of the graph.

Example Code (Recursive DFS):

```python
python

def dfs_recursive(graph, start, visited=None):
    """
    Recursive Depth-First Search (DFS) implementation.

    Parameters:
    - graph: A dictionary representing the graph, where keys
are node labels and
             values are lists of adjacent nodes.
    - start: The starting node for the DFS traversal.
    - visited: A set to keep track of visited nodes (default
is None).

    Returns:
    - visited: A set containing all nodes visited during the
traversal.
    """
    if visited is None:
```

```
        visited = set()
    visited.add(start)
    print(f"Visited: {start}")
    for neighbor in graph[start]:
        if neighbor not in visited:
            dfs_recursive(graph, neighbor, visited)
    return visited

# Example graph represented as an adjacency list
graph_example = {
    'A': ['B', 'C'],
    'B': ['D', 'E'],
    'C': ['F'],
    'D': [],
    'E': ['F'],
    'F': []
}

# Run DFS starting from node 'A'
dfs_recursive(graph_example, 'A')
```

Explanation:

- **Graph Representation:** The graph is represented as a dictionary where each key is a node, and its value is a list of adjacent nodes.
- **Recursive Call:** The function calls itself for every unvisited neighbor, ensuring the traversal goes as deep as possible before backtracking.
- **Visited Set:** This set keeps track of nodes that have been visited to prevent infinite loops in graphs with cycles.

Breadth-First Search (BFS)

Overview:
Breadth-First Search is another fundamental traversal method that explores all nodes at the present depth level before moving on to nodes at the next depth level. It uses a queue to maintain the order of nodes to be processed.

Key Characteristics:

- **Level-by-Level Exploration:** BFS visits all nodes at the current level before proceeding to the next level.

- **Shortest Path:** It is particularly useful in finding the shortest path in unweighted graphs.
- **Space Complexity:** BFS may require storing a significant number of nodes in the queue, especially in graphs with high branching factors.

Example Code (Iterative BFS):

```python
from collections import deque

def bfs_iterative(graph, start):
    """
    Iterative Breadth-First Search (BFS) implementation.

    Parameters:
    - graph: A dictionary representing the graph.
    - start: The starting node for the BFS traversal.

    Returns:
    - visited_order: A list containing nodes in the order
they were visited.
    """
    visited = set()
    queue = deque([start])
    visited_order = []

    while queue:
        node = queue.popleft()
        if node not in visited:
            visited.add(node)
            visited_order.append(node)
            print(f"Visited: {node}")
            # Enqueue all adjacent nodes that haven't been
visited
            for neighbor in graph[node]:
                if neighbor not in visited:
                    queue.append(neighbor)
    return visited_order

# Run BFS starting from node 'A'
bfs_iterative(graph_example, 'A')
```

Explanation:

- **Graph Representation:** Similar to DFS, the graph is a dictionary.

- **Queue Usage:** A deque (double-ended queue) is used to ensure FIFO (First-In-First-Out) behavior, which is essential for level-order traversal.
- **Visited Set:** Keeps track of visited nodes to avoid processing the same node multiple times.
- **Output Order:** The order in which nodes are visited is stored in a list, reflecting the level-order nature of BFS.

Comparison Table: DFS vs. BFS

Aspect	Depth-First Search (DFS)	Breadth-First Search (BFS)
Traversal Order	Deep into the graph before backtracking	Level-by-level, all nodes at one depth before moving deeper
Data Structure	Stack (explicit or recursive call stack)	Queue (FIFO)
Use Cases	Path finding, cycle detection, solving puzzles	Shortest path in unweighted graphs, level order traversal
Space Complexity	O(depth of graph)	O(width of graph)
Time Complexity	O(V + E) (V: vertices, E: edges)	O(V + E)

Additional Search Algorithms

While DFS and BFS are foundational, there are other search algorithms used in graphs, especially when dealing with weighted graphs or finding optimal paths:

1. **Dijkstra's Algorithm:**
   Used for finding the shortest path in weighted graphs where all weights are non-negative.
2. *A Search Algorithm:*
   An extension of Dijkstra's algorithm that uses heuristics to improve performance, particularly in pathfinding scenarios.

Note: Detailed explanations and code examples for Dijkstra's and A algorithms are provided in later sections of the book.

Summary

Graph traversal is a crucial technique in computer science, underpinning many algorithms used for search and analysis. In this section, we covered the two primary traversal methods—DFS and BFS—each with its unique characteristics and applications. The provided code examples and detailed explanations illustrate how these algorithms work in practice, ensuring a solid foundation for more advanced topics in graph theory and its applications in fields like natural language processing.

Understanding DFS and BFS will equip you with the tools necessary to explore graphs in various domains, from simple networks to complex, multi-layered systems. As you progress through this book, these foundational concepts will serve as building blocks for more sophisticated graph-based workflows and search algorithms.

2.4 Graph Data Structures in Python

When working with graphs in Python, selecting the right data structure to represent the graph is crucial for both efficiency and ease of implementation. Graph data structures allow you to store vertices (nodes) and edges (connections) in a way that facilitates common graph operations such as traversal, search, and modification. In this section, we explore various graph data structures in Python, including both built-in structures and object-oriented approaches, along with detailed code examples and explanations.

---

1. Using Dictionaries for Graph Representation

A common and flexible way to represent a graph in Python is by using dictionaries. There are two primary approaches:

- **Adjacency List Representation:**
  Each key in the dictionary represents a node, and its value is a list (or set) of neighbors. This method is efficient for sparse graphs.

- **Weighted Graph Representation:**
  The dictionary's values can also be dictionaries, where each inner key represents a neighboring node and its corresponding value is the weight of the edge connecting the nodes.

Example: Unweighted Graph (Adjacency List)

python

```python
# Define an unweighted graph using a dictionary (adjacency
list)
graph = {
    'A': ['B', 'C'],
    'B': ['A', 'D', 'E'],
    'C': ['A', 'F'],
    'D': ['B'],
    'E': ['B', 'F'],
    'F': ['C', 'E']
}

# Function to display the graph
def display_graph(g):
    for node, neighbors in g.items():
        print(f"{node}: {neighbors}")

print("Unweighted Graph (Adjacency List):")
display_graph(graph)
```

Explanation:

- **Dictionary Structure:**
  Each key represents a node. For example, node 'A' is connected to nodes 'B' and 'C'.
- **Display Function:**
  The function iterates over the dictionary items and prints each node with its list of neighbors.

Example: Weighted Graph

python

```python
# Define a weighted graph using a dictionary
weighted_graph = {
    'A': {'B': 5, 'C': 3},
    'B': {'A': 5, 'D': 2, 'E': 4},
    'C': {'A': 3, 'F': 7},
    'D': {'B': 2},
```

```python
    'E': {'B': 4, 'F': 1},
    'F': {'C': 7, 'E': 1}
}

# Function to display the weighted graph
def display_weighted_graph(g):
    for node, neighbors in g.items():
        neighbor_info = ", ".join([f"{neighbor}({weight})"
for neighbor, weight in neighbors.items()])
        print(f"{node}: {neighbor_info}")

print("\nWeighted Graph (Adjacency Dictionary):")
display_weighted_graph(weighted_graph)
```

Explanation:

- **Nested Dictionary:**
  Each node is a key, and its value is another dictionary that maps neighboring nodes to their edge weights.
- **Display Function:**
  The function constructs a string showing each neighbor along with its weight.

---

2. Using Lists for Graph Representation

Graphs can also be represented using lists, particularly when the nodes are labeled with integer indices. This approach is often used with adjacency matrices or lists.

Example: Graph as an Adjacency List Using Lists

python

```python
# Number of vertices
num_vertices = 4

# Create an empty adjacency list where each vertex has an
empty list of neighbors
graph_list = [[] for _ in range(num_vertices)]

# Function to add an edge in an undirected graph
def add_edge_list(adj_list, src, dest):
    adj_list[src].append(dest)
    adj_list[dest].append(src)
```

```
# Add some edges (using integer indices: 0, 1, 2, 3)
add_edge_list(graph_list, 0, 1)
add_edge_list(graph_list, 0, 2)
add_edge_list(graph_list, 1, 2)
add_edge_list(graph_list, 2, 3)

# Display the adjacency list
print("\nGraph Represented as an Adjacency List (Using
Lists):")
for index, neighbors in enumerate(graph_list):
    print(f"{index}: {neighbors}")
```

Explanation:

- **List of Lists:**
  The graph is represented as a list where the index represents the node, and the value is a list of adjacent nodes.
- **Edge Addition:**
  The `add_edge_list` function adds an edge between two nodes by updating both lists for an undirected graph.
- **Output:**
  Each index and its list of neighbors are printed.

---

3. Object-Oriented Graph Data Structures

For more complex projects, an object-oriented approach may be beneficial. This method uses classes to encapsulate the behavior and properties of graphs, nodes, and edges. Object-oriented design can make the code more modular, reusable, and easier to manage.

Example: Graph Class Using OOP

```python
python

class Node:
    def __init__(self, label):
        self.label = label
        self.neighbors = {}

    def add_neighbor(self, neighbor, weight=1):
        self.neighbors[neighbor] = weight

    def __str__(self):
```

```
            neighbor_str = ", ".join([f"{n.label}({w})" for n, w
in self.neighbors.items()])
        return f"{self.label}: {neighbor_str}"

class Graph:
    def __init__(self):
        self.nodes = {}

    def add_node(self, label):
        if label not in self.nodes:
            self.nodes[label] = Node(label)

    def add_edge(self, src_label, dest_label, weight=1):
        if src_label not in self.nodes:
            self.add_node(src_label)
        if dest_label not in self.nodes:
            self.add_node(dest_label)
        # Add edge in both directions for an undirected graph

self.nodes[src_label].add_neighbor(self.nodes[dest_label],
weight)

self.nodes[dest_label].add_neighbor(self.nodes[src_label],
weight)

    def display(self):
        for node in self.nodes.values():
            print(node)

# Create a graph instance and add nodes and edges
graph_obj = Graph()
graph_obj.add_edge('A', 'B', 5)
graph_obj.add_edge('A', 'C', 3)
graph_obj.add_edge('B', 'D', 2)
graph_obj.add_edge('C', 'D', 7)

print("\nGraph Represented with OOP:")
graph_obj.display()
```

Explanation:

- **Node Class:**
  Each Node instance holds a label and a dictionary of neighbors, where keys are neighboring node objects and values are weights.
- **Graph Class:**
  The Graph class manages a collection of nodes. It includes methods for adding nodes and edges and for displaying the graph.

- **Edge Addition:**
  The `add_edge` method ensures that nodes are created if they do not already exist and then updates both nodes' neighbor dictionaries.
- **Display Method:**
  The `display` method prints each node and its connected neighbors, showcasing the graph structure.

Comparison Table: Graph Data Structures in Python

Data Structure	Pros	Cons	Best Use Case
Dictionary (Adjacency List)	Flexible, efficient for sparse graphs, easy to add/remove edges	Edge existence check can be $O(d)O(d)O(d)$ where ddd is the node's degree	General-purpose graphs, weighted or unweighted
List (Adjacency List)	Simple implementation for graphs with integer labels	Less intuitive for graphs with non-integer labels	Graphs with consecutive integer nodes
Object-Oriented Approach	Modular, encapsulated behavior, easy to extend for complex operations	More overhead in code, can be more complex to implement	Large projects, graphs with rich metadata

Summary

Graph data structures in Python can be implemented using various methods, each with its own strengths and weaknesses.

- **Dictionaries** are versatile and particularly useful for representing both unweighted and weighted graphs using adjacency lists.
- **Lists** are simple and efficient when working with graphs whose nodes are indexed by integers.

- **Object-oriented designs** provide a robust framework for building more complex graph systems that require modularity and rich metadata.

By understanding these representations and their trade-offs, you can choose the most appropriate data structure for your graph-related tasks and projects. The examples and code provided here serve as a practical guide to help you implement and manipulate graphs effectively in Python.

2.5 Practical Exercises: Building Simple Graphs

In this section, we will work through a series of practical exercises designed to reinforce your understanding of graph theory fundamentals by building simple graphs in Python. These exercises will cover different types of graphs, such as undirected, directed, and weighted graphs, using various representations like dictionaries (adjacency lists) and lists. Each exercise includes complete code examples, detailed explanations, and, where appropriate, tables to summarize key concepts.

Exercise 1: Building an Undirected Graph Using an Adjacency List

Objective:
Create a simple undirected graph where each node is represented by a unique label and connected via an adjacency list. This exercise is ideal for understanding how nodes and edges are represented and manipulated.

Steps and Code:

1. **Initialize the Graph:**
   We start by creating an empty dictionary where keys will be node labels and values will be lists of adjacent nodes.
2. **Add Nodes and Edges:**
   Define a function to add nodes and another to add undirected edges between nodes.
3. **Display the Graph:**
   Write a function to iterate over the dictionary and print each node along with its neighbors.

python

```python
def create_graph():
    """
    Create an empty graph represented as an adjacency list
(dictionary).
    """
    return {}

def add_node(graph, node):
    """
    Add a node to the graph if it doesn't already exist.

    Parameters:
    - graph: The current graph (dictionary).
    - node: The node label to add.
    """
    if node not in graph:
        graph[node] = []

def add_edge(graph, node1, node2):
    """
    Add an undirected edge between node1 and node2.

    Parameters:
    - graph: The current graph (dictionary).
    - node1: The first node label.
    - node2: The second node label.
    """
    # Ensure both nodes exist in the graph
    add_node(graph, node1)
    add_node(graph, node2)

    # Add the edge (since the graph is undirected, add each
node to the other's list)
    graph[node1].append(node2)
    graph[node2].append(node1)

def display_graph(graph):
    """
    Display the graph: print each node and its list of
adjacent nodes.

    Parameters:
    - graph: The graph (dictionary) to display.
    """
    for node, neighbors in graph.items():
        print(f"{node}: {neighbors}")

# Exercise 1: Create and display an undirected graph
graph = create_graph()
add_edge(graph, 'A', 'B')
add_edge(graph, 'A', 'C')
```

```
add_edge(graph, 'B', 'D')
add_edge(graph, 'C', 'D')
add_edge(graph, 'D', 'E')

print("Exercise 1: Undirected Graph (Adjacency List)")
display_graph(graph)
```

Explanation:

- **Graph Initialization:**
  The `create_graph` function creates an empty dictionary to hold our graph.
- **Adding Nodes and Edges:**
  The `add_node` function ensures a node exists in the graph. The `add_edge` function adds an undirected edge by updating the list of neighbors for both nodes.
- **Displaying the Graph:**
  The `display_graph` function iterates over the graph and prints each node with its corresponding list of neighbors.

Exercise 2: Building a Weighted Graph

Objective:
Extend the undirected graph to include weights on edges. In this exercise, each edge will have an associated weight, which can represent distance, cost, or any other metric.

Steps and Code:

1. **Graph Representation:**
   Use a dictionary where each key is a node, and its value is another dictionary mapping neighboring nodes to their weights.
2. **Add Nodes and Weighted Edges:**
   Define functions to add nodes and weighted edges.
3. **Display the Weighted Graph:**
   Write a function to display each node with its neighbors and corresponding weights.

python

```
def create_weighted_graph():
```

```python
    """
    Create an empty weighted graph represented as an
adjacency dictionary.
    """
    return {}

def add_weighted_node(graph, node):
    """
    Add a node to the weighted graph if it doesn't already
exist.

    Parameters:
    - graph: The current weighted graph (dictionary).
    - node: The node label to add.
    """
    if node not in graph:
        graph[node] = {}

def add_weighted_edge(graph, node1, node2, weight):
    """
    Add a weighted undirected edge between node1 and node2.

    Parameters:
    - graph: The current weighted graph (dictionary).
    - node1: The first node label.
    - node2: The second node label.
    - weight: The weight of the edge.
    """
    add_weighted_node(graph, node1)
    add_weighted_node(graph, node2)

    graph[node1][node2] = weight
    graph[node2][node1] = weight  # For undirected graphs

def display_weighted_graph(graph):
    """
    Display the weighted graph: print each node and its
adjacent nodes with weights.

    Parameters:
    - graph: The weighted graph (dictionary) to display.
    """
    for node, neighbors in graph.items():
        neighbor_info = ", ".join([f"{neighbor}({weight})"
for neighbor, weight in neighbors.items()])
        print(f"{node}: {neighbor_info}")

# Exercise 2: Create and display a weighted graph
weighted_graph = create_weighted_graph()
add_weighted_edge(weighted_graph, 'A', 'B', 4)
add_weighted_edge(weighted_graph, 'A', 'C', 2)
```

```
add_weighted_edge(weighted_graph, 'B', 'D', 5)
add_weighted_edge(weighted_graph, 'C', 'D', 8)
add_weighted_edge(weighted_graph, 'D', 'E', 6)

print("\nExercise 2: Weighted Graph")
display_weighted_graph(weighted_graph)
```

Explanation:

- **Weighted Graph Initialization:**
  The `create_weighted_graph` function initializes an empty dictionary for the weighted graph.
- **Adding Weighted Edges:**
  The `add_weighted_edge` function updates the dictionary for both nodes, storing the edge weight.
- **Displaying the Graph:**
  The `display_weighted_graph` function prints each node with its neighbors, including the weights in parentheses.

Exercise 3: Building a Directed Graph

Objective:
Construct a directed graph where edges have a direction. This means that an edge from node A to node B does not imply an edge from node B to node A.

Steps and Code:

1. **Graph Representation:**
   Use a dictionary where keys are nodes, and values are lists of nodes to which there is a directed edge.
2. **Add Nodes and Directed Edges:**
   Create functions to add nodes and directed edges.
3. **Display the Directed Graph:**
   Write a function to display each node along with its outbound connections.

python

```
def create_directed_graph():
    """
    Create an empty directed graph represented as an
adjacency list (dictionary).
```

```python
    """
    return {}

def add_directed_node(graph, node):
    """
    Add a node to the directed graph if it doesn't already
exist.

    Parameters:
    - graph: The current directed graph (dictionary).
    - node: The node label to add.
    """
    if node not in graph:
        graph[node] = []

def add_directed_edge(graph, src, dest):
    """
    Add a directed edge from src to dest.

    Parameters:
    - graph: The current directed graph (dictionary).
    - src: The source node label.
    - dest: The destination node label.
    """
    add_directed_node(graph, src)
    add_directed_node(graph, dest)
    graph[src].append(dest)

def display_directed_graph(graph):
    """
    Display the directed graph: print each node and its list
of outbound nodes.

    Parameters:
    - graph: The directed graph (dictionary) to display.
    """
    for node, neighbors in graph.items():
        print(f"{node} -> {neighbors}")

# Exercise 3: Create and display a directed graph
directed_graph = create_directed_graph()
add_directed_edge(directed_graph, 'A', 'B')
add_directed_edge(directed_graph, 'A', 'C')
add_directed_edge(directed_graph, 'B', 'D')
add_directed_edge(directed_graph, 'C', 'D')
add_directed_edge(directed_graph, 'D', 'E')

print("\nExercise 3: Directed Graph")
display_directed_graph(directed_graph)
```

Explanation:

- **Directed Graph Initialization:**
  The `create_directed_graph` function initializes an empty dictionary for a directed graph.
- **Adding Directed Edges:**
  The `add_directed_edge` function ensures both source and destination nodes exist and adds an edge from the source node only.
- **Displaying the Graph:**
  The `display_directed_graph` function prints each node and its list of outbound (directed) neighbors.

Exercise 4: Visualizing Graphs Using NetworkX and Matplotlib

Objective:
Visualize a graph using the Python libraries `networkx` and `matplotlib` to better understand its structure. This exercise will take one of the previously built graphs and render it as a diagram.

Steps and Code:

1. **Install Required Libraries:**
   Ensure you have `networkx` and `matplotlib` installed.

   ```bash
   pip install networkx matplotlib
   ```

2. **Visualize an Undirected Graph:**
   Use `networkx` to create a graph from your adjacency list and then draw it using `matplotlib`.

```python
import networkx as nx
import matplotlib.pyplot as plt

def visualize_graph(graph):
    """
    Visualize an undirected graph using NetworkX and
Matplotlib.
```

```
    Parameters:
    - graph: An adjacency list representation of the graph
(dictionary).
    """
    G = nx.Graph()

    # Add nodes and edges from the dictionary
    for node, neighbors in graph.items():
        for neighbor in neighbors:
            G.add_edge(node, neighbor)

    # Draw the graph with a spring layout
    pos = nx.spring_layout(G)
    plt.figure(figsize=(6, 4))
    nx.draw(G, pos, with_labels=True, node_color='lightblue',
edge_color='gray', node_size=1500)
    plt.title("Graph Visualization")
    plt.show()

# Use the undirected graph from Exercise 1 for visualization
print("\nExercise 4: Visualizing the Undirected Graph")
visualize_graph(graph)
```

Explanation:

- **Graph Conversion:**
  The `visualize_graph` function converts the dictionary-based graph
  into a `networkx` graph by iterating through each node and its
  neighbors.
- **Graph Layout and Drawing:**
  The spring layout is used to position the nodes, and `nx.draw` renders
  the graph with labels, colors, and a title.
- **Visualization Outcome:**
  The graph appears as a visual diagram, making it easier to understand
  the structure and relationships between nodes.

Summary and Key Points

Exercise	Graph Type	Key Concepts Learned
Exercise 1	Undirected Graph	Building an adjacency list, adding nodes and undirected edges
Exercise 2	Weighted Graph	Incorporating edge weights using nested dictionaries

Exercise	Graph Type	Key Concepts Learned
Exercise 3	Directed Graph	Creating directed edges and understanding one-way relationships
Exercise 4	Graph Visualization	Converting a dictionary-based graph into a visual diagram using NetworkX and Matplotlib

Through these exercises, you have practiced building simple graphs in various forms. Each example reinforces fundamental graph data structures, preparing you for more advanced graph algorithms and applications later in this book.

By experimenting with these practical exercises, you can better understand how to represent, manipulate, and visualize graphs in Python—a crucial skill for many applications in computer science and data analysis.

Chapter 3: Introduction to Natural Language Processing (NLP)

3.1 NLP Fundamentals and Key Terminology

Natural Language Processing (NLP) is an interdisciplinary field that sits at the intersection of computer science, artificial intelligence, and linguistics. Its primary goal is to enable computers to understand, interpret, and generate human language in a meaningful way. In this section, we will cover the essential concepts and terminology that form the foundation of NLP. We will explain key tasks, techniques, and terms using clear definitions, illustrative tables, and practical code examples.

What is NLP?

At its core, NLP involves the interaction between computers and natural language. It encompasses a wide range of tasks, from simple text processing to complex language understanding. Some common applications include:

- **Machine Translation:** Converting text from one language to another.
- **Sentiment Analysis:** Determining the emotional tone behind a series of words.
- **Text Summarization:** Generating concise summaries of large documents.
- **Speech Recognition:** Converting spoken language into text.
- **Named Entity Recognition (NER):** Identifying and classifying key elements in text (such as names, dates, and locations).

Key Terminology in NLP

Understanding the fundamental terminology is crucial for anyone entering the field of NLP. Below is a table summarizing some of the most important terms and their definitions:

Term	Definition	Example
Tokenization	The process of breaking down text into individual words or tokens.	"Hello, world!" → ["Hello", ",", "world", "!"]
Stop Words	Commonly used words that are often filtered out before processing text.	"the", "is", "at", "which"
Stemming	Reducing words to their root form by removing suffixes.	"running", "runner" → "run"
Lemmatization	Reducing words to their base or dictionary form, considering the context.	"better" → "good"; "running" → "run"
Part-of-Speech (POS) Tagging	Assigning each token a grammatical category, such as noun, verb, adjective, etc.	"dog" (noun), "runs" (verb)
Named Entity Recognition (NER)	Identifying proper names or specific entities in text and classifying them into categories (person, location, etc.)	"Paris" → Location
Parsing	Analyzing the grammatical structure of sentences, often generating a parse tree.	Sentence structure analysis using dependency trees
Corpus	A large and structured set of texts used for statistical analysis and hypothesis testing in NLP.	The Brown Corpus, Wikipedia dump

Basic NLP Tasks and Techniques

1. **Text Preprocessing:**
   Before any analysis, raw text is usually preprocessed to remove noise and standardize the data. This may involve:
   - **Lowercasing:** Converting all text to lowercase to reduce variability.
   - **Tokenization:** Splitting text into words or sentences.
   - **Removing Punctuation and Special Characters:** Cleaning up the text.
   - **Stop Word Removal:** Eliminating common words that do not add significant meaning.

- o **Stemming or Lemmatization:** Converting words to their base forms.
2. **Feature Extraction:**
   After preprocessing, the next step is to extract features from the text. Common techniques include:
   - o **Bag-of-Words (BoW):** Representing text as a set of word counts.
   - o **TF-IDF (Term Frequency-Inverse Document Frequency):** Weighing words based on their importance.
   - o **Word Embeddings:** Mapping words into continuous vector spaces (e.g., Word2Vec, GloVe).
3. **Language Modeling and Parsing:**
   Language models predict the likelihood of a sequence of words and are used for applications like text generation. Parsing helps in understanding the structure of sentences.
4. **Named Entity Recognition (NER):**
   This task involves locating and classifying named entities in text into predefined categories such as names, organizations, dates, etc.

Practical Code Example: Text Preprocessing Using NLTK

Below is a complete and well-explained code example demonstrating basic text preprocessing using the Natural Language Toolkit (NLTK) library in Python.

```python
import nltk
from nltk.tokenize import word_tokenize, sent_tokenize
from nltk.corpus import stopwords
from nltk.stem import PorterStemmer, WordNetLemmatizer
import string

# Ensure necessary NLTK data is downloaded
nltk.download('punkt')
nltk.download('stopwords')
nltk.download('wordnet')

# Sample text for processing
text = "Natural Language Processing is an exciting field! It
combines computer science and linguistics."

# 1. Sentence Tokenization: Split text into sentences
```

```
sentences = sent_tokenize(text)
print("Sentences:")
print(sentences)

# 2. Word Tokenization: Split each sentence into words
words = word_tokenize(text)
print("\nWords:")
print(words)

# 3. Convert to lowercase and remove punctuation
words_cleaned = [word.lower() for word in words if word not
in string.punctuation]
print("\nCleaned Words (lowercase, no punctuation):")
print(words_cleaned)

# 4. Remove stop words
stop_words = set(stopwords.words('english'))
words_filtered = [word for word in words_cleaned if word not
in stop_words]
print("\nFiltered Words (stop words removed):")
print(words_filtered)

# 5. Stemming: Reduce words to their root form
ps = PorterStemmer()
words_stemmed = [ps.stem(word) for word in words_filtered]
print("\nStemmed Words:")
print(words_stemmed)

# 6. Lemmatization: Convert words to their dictionary form
lemmatizer = WordNetLemmatizer()
words_lemmatized = [lemmatizer.lemmatize(word) for word in
words_filtered]
print("\nLemmatized Words:")
print(words_lemmatized)
```

Explanation:

- **Sentence and Word Tokenization:**
  The text is first split into sentences using `sent_tokenize` and then into words using `word_tokenize`.
- **Cleaning and Lowercasing:**
  We convert all words to lowercase and remove punctuation using a list comprehension.
- **Stop Word Removal:**
  Common words that do not carry significant meaning are filtered out.
- **Stemming and Lemmatization:**
  The code demonstrates both stemming (using `PorterStemmer`) and

lemmatization (using `WordNetLemmatizer`) to reduce words to their base forms.

This example provides a hands-on look at the initial steps involved in processing text data, a critical foundation for any NLP project.

Summary

In this section, we covered the fundamental concepts and key terminology of NLP. We introduced the main tasks such as text preprocessing, tokenization, stop word removal, stemming, lemmatization, and parsing. A detailed table summarized important NLP terms, and a practical code example demonstrated how these techniques are applied in Python using the NLTK library.

By understanding these fundamentals, you are now equipped with the basic building blocks of NLP, setting the stage for more advanced topics such as language modeling, semantic analysis, and the integration of NLP with graph-based methods in later chapters.

3.2 Overview of Language Models and Their Evolution

Language models are at the heart of modern Natural Language Processing (NLP). They are designed to understand, generate, and manipulate human language by predicting the likelihood of a sequence of words. Over the years, language models have evolved dramatically, from simple statistical methods to complex deep learning architectures that power many of today's cutting-edge applications.

Early Language Models: N-gram Models

N-gram models are among the earliest language models. They work by predicting the next word in a sentence based on the previous $n-1n-1n-1$ words. For example, a bigram model ($n=2n=2n=2$) predicts the next word based solely on the current word, while a trigram model ($n=3n=3n=3$) considers the two preceding words.

Advantages:

- **Simplicity:** Easy to understand and implement.
- **Data-Driven:** Uses frequency counts from a corpus to estimate probabilities.

Limitations:

- **Context Window:** Limited to fixed-length context; cannot capture long-range dependencies.
- **Data Sparsity:** Requires large amounts of data to get reliable estimates, and many valid word sequences may not appear in the training corpus.

Neural Language Models: RNNs and LSTMs

With the advent of neural networks, language models began to incorporate more sophisticated architectures. **Recurrent Neural Networks (RNNs)** were among the first neural approaches. RNNs are designed to handle sequences by maintaining a hidden state that captures information from previous inputs.

Challenges with RNNs:

- **Vanishing/Exploding Gradients:** Difficulty in training over long sequences.
- **Limited Memory:** Struggle with long-range dependencies.

To address these issues, **Long Short-Term Memory (LSTM)** networks were developed. LSTMs include special gates that regulate the flow of information, making them capable of capturing longer contexts.

Advantages of LSTMs:

- **Improved Memory:** Better at retaining long-term dependencies compared to standard RNNs.
- **Flexibility:** Widely used in tasks like language translation, text generation, and more.

Transformers and the Modern Era

A significant breakthrough came with the introduction of the **Transformer** architecture in 2017. Transformers rely entirely on self-attention mechanisms to process input data in parallel, which allows them to capture dependencies regardless of their distance in the sequence.

Key Features of Transformers:

- **Self-Attention:** Allows the model to weigh the importance of different words in a sentence.
- **Parallel Processing:** Unlike RNNs, transformers can process all words simultaneously, significantly speeding up training.
- **Scalability:** Can be scaled to create very large models that perform exceptionally well on a wide range of tasks.

Notable Transformer-Based Models:

- **BERT (Bidirectional Encoder Representations from Transformers):** Focuses on understanding the context of words by considering both left and right contexts simultaneously.
- **GPT (Generative Pre-trained Transformer):** Excels at generating coherent and contextually relevant text, and is widely used in text generation tasks.
- **T5 (Text-to-Text Transfer Transformer):** Reformulates NLP tasks into a text-to-text format, making it highly versatile.

Table: Evolution of Language Models

Model Type	Architecture	Strengths	Limitations
N-gram Models	Statistical (fixed context)	Simple, interpretable	Limited context, data sparsity issues
RNNs	Recurrent Neural Networks	Captures sequence information	Struggles with long sequences
LSTMs	Enhanced RNN with memory gates	Better long-range dependency modeling	Computationally intensive for very long texts

Model Type	Architecture	Strengths	Limitations
Transformers	Self-Attention Mechanisms	Parallel processing, scalable, captures global context	Requires large datasets and high computational power

Practical Example: Text Generation with a Transformer

Below is a complete code example that demonstrates text generation using a pre-trained GPT model from the Hugging Face Transformers library. This example illustrates the power and ease-of-use of modern language models.

```python
# Import necessary libraries from Hugging Face Transformers
from transformers import pipeline

# Initialize the text generation pipeline with a pre-trained
GPT model
generator = pipeline('text-generation', model='gpt2')

# Generate text based on a prompt
prompt = "The future of AI in natural language processing is"
generated_text = generator(prompt, max_length=50,
num_return_sequences=1)

# Display the generated text
print("Generated Text:")
print(generated_text[0]['generated_text'])
```

Explanation:

- **Pipeline Initialization:**
  The `pipeline` function from Hugging Face initializes a text generation pipeline using the pre-trained GPT-2 model.
- **Text Generation:**
  The model generates text based on the prompt, with a maximum length of 50 tokens.
- **Output:**
  The generated text is printed, showcasing how modern language models can produce coherent and contextually appropriate language.

Summary

The evolution of language models reflects a journey from simple statistical methods to advanced deep learning architectures. Early models like n-grams laid the groundwork with basic probability estimates, while neural models like RNNs and LSTMs advanced the field by capturing sequential dependencies more effectively. The Transformer architecture revolutionized NLP by enabling parallel processing and more robust handling of long-range dependencies, leading to models like BERT and GPT that dominate modern NLP applications.

Understanding this evolution is crucial as it provides context for the current state of NLP and sets the stage for exploring more complex applications and integrations with graph-based methods later in this book.

3.3 Integrating NLP with Graph-Based Workflows

Integrating NLP with graph-based workflows brings together the strengths of two powerful paradigms: the ability of NLP to interpret, analyze, and generate human language, and the flexibility of graph structures to model complex relationships and processes. This integration enables the creation of systems that can not only understand language but also process it in a structured, dynamic, and interconnected manner.

Why Integrate NLP with Graph-Based Workflows?

Enhanced Data Flow and Modular Design:
Graph-based workflows allow you to decompose complex processes into smaller, manageable components (nodes) that can each handle specific NLP tasks. This modularity makes it easier to update, debug, and scale parts of the system.

Flexible and Dynamic Pipelines:
By representing the NLP pipeline as a graph, you can design workflows that adapt dynamically based on the content and context of the text. For example, different nodes might be activated depending on the detected language, sentiment, or topic.

Improved Interpretability and Debugging:
Visualizing the NLP workflow as a graph helps in understanding how data flows through the system. This clarity aids in diagnosing issues, optimizing performance, and ensuring that each component of the pipeline is functioning as expected.

Components of a Graph-Based NLP Workflow

A typical graph-based NLP workflow might consist of the following components:

1. **Input Node:**
   Captures the raw text data from various sources (e.g., user input, documents, social media feeds).
2. **Preprocessing Nodes:**
   These nodes handle tasks such as tokenization, lowercasing, stop word removal, stemming, and lemmatization. They prepare the text for further analysis.
3. **Feature Extraction and Analysis Nodes:**
   Nodes in this stage may compute TF-IDF scores, generate word embeddings, or perform sentiment analysis. They extract meaningful features from the text.
4. **Task-Specific Nodes:**
   Depending on the application, nodes may perform named entity recognition (NER), part-of-speech (POS) tagging, text summarization, or translation.
5. **Decision Nodes:**
   These nodes determine the subsequent path of the workflow. For instance, if sentiment analysis detects negative sentiment, the workflow might branch into a customer support escalation process.
6. **Output Node:**
   Aggregates the results from the various processing nodes and produces a final output, such as a report, a response message, or a visual dashboard.

Table: Example Components of an NLP Graph Workflow

Component	Function	Example Task
Input Node	Receives and initiates processing of raw text data	Collecting social media posts
Preprocessing Node	Cleans and tokenizes text	Tokenization, stop word removal
Feature Extraction Node	Derives meaningful features from text	TF-IDF computation, word embeddings
Analysis Node	Performs NLP tasks to extract insights	Sentiment analysis, NER
Decision Node	Routes workflow based on analysis results	Directing negative reviews to support team
Output Node	Consolidates and presents final results	Generating a summary report

Example: Building a Graph-Based NLP Workflow

Below is a comprehensive code example that demonstrates how to integrate NLP with a graph-based workflow using Python. In this example, we use a simplified version of a workflow framework where each node performs a specific NLP task. We will illustrate a workflow that:

1. **Receives input text.**
2. **Preprocesses the text (tokenization and cleaning).**
3. **Performs sentiment analysis.**
4. **Generates a final response based on the sentiment.**

```python
# Import necessary libraries
import nltk
from nltk.tokenize import word_tokenize
from nltk.corpus import stopwords
from transformers import pipeline
import string

# Ensure NLTK data is downloaded
nltk.download('punkt')
nltk.download('stopwords')
```

```python
# Define base Node class for the workflow
class Node:
    def __init__(self, name):
        self.name = name
        self.next_nodes = []

    def add_next(self, node):
        self.next_nodes.append(node)

    def run(self, data):
        raise NotImplementedError("Each node must implement
the run method.")

# Input Node: Receives raw text input
class InputNode(Node):
    def run(self, data=None):
        text = "I love the new features of this product, but
the battery life could be better."
        print(f"[{self.name}] Input Text: {text}")
        # Pass the raw text to the next nodes
        for node in self.next_nodes:
            node.run(text)

# Preprocessing Node: Tokenizes text, lowercases it, and
removes punctuation and stop words
class PreprocessingNode(Node):
    def run(self, data):
        # Tokenize the text
        tokens = word_tokenize(data)
        # Lowercase and remove punctuation
        tokens = [token.lower() for token in tokens if token
not in string.punctuation]
        # Remove stop words
        stop_words = set(stopwords.words('english'))
        filtered_tokens = [token for token in tokens if token
not in stop_words]
        processed_text = " ".join(filtered_tokens)
        print(f"[{self.name}] Processed Text:
{processed_text}")
        for node in self.next_nodes:
            node.run(processed_text)

# Sentiment Analysis Node: Analyzes the sentiment of the text
class SentimentAnalysisNode(Node):
    def __init__(self, name):
        super().__init__(name)
        # Initialize the sentiment analysis pipeline from
Hugging Face Transformers
        self.analyzer = pipeline("sentiment-analysis")

    def run(self, data):
```

```
        result = self.analyzer(data)
        sentiment = result[0]['label']
        score = result[0]['score']
        print(f"[{self.name}] Sentiment: {sentiment} (Score:
{score:.2f})")
        for node in self.next_nodes:
            node.run(sentiment)

# Decision Node: Generates a response based on the sentiment
class DecisionNode(Node):
    def run(self, data):
        if data == "NEGATIVE":
            response = "We are sorry to hear that. Our
support team will reach out to assist you."
        else:
            response = "Thank you for your positive
feedback!"
        print(f"[{self.name}] Final Response: {response}")

# Build the graph-based workflow
input_node = InputNode("InputNode")
preprocessing_node = PreprocessingNode("PreprocessingNode")
sentiment_node =
SentimentAnalysisNode("SentimentAnalysisNode")
decision_node = DecisionNode("DecisionNode")

# Connect the nodes to form the workflow
input_node.add_next(preprocessing_node)
preprocessing_node.add_next(sentiment_node)
sentiment_node.add_next(decision_node)

# Execute the workflow starting from the Input Node
print("Starting Graph-Based NLP Workflow...\n")
input_node.run()
```

Explanation:

- **Node Structure:**
  A base `Node` class is defined, and each node type (Input,
  Preprocessing, Sentiment Analysis, Decision) inherits from this base
  class and implements its own `run` method.
- **Input Node:**
  The `InputNode` simulates receiving raw text input. In a real-world
  application, this might come from a user interface or a file.
- **Preprocessing Node:**
  The `PreprocessingNode` tokenizes the text, converts it to lowercase,
  and removes punctuation and stop words. It then passes the cleaned
  text to the next node.

- **Sentiment Analysis Node:**
  The `SentimentAnalysisNode` utilizes a pre-trained transformer model (via the Hugging Face pipeline) to determine the sentiment of the text. It then passes the sentiment label onward.
- **Decision Node:**
  Based on the sentiment label received, the `DecisionNode` generates a final response. For negative sentiment, it triggers a support response; for positive sentiment, it thanks the user.
- **Workflow Execution:**
  Nodes are connected in a graph-like structure, and execution begins at the `InputNode`, which triggers the entire chain of processing.

Summary

Integrating NLP with graph-based workflows allows for the creation of dynamic, modular, and scalable systems that process text intelligently. By decomposing an NLP pipeline into discrete nodes—each handling tasks such as input processing, text cleaning, sentiment analysis, and decision-making—developers can build systems that are both flexible and easy to maintain. The example provided demonstrates how such a workflow can be implemented in Python, combining tools from NLTK and the Hugging Face Transformers library to process and analyze text.

This approach not only improves clarity and debugging but also lays a solid foundation for developing more complex systems where multiple NLP tasks interact within a graph-based framework. As you continue to explore this book, you will encounter more sophisticated applications that build upon these fundamental concepts.

3.4 Tools and Libraries in the NLP Ecosystem

The NLP ecosystem today is rich with tools and libraries that simplify the process of developing, testing, and deploying natural language processing applications. These resources cover a wide range of functionalities—from basic text preprocessing to complex tasks such as sentiment analysis, machine translation, and language generation. In this section, we will explore some of the most widely used tools and libraries in NLP, discussing their key features, use cases, and providing practical code examples to demonstrate their capabilities.

Popular NLP Libraries and Their Features

1. **NLTK (Natural Language Toolkit)**
   o **Overview:**
   NLTK is one of the earliest and most comprehensive libraries for NLP in Python. It provides a wealth of resources for text processing tasks such as tokenization, stemming, lemmatization, parsing, and corpus management.
   o **Key Features:**
     ▪ Extensive collection of corpora and lexical resources.
     ▪ Built-in algorithms for classification, clustering, and parsing.
     ▪ Educational resources and documentation, making it ideal for beginners.
   o **Use Cases:**
   Prototyping and teaching, basic NLP tasks, and research projects.

2. **spaCy**
   o **Overview:**
   spaCy is a modern, high-performance NLP library designed for production use. It offers fast and efficient processing for tasks such as tokenization, POS tagging, named entity recognition (NER), and dependency parsing.
   o **Key Features:**
     ▪ Pre-trained models for multiple languages.
     ▪ Industrial-strength performance and scalability.
     ▪ Easy integration with deep learning frameworks.
   o **Use Cases:**
   Real-time text processing, large-scale information extraction, and advanced NLP applications.

3. **Hugging Face Transformers**
   o **Overview:**
   The Transformers library by Hugging Face provides state-of-the-art pre-trained models for a variety of NLP tasks, including text generation, summarization, translation, and question answering. These models are based on architectures like BERT, GPT, and T5.
   o **Key Features:**
     ▪ A large repository of pre-trained models.
     ▪ Simplified APIs for inference and fine-tuning.

- Support for both TensorFlow and PyTorch.
  - **Use Cases:**
  Building cutting-edge NLP applications, research, and fine-tuning models for domain-specific tasks.
4. **Gensim**
   - **Overview:**
   Gensim is a library focused on topic modeling and document similarity analysis using unsupervised algorithms. It is particularly well-known for its implementation of Word2Vec and other vector space models.
   - **Key Features:**
     - Efficient and scalable for large text corpora.
     - Supports various topic modeling techniques such as Latent Dirichlet Allocation (LDA).
     - Provides tools for document similarity and clustering.
   - **Use Cases:**
   Topic extraction, document similarity analysis, and semantic search applications.
5. **Stanford CoreNLP**
   - **Overview:**
   Stanford CoreNLP is a robust NLP toolkit developed by Stanford University. It provides a comprehensive suite of tools for linguistic analysis, including tokenization, POS tagging, parsing, and sentiment analysis.
   - **Key Features:**
     - High accuracy and well-tested algorithms.
     - Support for multiple languages.
     - Available as a Java library, with Python wrappers available.
   - **Use Cases:**
   Academic research, large-scale linguistic analysis, and integration with Java-based systems.

Comparison Table: Key NLP Tools

Library/Tool	Language	Key Capabilities	Ideal Use Cases
NLTK	Python	Tokenization, stemming,	Education, prototyping, research

Library/Tool	Language	Key Capabilities	Ideal Use Cases
		lemmatization, parsing, corpora	
spaCy	Python	Fast tokenization, NER, POS tagging, dependency parsing	Production-grade applications, real-time processing
Hugging Face Transformers	Python	Pre-trained models for text generation, translation, summarization, QA	Cutting-edge NLP, fine-tuning, research
Gensim	Python	Topic modeling, document similarity, Word2Vec	Topic extraction, semantic search
Stanford CoreNLP	Java (with Python wrappers)	Comprehensive linguistic analysis, sentiment analysis, parsing	Academic research, multi-language processing

Practical Code Examples

Example 1: Basic Text Preprocessing with NLTK

```python
import nltk
from nltk.tokenize import word_tokenize, sent_tokenize
from nltk.corpus import stopwords
from nltk.stem import PorterStemmer
import string

# Ensure necessary NLTK data is downloaded
nltk.download('punkt')
nltk.download('stopwords')

text = "Natural Language Processing enables computers to
understand human language. It's fascinating!"

# Sentence Tokenization
sentences = sent_tokenize(text)
print("Sentences:", sentences)

# Word Tokenization
words = word_tokenize(text)
```

```
print("\nWords:", words)

# Remove punctuation and convert to lowercase
words_cleaned = [word.lower() for word in words if word not
in string.punctuation]
print("\nCleaned Words:", words_cleaned)

# Remove stop words
stop_words = set(stopwords.words('english'))
filtered_words = [word for word in words_cleaned if word not
in stop_words]
print("\nFiltered Words:", filtered_words)

# Stemming using PorterStemmer
ps = PorterStemmer()
stemmed_words = [ps.stem(word) for word in filtered_words]
print("\nStemmed Words:", stemmed_words)
```

Explanation:

- **Tokenization:** Splits the text into sentences and words.
- **Cleaning:** Converts words to lowercase and removes punctuation.
- **Stop Word Removal:** Filters out common words that add little value.
- **Stemming:** Reduces words to their root forms.

Example 2: Named Entity Recognition with spaCy

```python
import spacy

# Load the spaCy English model
nlp = spacy.load("en_core_web_sm")

text = "Apple is looking at buying U.K. startup for $1
billion."

# Process the text
doc = nlp(text)

# Print named entities
print("Named Entities:")
for ent in doc.ents:
    print(f"{ent.text} ({ent.label_})")
```

Explanation:

- **Model Loading:** The `en_core_web_sm` model is loaded for English.
- **Entity Extraction:** The text is processed, and entities such as organizations, locations, and monetary values are identified and printed.

Example 3: Text Generation with Hugging Face Transformers

```python
from transformers import pipeline

# Initialize text generation pipeline using a pre-trained
GPT-2 model
generator = pipeline("text-generation", model="gpt2")

prompt = "In the future, artificial intelligence will"
generated_text = generator(prompt, max_length=50,
num_return_sequences=1)

print("Generated Text:")
print(generated_text[0]['generated_text'])
```

Explanation:

- **Pipeline Initialization:** A text generation pipeline is created using GPT-2.
- **Text Generation:** The model generates text based on the prompt, illustrating the capabilities of modern language models.

Summary

The NLP ecosystem is supported by a diverse array of tools and libraries, each catering to different aspects of natural language processing. Whether you are just starting out or building complex, production-grade applications, there is a tool to meet your needs. In this section, we explored:

- **NLTK** for basic text processing and educational purposes.
- **spaCy** for high-performance NLP tasks in production environments.
- **Hugging Face Transformers** for state-of-the-art model applications.
- **Gensim** for topic modeling and semantic analysis.
- **Stanford CoreNLP** for comprehensive linguistic analysis.

By understanding the strengths and use cases of each library, you can select the most appropriate tools for your NLP projects. The provided code examples serve as practical demonstrations, ensuring you can implement these techniques effectively in your own work.

Part II: Diving into LangGraph Python

Chapter 4: Getting Started with LangGraph Python

4.1 Installation and Environment Setup

Before you can begin using LangGraph Python, it's important to set up your development environment correctly. In this section, we will guide you through the process of installing LangGraph Python, along with its dependencies, and configuring your environment for smooth development. This setup will ensure that you can follow along with the examples in this book and develop your own graph-based NLP applications without any issues.

Prerequisites

Before installing LangGraph Python, ensure you have the following:

- **Python 3.7 or Higher:**
  LangGraph Python is designed to work with Python 3.7 and above. You can check your Python version by running:

  ```bash
  python --version
  ```

- **Pip:**
  Pip is the package installer for Python. It is usually included with Python 3. If not, you can install it following the official guide.
- **Virtual Environment (Recommended):**
  It is best practice to use a virtual environment to manage dependencies for your projects. Tools such as `venv` (built into Python) or `conda` (from Anaconda) are excellent choices.

Step-by-Step Installation Guide

Step 1: Setting Up a Virtual Environment

Using a virtual environment ensures that dependencies for different projects remain isolated. Here's how to create and activate a virtual environment using Python's built-in `venv`:

1. **Create a Virtual Environment:**

   ```bash
   python -m venv langgraph-env
   ```

   This command creates a new directory called `langgraph-env` that contains the virtual environment.

2. **Activate the Virtual Environment:**
   - **On Windows:**

     ```bash
     langgraph-env\Scripts\activate
     ```

   - **On macOS and Linux:**

     ```bash
     source langgraph-env/bin/activate
     ```

3. Once activated, your terminal prompt will change to indicate that you are now working within the virtual environment.

Step 2: Installing LangGraph Python

With your virtual environment active, install LangGraph Python using pip. If LangGraph Python is available on PyPI, you can install it with the following command:

```bash
pip install langgraph
```

If the package is hosted on a repository (for example, GitHub), you might need to install it using:

```bash
bash
```

```bash
pip install git+https://github.com/yourusername/langgraph-python.git
```

Note: Replace the URL with the actual repository URL if necessary.

Step 3: Installing Additional Dependencies

LangGraph Python may depend on other libraries for graph visualization and NLP tasks. Common dependencies might include:

- **NetworkX:** For creating and manipulating graphs.
- **Matplotlib:** For visualizing graphs.
- **Transformers:** For NLP models.
- **NLTK or spaCy:** For text processing.

Install these dependencies using pip:

```bash
bash
```

```bash
pip install networkx matplotlib transformers nltk spacy
```

You may also need to download language models or corpora. For instance, to download the spaCy English model:

```bash
bash
```

```bash
python -m spacy download en_core_web_sm
```

And for NLTK, download the required datasets within your Python script or interactively:

```python
python
```

```python
import nltk
nltk.download('punkt')
nltk.download('stopwords')
```

Verifying the Installation

To ensure that everything is installed correctly, create a simple Python script called `test_langgraph.py` with the following content:

python

```python
# test_langgraph.py

from langgraph import Node, GraphManager

# Define a simple node class for demonstration
class PrintNode(Node):
    def __init__(self, message):
        super().__init__()
        self.message = message

    def run(self, data=None):
        print(f"PrintNode Output: {self.message}")
        return data

# Create nodes
node1 = PrintNode("Hello from LangGraph Python!")
node2 = PrintNode("This is a test node.")

# Instantiate the GraphManager and add nodes
graph_manager = GraphManager()
graph_manager.add_node("start", node1)
graph_manager.add_node("next", node2)

# Connect nodes to form a simple workflow
graph_manager.connect("start", "next")

# Run the workflow starting at the 'start' node
graph_manager.run("start")
```

Run the script from your terminal:

bash

```bash
python test_langgraph.py
```

If everything is set up correctly, you should see output similar to:

csharp

```csharp
PrintNode Output: Hello from LangGraph Python!
PrintNode Output: This is a test node.
```

Environment Setup Summary Table

Step	Command/Action	Purpose
Check Python Version	`python --version`	Ensure Python 3.7+ is installed
Create Virtual Environment	`python -m venv langgraph-env`	Isolate project dependencies
Activate Virtual Environment	`source langgraph-env/bin/activate` (macOS/Linux) or `langgraph-env\Scripts\activate` (Windows)	Activate the virtual environment
Install LangGraph Python	`pip install langgraph` or `pip install git+https://github.com/yourusername/langgraph-python.git`	Install LangGraph Python package
Install Additional Libraries	`pip install networkx matplotlib transformers nltk spacy`	Install required dependencies for graphs and NLP
Download Language Models/Datasets	`python -m spacy download en_core_web_sm` and `nltk.download('punkt')`	Ensure necessary NLP resources are available
Test Installation	Run a test script (`python test_langgraph.py`)	Verify that LangGraph Python and its dependenc

Step	Command/Action	Purpose
		ies work correctly

Setting up your environment correctly is the first step toward building robust and scalable NLP applications using LangGraph Python. By following the instructions above, you ensure that you have a clean, isolated workspace with all the necessary tools and libraries at your disposal. With this setup, you are now ready to dive deeper into LangGraph Python and explore its powerful features in constructing graph-based NLP workflows.

4.2 Core Architecture and Components

LangGraph Python is built on a modular architecture that seamlessly integrates graph theory concepts with the flexibility of Python programming. This design allows developers to create, manage, and execute complex workflows where each component of the process is encapsulated as a node in a graph. In this section, we will detail the core components of LangGraph Python, explain how they interact, and provide complete code examples and tables to illustrate the architecture.

1. Overview of the Architecture

At its heart, LangGraph Python divides a workflow into a collection of nodes and edges:

- **Nodes:**
  Represent discrete processing units. Each node performs a specific task, such as data input, text preprocessing, sentiment analysis, or output generation. Nodes are designed to be modular and reusable, making it easy to update or replace a component without affecting the entire workflow.
- **Edges:**
  Define the connections and data flow between nodes. An edge indicates that the output from one node becomes the input to another, establishing a clear and manageable sequence of operations.
- **Graph Manager:**
  Acts as the orchestrator of the workflow. It is responsible for

managing nodes, establishing connections between them, and executing the workflow in a controlled manner. The Graph Manager abstracts the complexity of workflow execution, enabling developers to focus on designing the process rather than handling low-level execution details.

---

2. Core Components

Below is an in-depth look at the key components of LangGraph Python.

a. Node Class

Each node in LangGraph Python is an instance of a class that inherits from a base `Node` class. This base class provides the structure and common functionality that all nodes share.

Key Attributes and Methods:

- **Attributes:**
    - `name`: A unique identifier for the node.
    - `next_nodes`: A list of nodes that should be executed after the current node.
- **Methods:**
    - `run(data)`: The method where the node's main functionality is implemented. It takes input data, processes it, and then passes the output to the next nodes.

Example Code:

python

```python
class Node:
    def __init__(self, name):
        self.name = name
        self.next_nodes = []

    def add_next(self, node):
        """
        Connects this node to the next node in the workflow.
        """
        self.next_nodes.append(node)
```

```
def run(self, data):
    """
    The run method must be overridden by each subclass to implement
    its specific functionality.
    """
    raise NotImplementedError("Subclasses must implement this method.")
```

Explanation:

- **Modularity:**
  The Node class is designed to be extended. Developers create custom nodes by subclassing Node and implementing the run method.
- **Connectivity:**
  The add_next method allows nodes to be linked together, forming the workflow graph.

---

b. Graph Manager

The Graph Manager is the central component that oversees the entire workflow. It is responsible for:

- Storing a registry of nodes.
- Creating connections (edges) between nodes.
- Initiating and controlling the execution of the workflow.

Key Attributes and Methods:

- **Attributes:**
  - nodes: A dictionary that maps node names to node instances.
- **Methods:**
  - add_node(name, node): Adds a node to the registry.
  - connect(source, destination): Establishes an edge from the source node to the destination node.
  - run(start_node, data=None): Initiates the workflow execution from the specified start node.

Example Code:

python

```python
class GraphManager:
    def __init__(self):
        self.nodes = {}

    def add_node(self, name, node):
        """
        Adds a node to the workflow.
        """
        self.nodes[name] = node

    def connect(self, source_name, destination_name):
        """
        Connects two nodes by name, indicating that the
        output of the source node
        will be passed to the destination node.
        """
        source_node = self.nodes.get(source_name)
        destination_node = self.nodes.get(destination_name)
        if source_node and destination_node:
            source_node.add_next(destination_node)
        else:
            raise ValueError("One or both nodes not found in
the graph.")

    def run(self, start_node_name, data=None):
        """
        Begins executing the workflow starting from the node
specified by start_node_name.
        """
        start_node = self.nodes.get(start_node_name)
        if start_node:
            start_node.run(data)
        else:
            raise ValueError("Start node not found in the
graph.")
```

Explanation:

- **Centralized Control:**
  The Graph Manager simplifies the execution of complex workflows
  by managing nodes and connections in one place.
- **Error Handling:**
  It includes error checking to ensure that nodes are properly connected
  and exist in the graph.

c. Specialized Nodes

In a typical workflow, nodes perform specific tasks such as data input, processing, and output. Here are examples of specialized nodes:

1. **Input Node:**
   Captures and supplies the initial data to the workflow.
2. **Processing Node:**
   Executes an NLP or data processing task.
3. **Output Node:**
   Consolidates the results and generates final output.

Example: Custom Print Node

python

```python
class PrintNode(Node):
    def __init__(self, name, message):
        super().__init__(name)
        self.message = message

    def run(self, data=None):
        """
        Prints a custom message and passes control to the
next nodes.
        """
        print(f"[{self.name}] {self.message}")
        # Pass data to each of the next nodes
        for node in self.next_nodes:
            node.run(data)
```

Explanation:

- **Custom Behavior:**
  The `PrintNode` subclass demonstrates how to implement a custom task—in this case, printing a message.
- **Workflow Propagation:**
  After processing, it forwards the data to its connected nodes.

---

3. Architecture Diagram

Below is a simplified diagram of LangGraph Python's core architecture:

pgsql

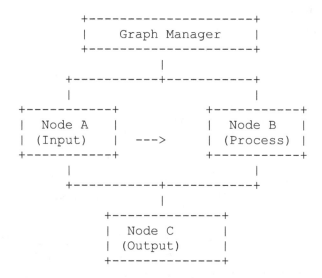

Explanation:

- **Nodes A, B, and C:**
  Represent various stages of a workflow. Node A could be an input node, Node B a processing node, and Node C an output node.
- **Graph Manager:**
  Orchestrates the connections and execution flow between nodes.

---

4. Summary Table

Component	Purpose	Key Methods/Attributes
Node Class	Base class for all workflow nodes	`run()`, `add_next()`, `name`, `next_nodes`
Graph Manager	Central orchestrator for managing nodes and execution	`add_node()`, `connect()`, `run()`, `nodes`
Specialized Nodes	Perform specific tasks (input, processing, output)	Custom implementations like `PrintNode`

The core architecture of LangGraph Python is designed to provide a flexible and modular framework for constructing graph-based workflows. By abstracting functionality into discrete nodes and managing these nodes through a centralized Graph Manager, the framework allows developers to build, modify, and extend complex processes with ease.

This modular design not only simplifies development but also enhances maintainability and scalability, making LangGraph Python an ideal tool for integrating graph-based processing with NLP and other data-driven applications.

4.3 Writing Your First LangGraph Application

In this section, we will guide you through creating your very first LangGraph application. This hands-on example will demonstrate how to combine the core components of LangGraph Python—nodes, edges, and the Graph Manager—to create a simple, yet fully functional, workflow. By the end of this section, you will understand how to build a modular application that processes data through a series of connected nodes.

Overview of the Application

Our sample application is designed to simulate a simple text-processing pipeline. The workflow consists of the following steps:

1. **Input Stage:**
   An Input Node that provides the raw text.
2. **Processing Stage:**
   A Preprocessing Node that cleans and tokenizes the text.
3. **Output Stage:**
   A Print Node that displays the final processed text.

The workflow will be orchestrated by the Graph Manager, which manages the nodes, establishes the connections (edges) between them, and executes the workflow.

Step 1: Define Custom Nodes

First, we need to define our custom nodes by extending the base `Node` class. Each node will implement its own `run` method to perform a specific task.

Code Example:

python

```python
# Define the base Node class (if not already defined)
class Node:
    def __init__(self, name):
        self.name = name
        self.next_nodes = []

    def add_next(self, node):
        """
        Connects this node to the next node in the workflow.
        """
        self.next_nodes.append(node)

    def run(self, data):
        """
        The run method must be overridden by each subclass to implement
        its specific functionality.
        """
        raise NotImplementedError("Subclasses must implement the run method.")

# Define an Input Node that supplies raw text
class InputNode(Node):
    def run(self, data=None):
        # In a real-world scenario, this might come from a file or user input.
        raw_text = "LangGraph Python makes creating graph-based workflows simple and powerful."
        print(f"[{self.name}] Raw Input: {raw_text}")
        # Pass the raw text to the next node
        for node in self.next_nodes:
            node.run(raw_text)

# Define a Preprocessing Node to tokenize and clean text
class PreprocessingNode(Node):
    def run(self, data):
        # For simplicity, we simulate tokenization by splitting on spaces.
        tokens = data.split()
        # Convert tokens to lowercase
```

```
        processed_tokens = [token.lower() for token in
tokens]
        processed_text = " ".join(processed_tokens)
        print(f"[{self.name}] Processed Text:
{processed_text}")
        # Pass the processed text to the next node
        for node in self.next_nodes:
            node.run(processed_text)

# Define a Print Node to output the final result
class PrintNode(Node):
    def __init__(self, name, message="Final Output:"):
        super().__init__(name)
        self.message = message

    def run(self, data):
        print(f"[{self.name}] {self.message} {data}")
        # End of workflow; no next nodes to run.
```

Explanation:

- **InputNode:**
  This node simulates obtaining raw text data. It prints the input and
  passes it along to connected nodes.
- **PreprocessingNode:**
  This node performs a simple preprocessing step: splitting the text into
  tokens, converting them to lowercase, and then rejoining them. In
  real applications, this could include more advanced processing such
  as removing punctuation, stop word filtering, or stemming.
- **PrintNode:**
  This node simply prints the final output. It demonstrates the endpoint
  of our workflow.

Step 2: Set Up the Graph Manager and Build the Workflow

The Graph Manager will handle the registration of nodes and the
establishment of connections (edges) between them.

Code Example:

python

```
# Define the Graph Manager
class GraphManager:
```

```python
    def __init__(self):
        self.nodes = {}

    def add_node(self, name, node):
        """
        Adds a node to the workflow.
        """
        self.nodes[name] = node

    def connect(self, source_name, destination_name):
        """
        Connects two nodes by name, passing the output of the
        source node to the destination node.
        """
        source_node = self.nodes.get(source_name)
        destination_node = self.nodes.get(destination_name)
        if source_node and destination_node:
            source_node.add_next(destination_node)
        else:
            raise ValueError("One or both nodes not found in
the graph.")

    def run(self, start_node_name, data=None):
        """
        Begins executing the workflow starting from the node
specified by start_node_name.
        """
        start_node = self.nodes.get(start_node_name)
        if start_node:
            start_node.run(data)
        else:
            raise ValueError("Start node not found in the
graph.")

# Create a Graph Manager instance
graph_manager = GraphManager()

# Create instances of our custom nodes
input_node = InputNode("InputNode")
preprocessing_node = PreprocessingNode("PreprocessingNode")
print_node = PrintNode("PrintNode", "Processed Text:")

# Add nodes to the Graph Manager
graph_manager.add_node("input", input_node)
graph_manager.add_node("preprocess", preprocessing_node)
graph_manager.add_node("print", print_node)

# Connect the nodes to form the workflow: Input ->
Preprocessing -> Print
graph_manager.connect("input", "preprocess")
graph_manager.connect("preprocess", "print")
```

Explanation:

- **GraphManager Class:**
  The Graph Manager class manages the nodes and their interconnections. Its methods `add_node`, `connect`, and `run` allow you to set up and execute the workflow.
- **Building the Workflow:**
  We create instances of our custom nodes and add them to the Graph Manager. Then, we establish the connections between them, forming a linear workflow: the raw text flows from the Input Node to the Preprocessing Node, and then to the Print Node.

Step 3: Execute the Workflow

Finally, run the workflow by calling the `run` method on the Graph Manager with the name of the starting node.

Code Example:

```python
python

# Execute the workflow starting from the Input Node
print("Starting LangGraph Application...\n")
graph_manager.run("input")
```

Expected Output:

```less
less

Starting LangGraph Application...

[InputNode] Raw Input: LangGraph Python makes creating graph-based workflows simple and powerful.
[PreprocessingNode] Processed Text: langgraph python makes creating graph-based workflows simple and powerful.
[PrintNode] Processed Text: langgraph python makes creating graph-based workflows simple and powerful.
```

Explanation:

- The workflow execution starts at the Input Node, which passes its output to the Preprocessing Node.

- The Preprocessing Node processes the text and forwards it to the Print Node.
- The Print Node outputs the final result, completing the workflow.

Summary Table: Workflow Components

Component	Function	Example
Input Node	Captures and supplies raw text	`"LangGraph Python makes creating graph-based workflows simple and powerful."`
Preprocessing Node	Tokenizes, cleans, and processes the text	Converts text to lowercase and splits/rejoins tokens
Print Node	Outputs the final processed text	Displays: `"Processed Text: langgraph python makes creating graph-based workflows simple and powerful."`
Graph Manager	Orchestrates node registration, connection, and execution	Manages the flow: Input → Preprocessing → Print

Writing your first LangGraph application involves understanding how to structure your workflow into modular nodes, how to connect these nodes with a Graph Manager, and how to execute the workflow effectively. This example provided a step-by-step guide—from defining custom nodes and building the workflow to running the application—demonstrating the core principles of LangGraph Python in a clear and practical manner.

With this foundation, you are now ready to explore more advanced applications and to integrate complex NLP tasks within your graph-based workflows. Happy coding, and enjoy harnessing the power of LangGraph Python!

4.4 Debugging and Testing Your Setup

Before diving deeper into application development with LangGraph Python, it is crucial to ensure that your development environment is set up correctly and that your LangGraph application runs smoothly. In this section, we will discuss various strategies and techniques for debugging and testing your LangGraph Python setup. This includes practical tips, common pitfalls, and code examples to help you troubleshoot and verify that each component of your workflow is functioning as expected.

1. Debugging Techniques

Debugging involves identifying, isolating, and fixing issues in your code. Here are some strategies you can use:

- **Print Debugging:**
  Use print statements at key points in your code to display variable values, node outputs, and execution flow. This simple method can quickly reveal where unexpected behavior occurs.
- **Logging:**
  Instead of using print statements, consider using Python's built-in `logging` module. Logging provides different levels of output (e.g., DEBUG, INFO, WARNING, ERROR) and is more flexible for larger projects.
- **Interactive Debugging:**
  Tools such as `pdb` (Python Debugger) allow you to set breakpoints, step through code, and inspect variables interactively. Many integrated development environments (IDEs) such as PyCharm or VS Code also provide robust debugging tools.
- **Unit Testing:**
  Writing tests for individual components (e.g., nodes, functions) can help verify that each part of your workflow works as intended. Unit tests also facilitate regression testing when modifications are made.

2. Testing Strategies for LangGraph Applications

Testing your LangGraph application ensures that every component is working correctly both in isolation and as part of the integrated workflow. Consider the following strategies:

- **Unit Tests for Individual Nodes:**
  Test each node independently to verify that its `run` method behaves as expected.
- **Integration Tests for Workflow Execution:**
  Verify that nodes are correctly connected, and data flows appropriately through the workflow managed by the Graph Manager.
- **Mock Data:**
  Use mock data to simulate various scenarios and edge cases, ensuring that your workflow can handle different inputs and conditions.
- **Automated Testing Tools:**
  Utilize frameworks like `unittest` or `pytest` to automate your testing process.

---

3. Practical Code Examples

Example 1: Using Print Statements for Debugging

Below is an example of modifying a node to include print statements that show the flow of data through the node.

```python
python

class DebugPreprocessingNode(Node):
    def run(self, data):
        print(f"[{self.name}] Received data: {data}")
        # Simulate tokenization and cleaning
        tokens = data.split()
        processed_tokens = [token.lower() for token in
tokens]
        processed_text = " ".join(processed_tokens)
        print(f"[{self.name}] Processed data:
{processed_text}")
        for node in self.next_nodes:
            node.run(processed_text)

# Usage in a simple workflow
```

```
debug_preprocessing_node =
DebugPreprocessingNode("DebugPreprocessing")
input_node = InputNode("InputNode")
print_node = PrintNode("PrintNode", "Final Output:")

# Build the graph
graph_manager = GraphManager()
graph_manager.add_node("input", input_node)
graph_manager.add_node("debug_preprocess",
debug_preprocessing_node)
graph_manager.add_node("print", print_node)
graph_manager.connect("input", "debug_preprocess")
graph_manager.connect("debug_preprocess", "print")

print("Running Debug Workflow...\n")
graph_manager.run("input")
```

Explanation:

- **Debug Statements:**
  The `DebugPreprocessingNode` prints the input data it receives and the output after processing. This helps you trace the data transformation step by step.
- **Workflow Execution:**
  Running this modified workflow provides clear output for each stage, helping you pinpoint where errors or unexpected behavior might occur.

Example 2: Basic Unit Test with Python's `unittest`

Create a test suite for verifying the functionality of a custom node. Below is an example using the `unittest` framework.

```python
import unittest

# Sample node to test: a simple node that returns a reversed
string
class ReverseNode(Node):
    def run(self, data):
        reversed_data = data[::-1]
        # Instead of printing, we return the value for
testing purposes.
        return reversed_data
```

```
class TestReverseNode(unittest.TestCase):
    def test_reverse(self):
        node = ReverseNode("ReverseNode")
        input_text = "Hello, LangGraph!"
        expected_output = "!hparGgnaL ,olleH"
        # Run the node and capture the output
        output = node.run(input_text)
        self.assertEqual(output, expected_output)

if __name__ == '__main__':
    unittest.main()
```

Explanation:

- **Custom ReverseNode:**
  This node reverses the input string.
- **Test Case:**
  The `TestReverseNode` class defines a test method `test_reverse`
  that asserts the node's output matches the expected reversed string.
- **Running Tests:**
  Executing this test script will verify that the ReverseNode works
  correctly, providing immediate feedback if changes cause
  regressions.

---

4. Common Debugging Issues and How to Resolve Them

Issue	Possible Cause	Suggested Resolution
Node Not Executing	Node not connected to the workflow properly	Verify that `add_next()` has been called and connections are set via Graph Manager
Data Not Passing Correctly	Incorrect data manipulation within a node	Add debug print/logging statements to inspect intermediate values
Runtime Errors (KeyError, ValueError)	Node names not found in the Graph Manager	Ensure that all nodes are added to the Graph Manager before connecting them
Unexpected Output	Logic errors in node's `run` method	Use unit tests to isolate and fix errors within individual nodes

5. Best Practices for Debugging and Testing

- **Write Tests Early:**
  Incorporate unit tests from the beginning to catch errors early.
- **Modular Design:**
  Design your nodes to perform single, well-defined tasks. This makes them easier to test and debug.
- **Use Logging for Production:**
  Replace print statements with logging for production code to maintain clean and manageable output.
- **Iterate and Refactor:**
  Regularly refactor your code and update tests to reflect changes. This iterative process helps maintain a robust codebase.

Debugging and testing are integral parts of developing a reliable LangGraph Python application. By using techniques like print debugging, logging, and unit testing, you can systematically identify and resolve issues in your workflow. The examples provided above demonstrate how to incorporate debugging output into your nodes and how to write unit tests using the `unittest` framework.

Following these best practices will not only help you build error-free applications but also ensure that your graph-based workflows are robust, scalable, and maintainable. With a well-tested foundation, you can confidently move forward to develop more complex and feature-rich applications using LangGraph Python.

Chapter 5: Designing Graph-Based Workflows

5.1 Building Blocks: Nodes, Edges, and Pipelines

Designing graph-based workflows begins with understanding its foundational building blocks: **nodes**, **edges**, and **pipelines**. These elements work together to create a structure that can model complex processes and data flows in a modular and scalable way. In this section, we will explain each building block in detail, discuss their roles within a workflow, and provide clear code examples and tables to illustrate how they work.

---

1. Nodes: The Fundamental Processing Units

Definition:
A **node** represents a discrete unit of work in your workflow. Each node is responsible for performing a specific task, such as data input, processing, or output generation. Nodes encapsulate functionality, allowing you to build modular systems where individual components can be easily modified or reused.

Key Characteristics of Nodes:

- **Modularity:** Each node performs a single, well-defined task.
- **Reusability:** Nodes can be reused in different parts of the workflow or across different projects.
- **Encapsulation:** The internal workings of a node are hidden, exposing only the input and output interfaces.

Example:
Consider a node that processes text by converting it to lowercase. This node takes a string as input, applies the transformation, and outputs the modified string.

Code Example:

```python
class Node:
    def __init__(self, name):
        self.name = name
        self.next_nodes = []

    def add_next(self, node):
        """Connects this node to the next node(s) in the
workflow."""
        self.next_nodes.append(node)

    def run(self, data):
        """Override this method to implement the node's
specific functionality."""
        raise NotImplementedError("Subclasses must implement
the run method.")

# Example of a custom node: LowerCaseNode
class LowerCaseNode(Node):
    def run(self, data):
        processed_data = data.lower()
        print(f"[{self.name}] Processed Data:
{processed_data}")
        # Propagate the processed data to the next nodes
        for node in self.next_nodes:
            node.run(processed_data)
```

Explanation:

- **Base Node Class:**
  The Node class defines a blueprint for creating custom nodes with a unique name and the ability to connect to other nodes via the add_next method.
- **LowerCaseNode:**
  This custom node inherits from Node and overrides the run method to convert input text to lowercase. It then prints the processed data and forwards it to any connected nodes.

---

2. Edges: Defining Relationships and Data Flow

Definition:
An **edge** represents a connection between two nodes. It defines the flow of data from one node (the source) to another (the destination). Edges determine

the structure of the workflow, establishing how data is passed, transformed, and aggregated.

Key Characteristics of Edges:

- **Directionality:**
  Edges are typically directed, meaning data flows from a source node to a destination node.
- **Connectivity:**
  They link nodes to form a complete pipeline or workflow.
- **Flexibility:**
  Edges can be used to implement branching (conditional workflows) and merging (combining multiple streams of data).

Table: Edge Characteristics

Characteristic	Description	Example
Direction	Data flows in a specified direction (source → destination)	Input Node → Processing Node
Connectivity	Links nodes to form a workflow	Edge from Node A to Node B
Flexibility	Supports branching and merging of data streams	Branching based on conditions

Explanation:
Edges, although not implemented as separate classes in many frameworks, are often implicit in the way nodes are connected using methods like `add_next`. They are critical for determining how data moves throughout the workflow.

---

3. Pipelines: Orchestrating the Workflow

Definition:
A **pipeline** is a complete workflow composed of interconnected nodes and edges. It represents the end-to-end process of data transformation from input to output. The pipeline is managed by a central orchestrator (often called a Graph Manager) that handles node registration, connection, and execution.

Key Characteristics of Pipelines:

- **End-to-End Flow:**
  Pipelines define the complete path that data follows from its initial state to its final processed form.
- **Modularity and Scalability:**
  By breaking the workflow into nodes, pipelines can be easily extended or modified.
- **Execution Control:**
  A Graph Manager or similar orchestrator controls the execution order and ensures that data flows correctly through the pipeline.

Code Example: Building a Simple Pipeline

python

```python
# Define a simple Graph Manager to manage the pipeline
class GraphManager:
    def __init__(self):
        self.nodes = {}

    def add_node(self, name, node):
        """Adds a node to the pipeline."""
        self.nodes[name] = node

    def connect(self, source_name, destination_name):
        """Connects two nodes by their names."""
        source_node = self.nodes.get(source_name)
        destination_node = self.nodes.get(destination_name)
        if source_node and destination_node:
            source_node.add_next(destination_node)
        else:
            raise ValueError("One or both nodes not found in
the pipeline.")

    def run(self, start_node_name, data=None):
        """Executes the pipeline starting from the specified
node."""
        start_node = self.nodes.get(start_node_name)
        if start_node:
            start_node.run(data)
        else:
            raise ValueError("Start node not found in the
pipeline.")

# Create instances of custom nodes
input_node = LowerCaseNode("LowerCaseNode")   # Using
LowerCaseNode as an example input node
```

```
# For demonstration, we can create another node that appends
extra text
class AppendTextNode(Node):
    def run(self, data):
        processed_data = data + " -- Processed by
AppendTextNode"
        print(f"[{self.name}] Processed Data:
{processed_data}")
        for node in self.next_nodes:
            node.run(processed_data)

append_node = AppendTextNode("AppendTextNode")

# Create a Graph Manager instance
graph_manager = GraphManager()

# Add nodes to the manager
graph_manager.add_node("lowercase", input_node)
graph_manager.add_node("append", append_node)

# Connect the nodes to form the pipeline: LowerCaseNode →
AppendTextNode
graph_manager.connect("lowercase", "append")

# Execute the pipeline starting from the LowerCaseNode
print("Running the Graph-Based Pipeline...\n")
initial_data = "Hello, LangGraph Python!"
graph_manager.run("lowercase", initial_data)
```

Explanation:

- **Graph Manager:**
  The GraphManager class is responsible for registering nodes,
  connecting them, and executing the workflow.
- **Pipeline Construction:**
  We add two nodes (LowerCaseNode and AppendTextNode) and
  connect them to form a pipeline.
- **Execution:**
  The pipeline starts with the LowerCaseNode, which processes the
  input text and passes it to the AppendTextNode. The final processed
  output is printed.

4. Summary Table: Building Blocks Overview

Component	Role	Key Characteristics	Example
Nodes	Fundamental processing units	Modular, reusable, encapsulate functionality; implement a `run` method	`LowerCaseNode`, `AppendTextNode`
Edges	Define connections and data flow	Directed, support branching/merging; implicitly defined via connections	Connection from `LowerCaseNode` to `AppendTextNode`
Pipelines	Orchestrate the entire workflow	End-to-end data flow; managed by a Graph Manager; scalable and modular	A workflow from input processing to final output

Understanding the building blocks of nodes, edges, and pipelines is essential for designing effective graph-based workflows. These components allow you to decompose complex processes into manageable, modular units that are easy to build, test, and maintain. The code examples provided demonstrate how to create custom nodes, connect them using implicit edges, and orchestrate a complete pipeline with a Graph Manager.

5.2 Workflow Design Patterns in LangGraph

Designing robust and scalable workflows in LangGraph Python involves more than simply connecting nodes. It requires understanding and applying common design patterns that address various real-world scenarios. In this section, we will explore several workflow design patterns that can be implemented using LangGraph Python. These patterns help you structure your pipelines in a way that is maintainable, flexible, and easy to extend. We will discuss each pattern in detail and provide complete code examples and tables for clarity.

1. Linear Workflows

Overview:
A linear workflow is the simplest form of workflow where nodes are connected sequentially. Data flows in one direction—from the start node through each intermediate node to the end node—without any branching or loops.

Characteristics:

- **Simplicity:** Easy to design and debug.
- **Deterministic Flow:** The order of execution is fixed.
- **Use Cases:** Simple data processing pipelines, sequential transformations, and one-off tasks.

Example Code:

```python
# Define custom nodes as previously demonstrated
class InputNode(Node):
    def run(self, data=None):
        raw_text = "LangGraph Python simplifies workflow design."
        print(f"[{self.name}] Raw Input: {raw_text}")
        for node in self.next_nodes:
            node.run(raw_text)

class ProcessingNode(Node):
    def run(self, data):
        processed_data = data.upper()   # Example processing: converting text to uppercase
        print(f"[{self.name}] Processed Data: {processed_data}")
        for node in self.next_nodes:
            node.run(processed_data)

class OutputNode(Node):
    def run(self, data):
        print(f"[{self.name}] Final Output: {data}")

# Build a linear workflow: Input -> Processing -> Output
graph_manager = GraphManager()
input_node = InputNode("InputNode")
processing_node = ProcessingNode("ProcessingNode")
output_node = OutputNode("OutputNode")
```

```
graph_manager.add_node("input", input_node)
graph_manager.add_node("process", processing_node)
graph_manager.add_node("output", output_node)

graph_manager.connect("input", "process")
graph_manager.connect("process", "output")

print("Running Linear Workflow...\n")
graph_manager.run("input")
```

Explanation:

- **Sequential Connection:** Data flows from the Input Node to the Processing Node and finally to the Output Node.
- **Simplicity:** The pattern is straightforward with a clear, linear progression.

---

2. Branching Workflows

Overview:
Branching workflows allow data to be processed in multiple paths based on specific conditions. This design pattern is useful when the workflow needs to handle different scenarios or routes based on the outcome of a particular node.

Characteristics:

- **Conditional Execution:** Nodes determine which branch to follow based on the data.
- **Flexibility:** Supports multiple outcomes and parallel processing.
- **Use Cases:** Decision-making processes, multi-path data analysis, dynamic routing.

Example Code:

```python
# Define a Decision Node that branches based on simple
condition
class DecisionNode(Node):
    def run(self, data):
        # Branch based on length of the text (for
demonstration purposes)
```

```python
        if len(data) > 40:
            branch = "long"
            print(f"[{self.name}] Routing to long text
branch")
        else:
            branch = "short"
            print(f"[{self.name}] Routing to short text
branch")
        # Forward the decision as part of the data
        for node in self.next_nodes:
            node.run((data, branch))

class LongTextNode(Node):
    def run(self, data):
        text, branch = data
        if branch == "long":
            result = f"LongTextNode processed: {text[::-1]}"
# Reverse the text as an example
            print(f"[{self.name}] {result}")

class ShortTextNode(Node):
    def run(self, data):
        text, branch = data
        if branch == "short":
            result = f"ShortTextNode processed:
{text.title()}"  # Convert to title case as an example
            print(f"[{self.name}] {result}")

# Build a branching workflow: Input -> Decision ->
[LongTextNode, ShortTextNode]
graph_manager = GraphManager()
input_node = InputNode("InputNode")
decision_node = DecisionNode("DecisionNode")
long_text_node = LongTextNode("LongTextNode")
short_text_node = ShortTextNode("ShortTextNode")

graph_manager.add_node("input", input_node)
graph_manager.add_node("decision", decision_node)
graph_manager.add_node("long", long_text_node)
graph_manager.add_node("short", short_text_node)

# Connect nodes: Input -> Decision, and Decision -> Long &
Decision -> Short
graph_manager.connect("input", "decision")
# Decision node sends to both long and short text nodes
decision_node.add_next(long_text_node)
decision_node.add_next(short_text_node)

print("\nRunning Branching Workflow...\n")
graph_manager.run("input")
```

Explanation:

- **Conditional Routing:**
  The Decision Node analyzes the text and routes data to either the LongTextNode or ShortTextNode.
- **Parallel Branches:**
  Both branches are connected to the Decision Node; however, only one branch will process the data based on the condition.
- **Dynamic Behavior:**
  This pattern illustrates how workflows can adapt based on runtime conditions.

---

3. Iterative or Looping Workflows

Overview:
Iterative workflows involve loops where a node or set of nodes is repeatedly executed until a certain condition is met. This is useful for tasks like iterative refinement, convergence-based algorithms, or processing batches of data.

Characteristics:

- **Repetition:**
  Allows for re-processing or refining data.
- **Conditional Termination:**
  Looping continues until a defined condition is satisfied.
- **Use Cases:**
  Convergence algorithms, iterative data cleaning, optimization routines.

Example Code:

python

```python
class LoopNode(Node):
    def __init__(self, name, max_iterations=3):
        super().__init__(name)
        self.iteration = 0
        self.max_iterations = max_iterations

    def run(self, data):
        if self.iteration < self.max_iterations:
            self.iteration += 1
```

```
            processed_data = f"{data} [Iteration
{self.iteration}]"
            print(f"[{self.name}] {processed_data}")
            # Loop: Call itself until max_iterations is
reached
            self.run(processed_data)
        else:
            # After looping, pass data to next nodes
            for node in self.next_nodes:
                node.run(data)

# Build an iterative workflow: Input -> Loop -> Output
graph_manager = GraphManager()
input_node = InputNode("InputNode")
loop_node = LoopNode("LoopNode", max_iterations=3)
output_node = OutputNode("OutputNode")

graph_manager.add_node("input", input_node)
graph_manager.add_node("loop", loop_node)
graph_manager.add_node("output", output_node)

graph_manager.connect("input", "loop")
graph_manager.connect("loop", "output")

print("\nRunning Iterative Workflow...\n")
graph_manager.run("input")
```

Explanation:

- **Looping Behavior:**
  The Loop Node repeatedly processes the input until it reaches a
  maximum number of iterations.
- **Termination Condition:**
  The loop stops after a specified number of iterations, and the
  processed data is then passed on.
- **Feedback Mechanism:**
  This pattern is essential when repeated processing is required for
  refinement.

---

4. Parallel Workflows

Overview:
Parallel workflows process data concurrently along different branches or
nodes. This design pattern is effective when tasks can be executed

independently and simultaneously, leading to improved performance and efficiency.

Characteristics:

- **Concurrent Processing:**
  Nodes execute in parallel rather than sequentially.
- **Synchronization:**
  Results from parallel branches can be merged or aggregated at a later stage.
- **Use Cases:**
  Batch processing, multi-modal data analysis, distributed computing tasks.

Example Code (Conceptual):

```python
class ParallelNode(Node):
    def run(self, data):
        # Simulate parallel processing by splitting the data
into parts
        part1 = data[:len(data)//2]
        part2 = data[len(data)//2:]
        print(f"[{self.name}] Processing in parallel:
'{part1}' and '{part2}'")
        # Pass results to next nodes; in a real scenario,
these might run concurrently using threading or async
        for node in self.next_nodes:
            node.run(part1 + " " + part2)

# Build a parallel workflow: Input -> ParallelNode -> Output
graph_manager = GraphManager()
input_node = InputNode("InputNode")
parallel_node = ParallelNode("ParallelNode")
output_node = OutputNode("OutputNode")

graph_manager.add_node("input", input_node)
graph_manager.add_node("parallel", parallel_node)
graph_manager.add_node("output", output_node)

graph_manager.connect("input", "parallel")
graph_manager.connect("parallel", "output")

print("\nRunning Parallel Workflow (Conceptual)...\n")
graph_manager.run("input")
```

Explanation:

- **Data Splitting:**
  The Parallel Node splits the data into two parts and simulates concurrent processing.
- **Merging:**
  After processing, results are merged and forwarded.
- **Concurrency Concept:**
  While this example runs sequentially, real-world implementations might use threading, multiprocessing, or asynchronous techniques for true parallelism.

5. Summary Table: Workflow Design Patterns

Pattern	Description	Key Use Cases	Example Nodes
Linear Workflow	Sequential execution with a fixed flow of data	Simple pipelines, sequential data transformations	InputNode → ProcessingNode → OutputNode
Branching Workflow	Conditional routing to different processing paths	Decision-making, multi-path analysis	DecisionNode → {LongTextNode, ShortTextNode}
Iterative Workflow	Looping nodes until a condition is met	Convergence algorithms, iterative refinement	LoopNode
Parallel Workflow	Concurrent processing of data along different branches	Batch processing, distributed tasks	ParallelNode (conceptual example)

Workflow design patterns are essential tools for creating efficient and scalable graph-based applications with LangGraph Python. By understanding and applying patterns like linear, branching, iterative, and parallel workflows, you can tailor your pipeline to meet the specific needs of your project. The modular nature of LangGraph Python makes it straightforward to implement these patterns, enabling you to design complex workflows that are both maintainable and extendable.

5.3 Visualizing Workflows: Tools and Techniques

Visualizing workflows is an essential aspect of designing, debugging, and communicating complex graph-based systems. A clear visual representation of your workflow helps you understand the structure, track data flow, and identify potential bottlenecks or errors. In LangGraph Python, visualizing workflows involves converting the abstract graph of nodes and edges into a diagram that is easy to interpret. In this section, we will discuss various tools and techniques for visualizing workflows, provide practical code examples, and include tables that summarize key points.

---

1. Importance of Visualization

Visualization serves several purposes in the context of graph-based workflows:

- **Clarification:**
  Diagrams provide a clear, concise view of how nodes connect and interact.
- **Debugging:**
  Visual representations help identify where data might be getting lost or misrouted.
- **Communication:**
  Flowcharts and diagrams make it easier to explain system architecture to team members or stakeholders.
- **Optimization:**
  Analyzing the graph can reveal inefficient paths or redundant nodes, guiding performance improvements.

---

2. Tools for Visualizing Workflows

Several Python libraries can be used to visualize workflows in LangGraph Python. Here are some popular ones:

- **NetworkX:**
  A comprehensive library for creating, manipulating, and studying the

structure of complex networks. When combined with Matplotlib, it can generate clear visualizations of graph structures.

- **Graphviz:**
  A powerful tool for rendering graph descriptions in various formats. The Python interface, `graphviz`, makes it straightforward to convert graph structures into diagrams.
- **Matplotlib:**
  A versatile plotting library that can be used along with NetworkX to display graphs with custom styling.
- **Plotly:**
  An interactive graphing library that allows you to create dynamic and interactive visualizations, which can be useful for exploring complex workflows.

---

3. Visualizing Workflows with NetworkX and Matplotlib

One of the simplest and most effective ways to visualize a LangGraph Python workflow is to use NetworkX for graph representation and Matplotlib for rendering the graph.

Step-by-Step Example:

1. **Install Dependencies:**

   Make sure you have the required libraries installed:

   ```bash
   pip install networkx matplotlib
   ```

2. **Build the Workflow Graph:**

   Assume you have a workflow composed of nodes connected by edges. We can use a simple dictionary-based representation (similar to an adjacency list) to define our graph structure.

3. **Render the Graph:**

   Use NetworkX to create a graph from the workflow data, and then use Matplotlib to draw the graph.

Complete Code Example:

```python
python

import networkx as nx
import matplotlib.pyplot as plt

# Define a simple workflow using a dictionary to represent
node connections
workflow = {
    'InputNode': ['PreprocessingNode'],
    'PreprocessingNode': ['ProcessingNode'],
    'ProcessingNode': ['DecisionNode', 'LoggingNode'],
    'DecisionNode': ['OutputNode'],
    'LoggingNode': ['OutputNode'],
    'OutputNode': []
}

def visualize_workflow(workflow):
    """
    Visualizes a workflow represented as a dictionary using
NetworkX and Matplotlib.

    Parameters:
    - workflow: A dictionary where keys are node names and
values are lists of connected node names.
    """
    # Create a directed graph
    G = nx.DiGraph()

    # Add nodes and edges from the workflow dictionary
    for node, neighbors in workflow.items():
        G.add_node(node)
        for neighbor in neighbors:
            G.add_edge(node, neighbor)

    # Use spring layout for positioning the nodes
    pos = nx.spring_layout(G, seed=42)  # Fixed seed for
reproducibility

    # Draw the nodes
    nx.draw_networkx_nodes(G, pos, node_size=1500,
node_color='lightblue')

    # Draw the edges
    nx.draw_networkx_edges(G, pos, arrowstyle='->',
arrowsize=20, edge_color='gray')

    # Draw the node labels
    nx.draw_networkx_labels(G, pos, font_size=10,
font_family="sans-serif")
```

```
# Set plot title and remove axis
plt.title("LangGraph Workflow Visualization")
plt.axis("off")
plt.tight_layout()
plt.show()

# Visualize the example workflow
visualize_workflow(workflow)
```

Explanation:

- **Graph Construction:**
  The workflow is defined as a dictionary where each key is a node name and each value is a list of nodes to which it is connected.
- **NetworkX Graph:**
  A directed graph (`DiGraph`) is created from this dictionary by adding nodes and edges accordingly.
- **Layout and Drawing:**
  The `spring_layout` is used to position nodes in a visually appealing manner. Nodes are drawn in light blue, edges are styled with arrows to indicate direction, and node labels are added for clarity.
- **Visualization:**
  Matplotlib renders the final diagram with an appropriate title, and axis ticks are removed for a cleaner look.

---

4. Visualizing Workflows with Graphviz

Graphviz offers another approach to visualize workflows, especially when you need publication-quality diagrams.

Step-by-Step Example:

1. **Install Graphviz and Its Python Interface:**

   bash

   ```
   pip install graphviz
   ```

   Additionally, ensure that the Graphviz software is installed on your system (download from Graphviz.org).

2. Create a Graphviz Diagram:

Complete Code Example:

```python
python

from graphviz import Digraph

def visualize_workflow_graphviz(workflow):
    """
    Visualizes a workflow using Graphviz.

    Parameters:
    - workflow: A dictionary where keys are node names and
values are lists of connected node names.
    """
    dot = Digraph(comment='LangGraph Workflow')

    # Add nodes
    for node in workflow.keys():
        dot.node(node, node)

    # Add edges
    for node, neighbors in workflow.items():
        for neighbor in neighbors:
            dot.edge(node, neighbor)

    # Render and display the graph (in PDF format or render
inline in Jupyter)
    dot.render('langgraph_workflow', view=True)
    print(dot.source)

# Visualize the example workflow using Graphviz
visualize_workflow_graphviz(workflow)
```

Explanation:

- **Graph Construction:**
  The `Digraph` class from Graphviz is used to construct a directed graph.
- **Node and Edge Addition:**
  Each node is added to the graph, and edges are created based on the workflow dictionary.
- **Rendering:**
  The graph is rendered and saved as a PDF file (`langgraph_workflow.pdf`) or viewed inline in Jupyter Notebook. The source code of the graph is also printed.

5. Comparison Table: Visualization Tools

Tool	Strengths	Use Cases	Example
NetworkX + Matplotlib	Easy to integrate with Python, highly customizable, suitable for interactive development	Quick prototyping, debugging, interactive visualization	Code example using `nx.DiGraph()` and `plt.show()`
Graphviz	Produces high-quality, publication-ready diagrams, excellent for static representations	Formal documentation, presentations, reports	Code example using `graphviz.Digraph()`
Plotly	Provides interactive, web-based visualizations	Dynamic dashboards, online sharing, data exploration	Not shown here but similar concepts apply

6. Best Practices and Techniques

- **Consistent Layouts:**
  Use fixed seeds in layout algorithms (e.g., `spring_layout(G, seed=42)`) to ensure reproducible visualizations.
- **Clear Labels and Colors:**
  Use distinct colors and labels for different node types to enhance readability.
- **Modular Visualization:**
  Break down complex workflows into smaller subgraphs if needed, then merge them into an overall diagram.
- **Interactive Tools:**
  Consider using interactive libraries like Plotly or Dash when real-time exploration of workflows is necessary.

Visualizing workflows in LangGraph Python is a powerful technique to understand and optimize your graph-based processes. Whether you choose to use NetworkX with Matplotlib for interactive development or Graphviz for high-quality static diagrams, these tools provide the flexibility needed to represent complex workflows clearly.

By integrating these visualization techniques into your development process, you can more easily debug, communicate, and enhance your workflows, ultimately leading to more efficient and robust applications. Happy visualizing, and may your workflows always be clear and well-organized!

5.4 Managing Data Flow and Dependencies

Managing data flow and dependencies is a crucial aspect of designing robust graph-based workflows. In a LangGraph Python application, data flows between nodes through well-defined connections (edges), while dependencies ensure that each node receives the correct input at the proper time. This section provides a detailed explanation of how to manage these aspects, along with practical techniques, complete code examples, and supporting tables to help you understand and implement effective data flow control in your workflows.

---

1. Understanding Data Flow in Graph-Based Workflows

Data Flow refers to the way data is transferred between nodes in a workflow. Each node processes its input and passes its output to one or more subsequent nodes. Effective data flow management involves:

- **Ensuring Correct Sequence:**
  Data must flow in the proper order so that each node receives the required input.
- **Handling Multiple Inputs/Outputs:**
  Some nodes may require input from several sources or send output to multiple nodes.
- **Maintaining Data Integrity:**
  Data should not be lost or corrupted as it moves between nodes.

---

2. Managing Dependencies

Dependencies describe the relationships between nodes where the output of one node is required by another. Managing dependencies involves:

- **Establishing Order of Execution:**
  Dependencies dictate that certain nodes must complete processing before others can begin.
- **Handling Parallel Processing:**
  When multiple nodes run concurrently, their dependencies must be managed to ensure that all necessary data is available when needed.
- **Error Propagation:**
  If a node fails to produce the expected output, dependent nodes should either be halted or provided with fallback logic.

Example Table: Data Flow and Dependency Considerations

Aspect	Consideration	Technique/Approach
Sequence of Execution	Ensuring nodes execute in the proper order	Use a Graph Manager to enforce node connections
Multiple Inputs	Nodes requiring data from several sources	Aggregate data before processing (e.g., merging lists)
Parallel Processing	Running nodes concurrently without violating dependencies	Synchronize results using dependency checks or callbacks
Error Handling	Propagation of errors or missing data in downstream nodes	Implement error handling and fallback mechanisms

3. Techniques for Managing Data Flow and Dependencies

a. Passing Data Through Nodes

Each node's `run` method should be designed to accept input data, process it, and then forward the output to the next node(s). This ensures a seamless flow of data through the workflow.

Code Example: Basic Data Passing

```python
class DataNode(Node):
    def run(self, data):
        # Process data (for example, appending node name)
        processed_data = f"{data} -> Processed by
{self.name}"
        print(f"[{self.name}] Output: {processed_data}")
        # Pass processed data to all connected next nodes
        for node in self.next_nodes:
            node.run(processed_data)

# Example usage:
input_text = "Initial Data"
node_A = DataNode("Node_A")
node_B = DataNode("Node_B")
node_C = DataNode("Node_C")

# Connect nodes linearly: Node_A -> Node_B -> Node_C
node_A.add_next(node_B)
node_B.add_next(node_C)

# Run the workflow starting from Node_A
node_A.run(input_text)
```

Explanation:

- **DataNode Class:**
  Inherits from the base `Node` class and processes data by appending a simple message.
- **Data Propagation:**
  After processing, the node iterates over its `next_nodes` and calls their `run` method, passing the updated data along.

b. Aggregating Data from Multiple Sources

When a node requires input from multiple sources, you may need to aggregate the data before processing. This can be achieved by storing the data until all expected inputs are received.

Code Example: Aggregating Data

```python
class AggregationNode(Node):
    def __init__(self, name, expected_inputs):
        super().__init__(name)
```

```
        self.expected_inputs = expected_inputs
        self.received_data = []

    def run(self, data):
        self.received_data.append(data)
        print(f"[{self.name}] Received: {data}")
        # Check if all expected data has been received
        if len(self.received_data) == self.expected_inputs:
            # Merge the data (e.g., concatenate strings)
            aggregated_data = " | ".join(self.received_data)
            print(f"[{self.name}] Aggregated Data:
{aggregated_data}")
            for node in self.next_nodes:
                node.run(aggregated_data)

# Example usage:
node_X = DataNode("Node_X")
node_Y = DataNode("Node_Y")
aggregator = AggregationNode("Aggregator", expected_inputs=2)
output_node = DataNode("OutputNode")

# Connect nodes: Node_X and Node_Y -> Aggregator ->
OutputNode
node_X.add_next(aggregator)
node_Y.add_next(aggregator)
aggregator.add_next(output_node)

# Run both input nodes independently (simulate parallel
inputs)
node_X.run("Data from X")
node_Y.run("Data from Y")
```

Explanation:

- **AggregationNode Class:**
  Inherits from Node and expects a certain number of inputs before
  processing.
- **Data Aggregation:**
  Once all expected inputs are received, the node aggregates the data
  (here, concatenates them) and forwards the result.

c. Handling Dependencies and Conditional Execution

Sometimes, the execution of a node depends on the outcome of previous
nodes. Conditional checks or decision nodes can control this flow.

Code Example: Conditional Execution

```python
class ConditionalNode(Node):
    def run(self, data):
        # Perform a conditional check (e.g., based on data length)
        if len(data) > 50:
            decision = "long"
            print(f"[{self.name}] Condition met: data is long")
        else:
            decision = "short"
            print(f"[{self.name}] Condition met: data is short")
        # Forward the decision along with the data
        for node in self.next_nodes:
            node.run((data, decision))

# Example usage:
conditional_node = ConditionalNode("ConditionalNode")
output_node = DataNode("OutputNode")

conditional_node.add_next(output_node)
# Pass data to the conditional node
conditional_node.run("Some example text that is being evaluated for its length.")
```

Explanation:

- **ConditionalNode Class:**
  Implements a condition to decide how to proceed based on the input data.
- **Decision Propagation:**
  The node forwards a tuple containing the data and the decision, allowing downstream nodes to handle different cases appropriately.

---

4. Summary Table: Managing Data Flow and Dependencies

Aspect	Technique	Example
Sequential Flow	Passing processed data through node run methods	DataNode processing and forwarding data to next_nodes

Aspect	Technique	Example
Aggregation	Storing multiple inputs until all expected data is received	AggregationNode collecting data from Node_X and Node_Y
Conditional Execution	Using decision nodes to branch based on input conditions	ConditionalNode checking data length and forwarding decision tuple
Error Handling	Implementing checks before propagating data	Verify received inputs in AggregationNode before processing

5. Best Practices

- **Design for Clarity:**
  Ensure that each node's purpose is clearly defined. This makes it easier to track data flow and debug issues.
- **Modular Aggregation:**
  When expecting multiple inputs, design nodes to aggregate data flexibly, handling missing or extra inputs gracefully.
- **Robust Error Checking:**
  Include error checks and logging at key points in the workflow to monitor data integrity and dependency resolution.
- **Document Dependencies:**
  Clearly document the dependencies between nodes so that anyone maintaining the code can understand the required order of execution.

Effective management of data flow and dependencies is key to building reliable and maintainable graph-based workflows in LangGraph Python. By designing nodes that pass, aggregate, and conditionally handle data, you can create complex workflows that are robust to changes and easy to debug. The provided code examples and summary tables illustrate common techniques and best practices that you can adapt to suit your specific project needs.

With these strategies in place, you are now well-equipped to manage data flow and dependencies in your LangGraph applications, paving the way for more advanced integrations and applications as you continue your development journey.

Chapter 6: Integrating Language Models and NLP Pipelines

6.1 Connecting LangGraph with Popular NLP Libraries

Integrating LangGraph Python with popular NLP libraries allows you to build advanced, graph-based applications that leverage state-of-the-art language models and processing pipelines. In this section, we will explain how to connect LangGraph with widely used libraries such as Hugging Face Transformers and LangChain. We will cover the following key areas:

- **Overview of NLP Libraries and Their Role:**
  A brief description of what these libraries offer and why they are beneficial for building robust NLP workflows.
- **Setting Up the Integration Environment:**
  Steps for installing necessary packages and setting up your development environment.
- **Implementing Integration in LangGraph:**
  Detailed code examples that illustrate how to create custom nodes in LangGraph Python that call functions from Hugging Face Transformers and LangChain.
- **Managing Data Flow Between LangGraph and NLP Pipelines:**
  Strategies for passing data between your graph nodes and NLP library functions effectively.

---

1. Overview of NLP Libraries and Their Role

Hugging Face Transformers:
Hugging Face provides an extensive collection of pre-trained models for various NLP tasks such as text generation, summarization, translation, and sentiment analysis. These models are built on modern architectures (e.g., BERT, GPT, T5) and can be easily integrated via the Transformers library. They allow you to add cutting-edge language understanding and generation capabilities to your workflow.

LangChain:
LangChain is designed to facilitate the development of applications that combine language models with external tools, data sources, or workflows. It offers utilities to chain together prompts, process outputs, and manage complex pipelines that leverage the power of large language models. LangChain is particularly useful when your application requires dynamic decision-making or interaction with multiple data sources.

Both libraries offer APIs that are straightforward to use and integrate. When combined with LangGraph Python, they allow you to design modular, graph-based workflows that incorporate advanced NLP functionalities.

---

2. Setting Up the Integration Environment

Before integrating, ensure that your environment includes all necessary packages. If you haven't already installed these libraries, you can do so using pip:

```bash
pip install langgraph transformers langchain
```

Additionally, you may need to download language models for Hugging Face. For example, to download the GPT-2 model, you would typically initialize it through the API, which downloads the model automatically if not already present.

---

3. Implementing Integration in LangGraph

The key idea is to create custom nodes in LangGraph that leverage functions from Hugging Face or LangChain. Below are two detailed examples:

Example A: Integrating with Hugging Face Transformers

In this example, we build a simple workflow that performs text generation using a pre-trained GPT-2 model.

Step 1: Create a Custom Node for Text Generation

python

```python
from langgraph import Node, GraphManager
from transformers import pipeline

class TextGenerationNode(Node):
    def __init__(self, name, model_name="gpt2",
max_length=50):
        super().__init__(name)
        # Initialize the text generation pipeline with the
specified model
        self.generator = pipeline("text-generation",
model=model_name)
        self.max_length = max_length

    def run(self, data):
        """
        Generates text based on the input prompt and passes
the generated text
        to the next nodes.
        """
        print(f"[{self.name}] Generating text for prompt:
'{data}'")
        # Generate text using the Hugging Face pipeline
        results = self.generator(data,
max_length=self.max_length, num_return_sequences=1)
        generated_text = results[0]['generated_text']
        print(f"[{self.name}] Generated Text:
{generated_text}")
        # Propagate the generated text to the next nodes
        for node in self.next_nodes:
            node.run(generated_text)

# Test the TextGenerationNode independently
if __name__ == "__main__":
    # Create an instance of the node
    text_gen_node = TextGenerationNode("TextGen")
    # Run the node with a sample prompt
    text_gen_node.run("Once upon a time, in a land far
away,")
```

Explanation:

- **Node Initialization:**
  The custom TextGenerationNode inherits from the base Node class.
  During initialization, it creates a Hugging Face text generation
  pipeline using GPT-2.

- **Run Method:**
  The `run` method receives an input prompt, generates text using the pipeline, prints the result, and then passes the generated text to the next node(s) in the workflow.
- **Integration:**
  This node can be incorporated into a larger LangGraph workflow where text generation is one step in the overall pipeline.

Example B: Integrating with LangChain

In this example, we create a custom node that uses LangChain to chain multiple prompts or tasks. Suppose we want to perform a two-step process: first, summarize a piece of text, and then generate a response based on the summary.

Step 1: Create Custom Nodes for Summarization and Response Generation

python

```python
from langgraph import Node, GraphManager
import langchain  # This is a placeholder import; actual
usage depends on LangChain's API

# Assuming LangChain provides a simple interface for
summarization
class SummarizationNode(Node):
    def __init__(self, name):
        super().__init__(name)
        # Initialize a summarization component (pseudo-code;
adjust as per LangChain's API)
        self.summarizer = langchain.Summarizer(model="some-
summarization-model")

    def run(self, data):
        print(f"[{self.name}] Summarizing text: '{data}'")
        summary = self.summarizer.summarize(data)
        print(f"[{self.name}] Summary: {summary}")
        for node in self.next_nodes:
            node.run(summary)

# A node for generating a response based on the summary
class ResponseGenerationNode(Node):
    def __init__(self, name):
        super().__init__(name)
```

```
        # Initialize a response generator (pseudo-code)
        self.response_generator =
langchain.ResponseGenerator(model="some-response-model")

    def run(self, data):
        print(f"[{self.name}] Generating response for
summary: '{data}'")
        response =
self.response_generator.generate_response(data)
        print(f"[{self.name}] Generated Response:
{response}")
        for node in self.next_nodes:
            node.run(response)

# Test the LangChain integration nodes independently
if __name__ == "__main__":
    # Create instances of the nodes
    summarization_node = SummarizationNode("Summarizer")
    response_node = ResponseGenerationNode("Responder")

    # Build the workflow: Summarization -> Response
Generation
    graph_manager = GraphManager()
    graph_manager.add_node("summarizer", summarization_node)
    graph_manager.add_node("responder", response_node)
    graph_manager.connect("summarizer", "responder")

    # Run the workflow with sample text
    sample_text = "LangGraph Python provides a powerful way
to integrate NLP pipelines into graph-based workflows."
    print("\nRunning LangChain-Based Workflow...\n")
    graph_manager.run("summarizer", sample_text)
```

Explanation:

- **SummarizationNode:**
  This node uses a summarization component from LangChain to
  condense the input text. It then passes the summary to the next node.
- **ResponseGenerationNode:**
  Based on the summary, this node generates an appropriate response.
- **Workflow Integration:**
  The Graph Manager is used to add these nodes to the workflow and
  connect them so that the summary flows into the response generator.
- **Pseudo-Code Notice:**
  Since LangChain's API may vary, adjust the node implementation
  according to the actual functions and model names provided by
  LangChain.

4. Managing Data Flow Between LangGraph and NLP Pipelines

When integrating external NLP libraries, it is important to ensure that the data passed between nodes is in the expected format. Here are a few best practices:

- **Input Validation:**
  Validate and, if necessary, preprocess the data before passing it to NLP library functions.
- **Consistent Data Formats:**
  Ensure that each node outputs data in a format that is compatible with the input requirements of downstream nodes.
- **Error Handling:**
  Implement try-except blocks within nodes to handle exceptions raised by external libraries gracefully.

Example: Adding Input Validation

```python
class ValidatedTextGenerationNode(TextGenerationNode):
    def run(self, data):
        # Validate that the input is a non-empty string
        if not isinstance(data, str) or not data.strip():
            print(f"[{self.name}] Invalid input data:
{data}")
            return
        super().run(data)

# Test the validated node
validated_node =
ValidatedTextGenerationNode("ValidatedTextGen")
validated_node.run("Hello, world!")   # Valid input
validated_node.run("")                # Invalid input, will
trigger validation check
```

Explanation:

- **ValidatedTextGenerationNode:**
  Extends the TextGenerationNode by adding a validation step that checks whether the input data is a non-empty string.

- **Error Handling:**
  If the input is invalid, the node logs an error and does not attempt to call the external NLP library.

---

5. Summary Table: Integration Components

Component/Node	Library/Tool	Functionality	Key Methods/Attributes
TextGenerationNode	Hugging Face Transformers	Generates text from a prompt using a pre-trained model	`pipeline("text-generation")`, `max_length`, `run(data)`
SummarizationNode	LangChain (example)	Summarizes input text using LangChain's summarizer	`self.summarizer.summarize(data)`, `run(data)`
ResponseGenerationNode	LangChain (example)	Generates responses based on summarized text	`self.response_generator.generate_response(data)`, `run(data)`
Graph Manager	LangGraph Python	Orchestrates node registrat	`add_node()`, `connect()`, `run(start_node, data)`

Component/Node	Library/Tool	Functionality	Key Methods/Attributes
		ion, connection, and execution	
ValidatedTextGenerationNode	Extension of TextGenerationNode	Adds input validation to ensure correct data flow	Overridden `run(data)` with input checks

Connecting LangGraph Python with popular NLP libraries like Hugging Face Transformers and LangChain unlocks the potential to build sophisticated, graph-based NLP applications. By creating custom nodes that encapsulate calls to these libraries, you can seamlessly integrate advanced language models and processing pipelines into your workflow.

This section provided detailed explanations, complete code examples, and practical tips for managing data flow, validating inputs, and orchestrating node execution within your LangGraph applications. With these integration techniques, you are well-equipped to harness state-of-the-art NLP capabilities and build powerful, modular systems.

6.2 Building Conversational Agents and Chatbots

Conversational agents and chatbots are among the most popular applications of natural language processing (NLP). They allow machines to interact with users in natural language, providing responses, recommendations, and support. In LangGraph Python, building such systems becomes manageable by decomposing the process into modular nodes and connecting them in a workflow. In this section, we'll explore how to design, implement, and integrate components for conversational agents and chatbots using LangGraph Python along with popular NLP libraries.

1. Overview of Conversational Agents and Chatbots

Definition:
A conversational agent (or chatbot) is a software application that communicates with users through text or speech. It processes input, determines intent, retrieves or generates an appropriate response, and returns that response to the user.

Key Components in a Chatbot Workflow:

- **Input Handling:**
  Captures user input from text, speech, or another source.
- **Preprocessing:**
  Cleans and tokenizes the input, removing noise and standardizing the text.
- **Intent Detection:**
  Analyzes the input to determine the user's intent using techniques like classification or entity recognition.
- **Dialogue Management:**
  Decides the appropriate response or action based on the detected intent and context.
- **Response Generation:**
  Constructs a response, which can be rule-based or generated using advanced language models.
- **Output Delivery:**
  Sends the response back to the user through the appropriate channel.

Table: Chatbot Workflow Components

Component	Function	Example Task
Input Handling	Captures raw user input	Receiving a text query via chat
Preprocessing	Cleans and tokenizes the input text	Removing punctuation, lowercasing
Intent Detection	Determines user intent and extracts key entities	Classifying input as a "booking" request
Dialogue Management	Manages conversation flow and decision-making	Routing to a FAQ module or support agent

Component	Function	Example Task
Response Generation	Produces an answer or action based on the input	Generating a response using a language model
Output Delivery	Presents the response to the user	Displaying the answer in a chat interface

2. Designing a Chatbot Workflow with LangGraph Python

Using LangGraph Python, you can model each component as a node in a graph, connecting them to form a complete conversational workflow. The following is an example of a simplified chatbot that processes text input, detects intent, generates a response, and outputs the result.

Step-by-Step Architecture:

1. **Input Node:** Captures user input.
2. **Preprocessing Node:** Normalizes and tokenizes the text.
3. **Intent Detection Node:** Uses an NLP library (e.g., Hugging Face Transformers) to detect intent.
4. **Response Generation Node:** Generates a response based on the detected intent.
5. **Output Node:** Delivers the final response to the user.

3. Implementation: Code Examples

Below is a complete code example demonstrating how to build a simple conversational agent using LangGraph Python. We will use custom nodes that integrate with Hugging Face's Transformers for intent detection and response generation.

Step 1: Define the Custom Nodes

```python
python

from langgraph import Node, GraphManager
from transformers import pipeline

# Input Node: Simulate capturing user input
class ChatInputNode(Node):
```

```python
    def run(self, data=None):
        # In a real scenario, this could come from a web
interface or messaging API.
        user_input = "I need help booking a flight."
        print(f"[{self.name}] User Input: {user_input}")
        for node in self.next_nodes:
            node.run(user_input)


# Preprocessing Node: Normalize and tokenize the text (simple
simulation)
class ChatPreprocessingNode(Node):
    def run(self, data):
        # For demonstration, we simply lower-case the text
        processed_text = data.lower().strip()
        print(f"[{self.name}] Processed Text:
{processed_text}")
        for node in self.next_nodes:
            node.run(processed_text)


# Intent Detection Node: Uses a pre-trained model to classify
the intent
class IntentDetectionNode(Node):
    def __init__(self, name):
        super().__init__(name)
        # Initialize a text classification pipeline (simulate
intent detection)
        self.classifier = pipeline("zero-shot-
classification", model="facebook/bart-large-mnli")
        # Define candidate labels for intents
        self.intents = ["booking", "cancellation", "inquiry",
"complaint"]

    def run(self, data):
        print(f"[{self.name}] Detecting intent for:
'{data}'")
        # Zero-shot classification to determine the intent
        result = self.classifier(data,
candidate_labels=self.intents)
        # Select the top intent
        top_intent = result["labels"][0]
        print(f"[{self.name}] Detected Intent: {top_intent}")
        # Pass both text and detected intent to the next node
        for node in self.next_nodes:
            node.run((data, top_intent))


# Response Generation Node: Generates a response based on
intent
class ResponseGenerationNode(Node):
    def __init__(self, name):
        super().__init__(name)
```

```python
        # Initialize a text generation pipeline (using GPT-2
for demonstration)
        self.generator = pipeline("text-generation",
model="gpt2")

    def run(self, data):
        text, intent = data
        # Customize prompt based on intent
        prompt = f"User said: '{text}'. Provide a helpful
response regarding {intent}."
        print(f"[{self.name}] Generating response with
prompt: '{prompt}'")
        result = self.generator(prompt, max_length=60,
num_return_sequences=1)
        response = result[0]['generated_text']
        print(f"[{self.name}] Generated Response:
{response}")
        for node in self.next_nodes:
            node.run(response)

# Output Node: Delivers the response to the user
class ChatOutputNode(Node):
    def run(self, data):
        print(f"[{self.name}] Final Chatbot Response:
{data}")
        # In a real application, this could be returned to a
web interface or messaging service.

# For demonstration, create a Graph Manager instance and set
up the workflow
graph_manager = GraphManager()

# Create instances of the nodes
input_node = ChatInputNode("ChatInput")
preprocessing_node = ChatPreprocessingNode("Preprocessing")
intent_node = IntentDetectionNode("IntentDetection")
response_node = ResponseGenerationNode("ResponseGeneration")
output_node = ChatOutputNode("ChatOutput")

# Register nodes with the Graph Manager
graph_manager.add_node("input", input_node)
graph_manager.add_node("preprocess", preprocessing_node)
graph_manager.add_node("intent", intent_node)
graph_manager.add_node("response", response_node)
graph_manager.add_node("output", output_node)

# Connect nodes to form the chatbot workflow:
# ChatInput -> Preprocessing -> IntentDetection ->
ResponseGeneration -> ChatOutput
graph_manager.connect("input", "preprocess")
graph_manager.connect("preprocess", "intent")
```

```
graph_manager.connect("intent", "response")
graph_manager.connect("response", "output")

# Execute the workflow starting at the ChatInput node
print("Starting Conversational Agent Workflow...\n")
graph_manager.run("input")
```

Explanation:

- **ChatInputNode:**
  Simulates the collection of user input and passes it to the preprocessing stage.
- **ChatPreprocessingNode:**
  Normalizes the input text (e.g., lowercasing and trimming whitespace) and forwards it to the intent detection node.
- **IntentDetectionNode:**
  Uses Hugging Face's zero-shot classification pipeline to determine the most likely intent from predefined candidate labels. It then passes both the processed text and the detected intent to the next node.
- **ResponseGenerationNode:**
  Generates a response using a text generation model (GPT-2 in this case). It customizes the prompt based on the detected intent to produce a contextually appropriate reply.
- **ChatOutputNode:**
  Outputs the final response. In a production system, this might send the response to a chat interface, mobile app, or web application.
- **Graph Manager:**
  Orchestrates the nodes, ensuring that data flows correctly from the input through preprocessing, intent detection, response generation, and finally to output.

---

4. Managing Data Flow and Dependencies in the Chatbot Workflow

Proper data flow is crucial in a conversational agent. Notice how each node in the workflow:

- Receives the output from the previous node.
- Processes the data accordingly.
- Passes the result to the next node using the `run` method.

This structure ensures that all components work in unison, and dependencies are maintained. For example, the ResponseGenerationNode waits until it receives both the text and the detected intent from the IntentDetectionNode before generating a response.

Table: Data Flow in Chatbot Workflow

Node	Input	Output	Dependency
ChatInputNode	None (simulated user input)	Raw text	Starts the workflow
ChatPreprocessingNode	Raw text	Cleaned and normalized text	Depends on ChatInputNode
IntentDetectionNode	Processed text	Tuple (processed text, detected intent)	Depends on ChatPreprocessingNode
ResponseGenerationNode	Tuple (processed text, detected intent)	Generated response	Depends on IntentDetectionNode
ChatOutputNode	Generated response	Final output to the user	Depends on ResponseGenerationNode

5. Best Practices for Building Conversational Agents

- **Modular Design:**
  Build each component as a separate node. This makes it easier to debug, update, or replace individual parts of the workflow.
- **Clear Data Contracts:**
  Ensure that each node clearly defines the format of its input and output. For example, when passing a tuple (text, intent), document what each element represents.

- **Error Handling:**
  Implement error handling within each node to manage exceptions from external libraries (e.g., handling model inference errors).
- **Scalability:**
  Consider parallelizing components where possible, especially for high-traffic applications. For instance, intent detection can be scaled horizontally.
- **Testing:**
  Create unit tests for individual nodes and integration tests for the complete workflow to ensure reliability and robustness.

Building conversational agents and chatbots with LangGraph Python involves decomposing the task into discrete, manageable nodes and orchestrating them into a cohesive workflow. By integrating popular NLP libraries such as Hugging Face Transformers for intent detection and text generation, you can leverage state-of-the-art models to deliver contextually relevant responses.

This comprehensive example demonstrated how to define custom nodes, manage data flow and dependencies, and connect everything using a Graph Manager. As you extend these concepts, you can add more sophisticated dialogue management, context retention, and multi-turn conversation capabilities to create even more robust conversational agents.

6.3 Designing Q&A and Recommendation Systems

Designing Q&A (Question & Answer) and recommendation systems with LangGraph Python involves leveraging graph-based workflows to structure complex processing pipelines. These systems share some common architectural elements, such as data ingestion, natural language processing (NLP), ranking or selection algorithms, and output generation. However, they serve distinct purposes:

- **Q&A Systems:** Aim to understand a user's question and retrieve or generate the correct answer.
- **Recommendation Systems:** Provide personalized suggestions (e.g., products, content, or services) based on user preferences, behavior, or item similarities.

In this section, we will explore the building blocks for designing these systems, discuss their key components and data flow, and provide complete code examples with explanations.

---

1. Overview and Key Components

Q&A Systems typically include:

- **Input Handling:** Capturing user queries.
- **Preprocessing:** Cleaning and tokenizing questions.
- **Question Understanding:** Analyzing the query to extract intent and key entities.
- **Knowledge Retrieval/Inference:** Searching a database or knowledge graph, or generating answers using language models.
- **Response Generation:** Composing a coherent answer.

Recommendation Systems typically include:

- **User Data and Item Data Ingestion:** Collecting information on user behavior, preferences, and item features.
- **Feature Extraction and Embedding:** Transforming textual or structured data into numerical representations.
- **Similarity/Ranking Algorithms:** Comparing users or items and ranking recommendations.
- **Output Delivery:** Presenting personalized recommendations.

Both systems can be designed as graph-based workflows where each functional block is encapsulated as a node. The **Graph Manager** orchestrates data flow between nodes, ensuring dependencies are met.

---

2. Workflow Design Patterns

Below is a high-level view of the workflows for each system:

Q&A Workflow:

1. **Input Node:** Captures the user's question.
2. **Preprocessing Node:** Cleans and tokenizes the query.

3. **Question Analysis Node:** Uses an NLP model (e.g., a transformer-based classifier) to extract intent and key entities.
4. **Knowledge Retrieval/Inference Node:** Searches a knowledge base or uses a language model to generate an answer.
5. **Response Generation Node:** Formats and outputs the answer.

Recommendation Workflow:

1. **Input Node:** Captures user profile and context.
2. **Item Data Node:** Loads item features (e.g., product descriptions).
3. **Feature Extraction Node:** Converts text into embeddings using an NLP library (e.g., Hugging Face Transformers, Sentence Transformers).
4. **Similarity Calculation/Ranking Node:** Compares user preferences with item embeddings.
5. **Recommendation Output Node:** Displays a ranked list of recommendations.

Table: Workflow Components Comparison

Component	Q&A Systems	Recommendation Systems
Input Handling	User question capture	User profile and context capture
Preprocessing	Tokenization, normalization of the question	Text cleaning and embedding of item data
Analysis/Retrieval	Intent and entity extraction; answer retrieval	Feature extraction; similarity computation; ranking
Response/Output	Formatted answer generation	Ranked list of personalized recommendations

3. Code Example: Building a Q&A System

Below is a simplified example using LangGraph Python that demonstrates a Q&A workflow. This example integrates Hugging Face Transformers for question analysis and answer generation.

```
python
```

```python
# Import necessary libraries from LangGraph Python and
Hugging Face
from langgraph import Node, GraphManager
from transformers import pipeline

# Define a Node to capture the user question
class QAInputNode(Node):
    def run(self, data=None):
        question = "What is the capital of France?"
        print(f"[{self.name}] Captured Question: {question}")
        for node in self.next_nodes:
            node.run(question)

# Define a Preprocessing Node for cleaning the question
class QAPreprocessingNode(Node):
    def run(self, data):
        # Simple preprocessing: lowercase and strip extra
spaces
        processed_question = data.lower().strip()
        print(f"[{self.name}] Preprocessed Question:
{processed_question}")
        for node in self.next_nodes:
            node.run(processed_question)

# Define a Node for Question Analysis using a zero-shot
classifier to extract intent/entities
class QAAnalysisNode(Node):
    def __init__(self, name):
        super().__init__(name)
        self.classifier = pipeline("zero-shot-
classification", model="facebook/bart-large-mnli")
        self.candidate_labels = ["capital", "population",
"area", "history"]

    def run(self, data):
        print(f"[{self.name}] Analyzing question: '{data}'")
        result = self.classifier(data,
candidate_labels=self.candidate_labels)
        # Assume the top label indicates the type of answer
needed
        intent = result["labels"][0]
        print(f"[{self.name}] Detected Intent: {intent}")
        for node in self.next_nodes:
            node.run((data, intent))

# Define a Node for Answer Retrieval/Generation
class QAAnswerNode(Node):
    def __init__(self, name):
        super().__init__(name)
```

```
            # For demonstration, using a text generation pipeline
(GPT-2)
            self.generator = pipeline("text-generation",
model="gpt2")

    def run(self, data):
        question, intent = data
        prompt = f"Question: {question}\nAnswer regarding
{intent}:"
        print(f"[{self.name}] Generating answer with prompt:
'{prompt}'")
        result = self.generator(prompt, max_length=60,
num_return_sequences=1)
        answer = result[0]['generated_text']
        print(f"[{self.name}] Generated Answer: {answer}")
        for node in self.next_nodes:
            node.run(answer)

# Define a Node to output the final answer
class QAOutputNode(Node):
    def run(self, data):
        print(f"[{self.name}] Final Answer: {data}")

# Build the Q&A workflow using GraphManager
qa_graph = GraphManager()
input_node = QAInputNode("QA_Input")
preprocess_node = QAPreprocessingNode("QA_Preprocess")
analysis_node = QAAnalysisNode("QA_Analysis")
answer_node = QAAnswerNode("QA_Answer")
output_node = QAOutputNode("QA_Output")

qa_graph.add_node("input", input_node)
qa_graph.add_node("preprocess", preprocess_node)
qa_graph.add_node("analysis", analysis_node)
qa_graph.add_node("answer", answer_node)
qa_graph.add_node("output", output_node)

qa_graph.connect("input", "preprocess")
qa_graph.connect("preprocess", "analysis")
qa_graph.connect("analysis", "answer")
qa_graph.connect("answer", "output")

print("Starting Q&A Workflow...\n")
qa_graph.run("input")
```

Explanation:

- **QAInputNode:** Simulates capturing a user's question.
- **QAPreprocessingNode:** Performs simple text cleaning.

- **QAAnalysisNode:** Uses a zero-shot classification model to detect the intent (e.g., identifying the topic "capital").
- **QAAnswerNode:** Generates an answer using a text generation model, constructing a prompt that includes both the question and detected intent.
- **QAOutputNode:** Outputs the final answer.
- **Graph Manager:** Orchestrates the nodes, ensuring a smooth data flow from input to output.

4. Code Example: Building a Recommendation System

Below is an example demonstrating a recommendation workflow. In this scenario, we simulate a system that recommends items based on user preferences. For simplicity, we'll use placeholder functions to mimic feature extraction and similarity calculation.

```python
python

from langgraph import Node, GraphManager

# Define a Node to capture user profile or preferences
class RecInputNode(Node):
    def run(self, data=None):
        # Simulated user profile: a list of liked genres
        user_profile = {"user_id": "123", "preferences":
["sci-fi", "thriller"]}
        print(f"[{self.name}] Captured User Profile:
{user_profile}")
        for node in self.next_nodes:
            node.run(user_profile)

# Define a Node to load item data (e.g., product or movie
details)
class ItemDataNode(Node):
    def run(self, data):
        # Simulated item data: a list of items with their
genres
        items = [
            {"item_id": "A", "title": "Space Odyssey",
"genre": "sci-fi"},
            {"item_id": "B", "title": "Mystery Manor",
"genre": "thriller"},
            {"item_id": "C", "title": "Romantic Escape",
"genre": "romance"}
        ]
```

```
        print(f"[{self.name}] Loaded Item Data: {items}")
        # Combine user profile with item data for further
processing
        for node in self.next_nodes:
            node.run((data, items))

# Define a Node for Feature Extraction and Similarity
Calculation
class RecProcessingNode(Node):
    def run(self, data):
        user_profile, items = data
        # Simulated recommendation logic: recommend items
matching user preferences
        recommendations = [item for item in items if
item["genre"] in user_profile["preferences"]]
        print(f"[{self.name}] Recommendations:
{recommendations}")
        for node in self.next_nodes:
            node.run(recommendations)

# Define a Node to output recommendations
class RecOutputNode(Node):
    def run(self, data):
        print(f"[{self.name}] Final Recommendations: {data}")

# Build the Recommendation workflow using GraphManager
rec_graph = GraphManager()
input_node = RecInputNode("Rec_Input")
item_node = ItemDataNode("Item_Data")
processing_node = RecProcessingNode("Rec_Processing")
output_node = RecOutputNode("Rec_Output")

rec_graph.add_node("input", input_node)
rec_graph.add_node("item", item_node)
rec_graph.add_node("processing", processing_node)
rec_graph.add_node("output", output_node)

rec_graph.connect("input", "item")
rec_graph.connect("item", "processing")
rec_graph.connect("processing", "output")

print("\nStarting Recommendation Workflow...\n")
rec_graph.run("input")
```

Explanation:

- **RecInputNode:** Captures a simulated user profile with preferences.
- **ItemDataNode:** Loads a list of items with attributes such as genre.
- **RecProcessingNode:** Filters items based on matching genres to user preferences, simulating a recommendation algorithm.

- **RecOutputNode:** Outputs the final recommendations.
- **Graph Manager:** Ensures the proper sequencing and data flow between nodes.

---

5. Best Practices and Considerations

- **Modular Nodes:**
  Design each node to perform a single task (e.g., preprocessing, analysis, response generation). This improves maintainability and testing.
- **Clear Data Contracts:**
  Define and document the input and output formats of each node to ensure smooth data flow and proper dependency management.
- **Error Handling:**
  Implement robust error checking within nodes to handle unexpected input or failures in external library calls.
- **Scalability:**
  Consider parallelizing parts of the workflow where appropriate. For recommendation systems, batch processing or asynchronous execution can improve performance.
- **Evaluation:**
  Continuously test the Q&A or recommendation system with real-world data and user feedback. Use unit and integration tests to ensure reliability.

---

6. Summary Table: Q&A vs. Recommendation Workflows

Aspect	Q&A System	Recommendation System
Primary Input	User question (text)	User profile and item data
Preprocessing	Text normalization, tokenization	Data cleaning, embedding extraction
Core Task	Intent detection, knowledge retrieval/generation	Similarity calculation, ranking
Output	Generated answer or explanation	Ranked list of recommended items

Aspect	Q&A System	Recommendation System
Key Libraries	Hugging Face Transformers, LangChain	NLP libraries for embedding (e.g., Sentence Transformers)

Designing Q&A and recommendation systems using LangGraph Python enables you to build sophisticated applications by decomposing complex tasks into modular nodes. By integrating popular NLP libraries and defining clear data flows and dependencies, you can create workflows that are both robust and scalable.

The detailed code examples above demonstrate how to construct and orchestrate a Q&A workflow and a recommendation workflow, highlighting best practices in data management and node design. With these foundations, you can further extend your systems to incorporate more advanced processing, richer dialogue management, and personalized recommendations.

6.4 Case Study: End-to-End NLP Pipeline with LangGraph

In this case study, we will build an end-to-end NLP pipeline using LangGraph Python. This comprehensive example will demonstrate how to integrate various NLP components into a cohesive workflow that processes raw text, extracts information, and generates an output. We will cover every step from data ingestion to final output generation, and include detailed code examples, explanations, and supporting tables.

Overview of the Pipeline

The end-to-end NLP pipeline in this case study consists of the following stages:

1. **Data Ingestion:**
   Captures raw text input from a user or data source.
2. **Preprocessing:**
   Cleans and tokenizes the input text.

3. **Named Entity Recognition (NER):**
    Identifies and classifies key entities in the text (e.g., names, organizations, locations).
4. **Sentiment Analysis:**
    Evaluates the emotional tone of the text.
5. **Response Generation:**
    Uses the processed information to generate a customized response.
6. **Output Delivery:**
    Displays or sends the final output.

Each of these stages will be implemented as a separate node in our LangGraph workflow, and a Graph Manager will orchestrate the data flow between nodes.

Pipeline Architecture Diagram

Below is a simplified diagram representing the structure of our end-to-end NLP pipeline:

pgsql

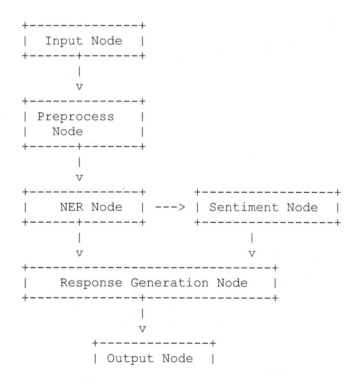

```
         +--------------+
         |  Input Node  |
         +------+-------+
                |
                v
         +--------------+
         |  Preprocess  |
         |    Node      |
         +------+-------+
                |
                v
         +--------------+        +-----------------+
         |   NER Node   | --->   | Sentiment Node  |
         +------+-------+        +-----------------+
                |                         |
                v                         v
         +-------------------------------------+
         |     Response Generation Node        |
         +----------------+--------------------+
                          |
                          v
               +--------------+
               | Output Node  |
```

```
                   +--------------+
```

Explanation:

- **Input Node:** Captures the raw text.
- **Preprocess Node:** Cleans and tokenizes the text.
- **NER Node:** Extracts named entities.
- **Sentiment Node:** Determines the sentiment of the text.
- **Response Generation Node:** Uses information from the NER and Sentiment nodes to generate a tailored response.
- **Output Node:** Displays or returns the final output.

Detailed Code Example

Below is a complete, detailed code example that implements this NLP pipeline using LangGraph Python. We assume that you have installed the necessary packages (e.g., `langgraph`, `transformers`, `spacy`, and any additional NLP libraries).

```python
python

# Import necessary libraries and modules
from langgraph import Node, GraphManager
from transformers import pipeline
import spacy

# Load spaCy's English model for NER
nlp_spacy = spacy.load("en_core_web_sm")

# --- Node Definitions ---

# 1. Input Node: Captures raw text input.
class InputNode(Node):
    def run(self, data=None):
        # For demonstration, using a fixed input text.
        raw_text = ("Apple Inc. announced a new product today
in Cupertino, "
                    "and many are excited about its
innovative features.")
        print(f"[{self.name}] Raw Input: {raw_text}")
        for node in self.next_nodes:
            node.run(raw_text)

# 2. Preprocessing Node: Cleans and tokenizes the text.
class PreprocessNode(Node):
```

```python
    def run(self, data):
        # Simple preprocessing: lowercasing and stripping
whitespace.
        processed_text = data.lower().strip()
        print(f"[{self.name}] Processed Text:
{processed_text}")
        for node in self.next_nodes:
            node.run(processed_text)

# 3. NER Node: Extracts named entities using spaCy.
class NERNode(Node):
    def run(self, data):
        doc = nlp_spacy(data)
        # Extract entities as a list of tuples: (entity_text,
entity_label)
        entities = [(ent.text, ent.label_) for ent in
doc.ents]
        print(f"[{self.name}] Detected Entities: {entities}")
        # Pass both original text and entities to the next
node
        for node in self.next_nodes:
            node.run((data, entities))

# 4. Sentiment Analysis Node: Analyzes sentiment using a
Hugging Face pipeline.
class SentimentNode(Node):
    def __init__(self, name):
        super().__init__(name)
        # Initialize sentiment analysis pipeline; using a
common model.
        self.sentiment_analyzer = pipeline("sentiment-
analysis", model="distilbert-base-uncased-finetuned-sst-2-
english")

    def run(self, data):
        # 'data' is a tuple (text, entities)
        text, entities = data
        sentiment_result = self.sentiment_analyzer(text)[0]
        sentiment = sentiment_result["label"]
        score = sentiment_result["score"]
        print(f"[{self.name}] Sentiment: {sentiment} (Score:
{score:.2f})")
        # Pass the text, entities, and sentiment to the next
node
        for node in self.next_nodes:
            node.run((text, entities, sentiment))

# 5. Response Generation Node: Generates a response based on
processed info.
class ResponseGenerationNode(Node):
    def __init__(self, name):
```

```python
        super().__init__(name)
        # Initialize a text generation pipeline using GPT-2
        self.generator = pipeline("text-generation",
model="gpt2")

    def run(self, data):
        text, entities, sentiment = data
        # Create a prompt that includes key extracted info
        prompt = (f"Based on the following information:\n"
                  f"Text: {text}\n"
                  f"Entities: {entities}\n"
                  f"Sentiment: {sentiment}\n"
                  "Provide a concise summary and a
recommendation.")
        print(f"[{self.name}] Generating response with
prompt:\n{prompt}")
        result = self.generator(prompt, max_length=100,
num_return_sequences=1)
        response = result[0]['generated_text']
        print(f"[{self.name}] Generated Response:
{response}")
        for node in self.next_nodes:
            node.run(response)

# 6. Output Node: Delivers the final output.
class OutputNode(Node):
    def run(self, data):
        print(f"[{self.name}] Final Output:\n{data}")

# --- Build the Graph-Based Pipeline ---

# Instantiate the Graph Manager.
graph_manager = GraphManager()

# Create node instances.
input_node = InputNode("InputNode")
preprocess_node = PreprocessNode("PreprocessNode")
ner_node = NERNode("NERNode")
sentiment_node = SentimentNode("SentimentNode")
response_node =
ResponseGenerationNode("ResponseGenerationNode")
output_node = OutputNode("OutputNode")

# Register nodes with the Graph Manager.
graph_manager.add_node("input", input_node)
graph_manager.add_node("preprocess", preprocess_node)
graph_manager.add_node("ner", ner_node)
graph_manager.add_node("sentiment", sentiment_node)
graph_manager.add_node("response", response_node)
graph_manager.add_node("output", output_node)
```

```
# Connect nodes to form the pipeline.
graph_manager.connect("input", "preprocess")
graph_manager.connect("preprocess", "ner")
graph_manager.connect("ner", "sentiment")
graph_manager.connect("sentiment", "response")
graph_manager.connect("response", "output")

# --- Execute the Pipeline ---
print("Starting End-to-End NLP Pipeline...\n")
graph_manager.run("input")
```

Explanation

1. **Input Node:**
   - **Purpose:** Simulates capturing raw text from a source.
   - **Functionality:** Provides a fixed example sentence for demonstration.
2. **Preprocessing Node:**
   - **Purpose:** Normalizes text by converting it to lowercase and trimming whitespace.
   - **Functionality:** Ensures consistency in further processing steps.
3. **NER Node:**
   - **Purpose:** Extracts named entities from the text using spaCy.
   - **Functionality:** Identifies entities (e.g., "Apple Inc.", "Cupertino") and passes both the text and entities to the next node.
4. **Sentiment Node:**
   - **Purpose:** Analyzes the sentiment of the text using a Hugging Face pipeline.
   - **Functionality:** Outputs sentiment (e.g., "POSITIVE" or "NEGATIVE") along with a score and passes the data onward.
5. **Response Generation Node:**
   - **Purpose:** Generates a custom response using GPT-2, incorporating the text, entities, and sentiment.
   - **Functionality:** Constructs a detailed prompt and produces a generated response.
6. **Output Node:**
   - **Purpose:** Delivers the final output to the user.
   - **Functionality:** Simply prints the final response.
7. **Graph Manager:**

- o **Purpose:** Orchestrates the entire pipeline by registering nodes, connecting them, and initiating execution.
- o **Functionality:** Ensures the correct data flow through the pipeline.

Summary Table: Pipeline Components

Node	Input	Processing	Output
Input Node	None (raw text source)	Captures raw text	Raw text
Preprocess Node	Raw text	Lowercases and trims text	Processed text
NER Node	Processed text	Uses spaCy to extract named entities	Tuple: (Processed text, List of entities)
Sentiment Node	Tuple: (Processed text, List of entities)	Analyzes sentiment with a Hugging Face pipeline	Tuple: (Text, Entities, Sentiment)
Response Generation Node	Tuple: (Text, Entities, Sentiment)	Generates a response using a text generation model (GPT-2)	Generated response
Output Node	Generated response	Outputs the final result	Final output displayed

This case study demonstrates how to build an end-to-end NLP pipeline using LangGraph Python. By decomposing the overall task into modular nodes, each responsible for a specific function, you can create a flexible, maintainable, and scalable workflow. The integration of popular NLP libraries—spaCy for NER and Hugging Face Transformers for sentiment analysis and text generation—shows how to leverage state-of-the-art models within your graph-based pipeline.

By following this example, you now have a blueprint for developing more complex NLP applications that incorporate multiple processing steps and data dependencies. This approach not only improves modularity and reusability but also makes it easier to debug, test, and extend your pipeline as requirements evolve.

Part III: Advanced Concepts and Customization

Chapter 7: Advanced Workflow Techniques

7.1 Custom Node Development

Custom node development is a critical skill when working with LangGraph Python. While the framework provides basic node classes to get started quickly, building advanced, production-ready workflows often requires creating custom nodes tailored to your application's specific needs. In this chapter, we will explore how to design, develop, and integrate custom nodes into your LangGraph workflows.

Custom nodes allow you to encapsulate unique functionality, whether it's an intricate NLP task, a specialized data transformation, or integrating with external services. By creating custom nodes, you can keep your workflow modular, maintainable, and reusable across different projects.

---

1. Understanding the Base Node Class

Before creating a custom node, it's essential to understand the base `Node` class provided by LangGraph Python. The base class offers the following key features:

- **Name Attribute:**
  Each node is identified by a unique name.
- **Next Nodes List:**
  A node can be connected to one or more subsequent nodes using an `add_next()` method. This list represents the outgoing edges from the node.
- **Run Method:**
  The core functionality of a node is defined in its `run(data)` method. This method processes the input data and passes the result to the next connected node(s).

Base Node Class Example:

```python
```

```
class Node:
    def __init__(self, name):
        self.name = name
        self.next_nodes = []

    def add_next(self, node):
        """
        Connect this node to another node.

        Parameters:
        - node (Node): The node to connect as a downstream
node.
        """
        self.next_nodes.append(node)

    def run(self, data):
        """
        Process input data. This method should be overridden
by custom nodes.

        Parameters:
        - data: The input data for the node.

        Raises:
        - NotImplementedError: Indicates that the subclass
must implement this method.
        """
        raise NotImplementedError("Subclasses must implement
the run method.")
```

Explanation:

- The constructor initializes the node with a name and an empty list for next nodes.
- The `add_next()` method provides a simple interface for connecting nodes.
- The `run()` method is defined as a placeholder to enforce that any custom node must implement its own processing logic.

---

2. Designing a Custom Node

When designing a custom node, consider the following:

- **Single Responsibility Principle:**
  Each node should perform one well-defined task. This simplifies testing and debugging.
- **Input/Output Contract:**
  Clearly define what data the node expects as input and what it will output. Consistency in data formats is critical for ensuring smooth integration with other nodes.
- **Error Handling:**
  Implement robust error handling within the node to manage exceptions, especially when integrating with external APIs or performing complex computations.
- **Reusability:**
  Structure the node's code so that it can be reused in different workflows without significant modifications.

---

3. Creating a Custom Node: A Step-by-Step Example

Let's create a custom node that performs a specific NLP task—extracting key phrases from text using a simple algorithm. In this example, the custom node will:

- Accept a string as input.
- Tokenize the string.
- Identify key phrases (for simplicity, let's assume key phrases are tokens longer than 4 characters).
- Output the list of key phrases.

Step 1: Define the Custom KeyPhraseExtractionNode

python

```python
class KeyPhraseExtractionNode(Node):
    def __init__(self, name):
        super().__init__(name)

    def run(self, data):
        """
        Extracts key phrases from the input text.

        Parameters:
        - data (str): The input text.
```

```
        Process:
        1. Split the text into tokens.
        2. Identify tokens longer than 4 characters as key
phrases.
        3. Print and propagate the list of key phrases.
        """
        if not isinstance(data, str):
            raise ValueError(f"[{self.name}] Expected input
data to be a string, got {type(data)}")

        # Tokenize the text by splitting on whitespace.
        tokens = data.split()
        # Identify key phrases (tokens longer than 4
characters).
        key_phrases = [token for token in tokens if
len(token) > 4]

        print(f"[{self.name}] Extracted Key Phrases:
{key_phrases}")
        # Pass the list of key phrases to the next connected
nodes.
        for node in self.next_nodes:
            node.run(key_phrases)
```

Explanation:

- **Input Validation:**
  The node checks if the input is a string and raises an error if it isn't.
- **Tokenization:**
  The node splits the input text into tokens using Python's built-in
  string `split()` method.
- **Key Phrase Extraction:**
  It filters tokens to include only those longer than 4 characters,
  treating them as key phrases.
- **Data Propagation:**
  The extracted key phrases are printed for debugging purposes and
  then forwarded to any connected nodes.

---

4. Integrating Custom Nodes into a Workflow

Now that we have our custom node, let's integrate it into a simple
LangGraph workflow. This workflow will consist of:

1. An Input Node that supplies raw text.

2. Our custom KeyPhraseExtractionNode.
3. An Output Node that displays the final output.

Step 2: Define Additional Nodes

We can reuse a basic Input Node and Output Node for this example.

python

```
# Define a simple Input Node
class SimpleInputNode(Node):
    def run(self, data=None):
        # Provide a sample input text.
        text = "LangGraph Python simplifies complex workflow
development."
        print(f"[{self.name}] Input Text: {text}")
        for node in self.next_nodes:
            node.run(text)

# Define a simple Output Node
class SimpleOutputNode(Node):
    def run(self, data):
        print(f"[{self.name}] Final Output: {data}")
```

Step 3: Build the Workflow Using GraphManager

python

```
# Define the Graph Manager class (as provided in previous
chapters)
class GraphManager:
    def __init__(self):
        self.nodes = {}

    def add_node(self, name, node):
        self.nodes[name] = node

    def connect(self, source_name, destination_name):
        source_node = self.nodes.get(source_name)
        destination_node = self.nodes.get(destination_name)
        if source_node and destination_node:
            source_node.add_next(destination_node)
        else:
            raise ValueError("One or both nodes not found in
the workflow.")

    def run(self, start_node_name, data=None):
        start_node = self.nodes.get(start_node_name)
        if start_node:
```

```
            start_node.run(data)
        else:
            raise ValueError("Start node not found in the
workflow.")

# Build the workflow
graph_manager = GraphManager()

# Create node instances
input_node = SimpleInputNode("InputNode")
keyphrase_node =
KeyPhraseExtractionNode("KeyPhraseExtractor")
output_node = SimpleOutputNode("OutputNode")

# Register nodes with the Graph Manager
graph_manager.add_node("input", input_node)
graph_manager.add_node("extractor", keyphrase_node)
graph_manager.add_node("output", output_node)

# Connect the nodes to form the workflow: Input ->
KeyPhraseExtraction -> Output
graph_manager.connect("input", "extractor")
graph_manager.connect("extractor", "output")

# Execute the workflow
print("Starting Custom Node Workflow...\n")
graph_manager.run("input")
```

Expected Output:

```
less

Starting Custom Node Workflow...

[InputNode] Input Text: LangGraph Python simplifies complex
workflow development.
[KeyPhraseExtractor] Extracted Key Phrases: ['LangGraph',
'Python', 'simplifies', 'complex', 'workflow',
'development.']
[OutputNode] Final Output: ['LangGraph', 'Python',
'simplifies', 'complex', 'workflow', 'development.']
```

Explanation:

- **Workflow Construction:**
  The Graph Manager registers and connects nodes, creating a simple
  linear workflow.
- **Data Flow:**
  The Input Node provides raw text, which is processed by the

KeyPhraseExtractionNode to extract key phrases. The Output Node then displays the list of key phrases.

- **Custom Node Role:**
  Our custom node successfully encapsulates the key phrase extraction logic, and its integration into the workflow demonstrates modularity and reusability.

5. Best Practices for Custom Node Development

Best Practice	Description	Example
Single Responsibility	Each custom node should perform one well-defined task to maintain clarity and simplicity.	KeyPhraseExtractionNode focuses only on key phrase extraction.
Clear Input/Output Contracts	Define and document the expected input and output for each node to avoid data mismatch errors.	The node expects a string input and outputs a list of key phrases.
Robust Error Handling	Implement error checking within the node to handle invalid inputs or exceptions from external libraries gracefully.	Validate input type and raise descriptive errors if needed.
Modularity and Reusability	Write nodes in a modular fashion so they can be easily reused in different workflows without modification.	Use base Node class and follow consistent design patterns.

Custom node development in LangGraph Python empowers you to extend the framework's capabilities and tailor workflows to meet specific requirements. By creating modular nodes with well-defined responsibilities, you can build robust, maintainable, and scalable workflows. The examples provided in this chapter demonstrate how to design a custom node—from understanding the base class and implementing the `run()` method to integrating the node into a complete workflow managed by a Graph Manager.

7.2 Dynamic Workflow Adaptation and Conditional Branching

Dynamic workflow adaptation and conditional branching are advanced techniques that enable your LangGraph Python workflows to adjust their execution paths in real time based on the data being processed. Rather than following a fixed, linear path, these techniques allow the workflow to make decisions—executing different nodes or branches—depending on conditions evaluated during runtime. This flexibility is particularly valuable in applications where decisions must be made dynamically, such as adaptive data processing, interactive conversational agents, or real-time monitoring systems.

In this section, we will explore the concepts behind dynamic workflow adaptation and conditional branching, discuss their importance, and provide detailed, step-by-step code examples and supporting tables.

---

1. Understanding Dynamic Workflow Adaptation

Dynamic workflow adaptation involves modifying the execution flow of a workflow during runtime based on changing data, external triggers, or conditional logic. This approach is useful when:

- **Data Variability:** The input data varies significantly, requiring different processing strategies.
- **Real-Time Decision Making:** The system must make decisions on the fly (e.g., routing a request based on detected sentiment or error conditions).
- **Adaptive Processing:** The workflow can optimize itself by choosing the best processing route depending on current conditions.

Key Aspects:

- **Conditional Checks:** Nodes evaluate conditions based on the input data.

- **Branch Selection:** Depending on the outcome of the conditions, different branches (sub-workflows) are executed.
- **Reconfiguration:** The workflow may add, remove, or reorder nodes dynamically if needed.

2. Conditional Branching in Workflows

Conditional branching is a specific form of dynamic adaptation where the workflow splits into different paths based on a condition. Each branch handles a particular scenario, and the correct branch is chosen at runtime. For example, in a chatbot, if the user's query is classified as a "complaint," the workflow might route the conversation to a support team; otherwise, it might proceed with standard responses.

Table: Key Elements of Conditional Branching

Element	Description	Example
Condition Evaluation	Check input data to determine which branch to follow.	If sentiment is "negative," then route to support branch.
Branch Node	A node that makes a decision and routes data accordingly.	A DecisionNode that directs data to either a complaint handler or a general response generator.
Multiple Branches	Different paths that handle various conditions.	One branch for positive sentiment, another for negative sentiment.
Fallback Mechanism	Default path or error handling when conditions are not met.	A default branch that logs an error or provides a generic response.

3. Implementing Dynamic Workflow Adaptation and Conditional Branching

Let's create an example that demonstrates dynamic workflow adaptation. In this example, we'll build a simplified workflow for a sentiment-based routing system. The workflow will include:

- **Input Node:** Captures the user input.
- **Sentiment Analysis Node:** Analyzes the sentiment of the text.
- **Decision Node:** Routes the data to different branches based on the sentiment.
- **Positive Branch Node:** Processes positive sentiment.
- **Negative Branch Node:** Processes negative sentiment.
- **Fallback Node:** Handles cases when sentiment is neutral or cannot be determined.
- **Output Node:** Delivers the final output.

---

4. Detailed Code Example

Below is a complete code example illustrating how to implement dynamic workflow adaptation and conditional branching using LangGraph Python.

python

```python
# Import necessary modules
from langgraph import Node, GraphManager
from transformers import pipeline

# Define a basic Input Node to simulate user input
class ChatInputNode(Node):
    def run(self, data=None):
        # Simulate capturing user input
        user_input = "I am really disappointed with the
service."
        print(f"[{self.name}] User Input: {user_input}")
        for node in self.next_nodes:
            node.run(user_input)

# Define a Sentiment Analysis Node using Hugging Face
Transformers
class SentimentAnalysisNode(Node):
    def __init__(self, name):
        super().__init__(name)
        # Use a pre-trained sentiment analysis pipeline
        self.analyzer = pipeline("sentiment-analysis",
model="distilbert-base-uncased-finetuned-sst-2-english")

    def run(self, data):
        print(f"[{self.name}] Analyzing sentiment for:
'{data}'")
        result = self.analyzer(data)[0]
```

```python
        sentiment = result["label"]  # Expected to be
"POSITIVE" or "NEGATIVE"
        score = result["score"]
        print(f"[{self.name}] Detected Sentiment: {sentiment}
(Score: {score:.2f})")
        # Forward the original data along with the sentiment
label
        for node in self.next_nodes:
            node.run((data, sentiment))

# Define a Decision Node for Conditional Branching based on
sentiment
class DecisionNode(Node):
    def run(self, data):
        # Data is a tuple (input_text, sentiment)
        input_text, sentiment = data
        print(f"[{self.name}] Evaluating condition with
sentiment: {sentiment}")
        # Choose branch based on sentiment
        if sentiment == "NEGATIVE":
            print(f"[{self.name}] Routing to Negative
Branch")
            for node in self.next_nodes:
                if isinstance(node, NegativeBranchNode):
                    node.run(input_text)
        elif sentiment == "POSITIVE":
            print(f"[{self.name}] Routing to Positive
Branch")
            for node in self.next_nodes:
                if isinstance(node, PositiveBranchNode):
                    node.run(input_text)
        else:
            print(f"[{self.name}] Routing to Fallback
Branch")
            for node in self.next_nodes:
                if isinstance(node, FallbackNode):
                    node.run(input_text)

# Define Positive Branch Node: processes positive sentiment
class PositiveBranchNode(Node):
    def run(self, data):
        # Simulate processing for positive feedback
        response = f"Thank you for your positive feedback! We
are glad you had a great experience."
        print(f"[{self.name}] Response: {response}")
        for node in self.next_nodes:
            node.run(response)

# Define Negative Branch Node: processes negative sentiment
class NegativeBranchNode(Node):
    def run(self, data):
```

```
        # Simulate processing for negative feedback
        response = f"We're sorry to hear about your
experience. Our support team will reach out to assist you."
        print(f"[{self.name}] Response: {response}")
        for node in self.next_nodes:
            node.run(response)

# Define Fallback Node: handles neutral or undefined
sentiment cases
class FallbackNode(Node):
    def run(self, data):
        # Default response for neutral or undefined cases
        response = f"Thank you for your input. Could you
please provide more details?"
        print(f"[{self.name}] Response: {response}")
        for node in self.next_nodes:
            node.run(response)

# Define Output Node: delivers the final response
class ChatOutputNode(Node):
    def run(self, data):
        print(f"[{self.name}] Final Output: {data}")

# Build the workflow using GraphManager
graph_manager = GraphManager()

# Create node instances
input_node = ChatInputNode("ChatInput")
sentiment_node = SentimentAnalysisNode("SentimentAnalysis")
decision_node = DecisionNode("Decision")
positive_node = PositiveBranchNode("PositiveBranch")
negative_node = NegativeBranchNode("NegativeBranch")
fallback_node = FallbackNode("Fallback")
output_node = ChatOutputNode("ChatOutput")

# Register nodes with the Graph Manager
graph_manager.add_node("input", input_node)
graph_manager.add_node("sentiment", sentiment_node)
graph_manager.add_node("decision", decision_node)
graph_manager.add_node("positive", positive_node)
graph_manager.add_node("negative", negative_node)
graph_manager.add_node("fallback", fallback_node)
graph_manager.add_node("output", output_node)

# Connect nodes to form the dynamic workflow:
# ChatInput -> SentimentAnalysis -> DecisionNode
graph_manager.connect("input", "sentiment")
graph_manager.connect("sentiment", "decision")

# DecisionNode connects to multiple branches
# Each branch node then connects to the ChatOutput node
```

```
decision_node.add_next(positive_node)
decision_node.add_next(negative_node)
decision_node.add_next(fallback_node)
positive_node.add_next(output_node)
negative_node.add_next(output_node)
fallback_node.add_next(output_node)

# Execute the workflow starting from the ChatInput node
print("Starting Dynamic Workflow with Conditional
Branching...\n")
graph_manager.run("input")
```

5. Explanation

- **Input and Sentiment Analysis:**
  - The **ChatInputNode** simulates capturing a user message.
  - The **SentimentAnalysisNode** analyzes the input text using a Hugging Face sentiment pipeline, determining whether the sentiment is "POSITIVE" or "NEGATIVE".
- **Decision Node:**
  - The **DecisionNode** receives the original text and sentiment. It then evaluates the condition to decide which branch to execute.
  - It checks the sentiment and routes the data to either the **PositiveBranchNode**, **NegativeBranchNode**, or **FallbackNode**.
- **Branch Nodes:**
  - The **PositiveBranchNode** and **NegativeBranchNode** simulate generating different responses based on the sentiment.
  - The **FallbackNode** handles cases that are not clearly positive or negative.
- **Output:**
  - Finally, the **ChatOutputNode** outputs the final response generated by the branch nodes.
- **Dynamic Adaptation:**
  - The workflow dynamically adapts based on the sentiment analysis result, demonstrating conditional branching.

6. Summary Table: Dynamic Workflow Adaptation

Component	Role	Key Logic/Condition	Example Action
Input Node	Captures initial user input	N/A	"I am really disappointed with the service."
Sentiment Analysis Node	Analyzes the sentiment of the text	Uses pre-trained sentiment analysis model	Returns "NEGATIVE" with a confidence score
Decision Node	Evaluates conditions and routes data to branches	If sentiment == "NEGATIVE", route to Negative Branch; if "POSITIVE", route to Positive Branch; otherwise, Fallback	Routes negative sentiment to support branch
Branch Nodes	Process data based on specific conditions	Conditional processing based on branch type	Negative branch generates an apology and support message
Output Node	Delivers the final output	N/A	Displays the final response from the selected branch

Dynamic workflow adaptation and conditional branching are powerful techniques for building flexible, responsive systems with LangGraph Python. By evaluating conditions at runtime, you can direct the flow of data to different branches and customize processing based on specific criteria. This approach is especially useful for applications like conversational agents, monitoring systems, and any scenario where the processing path must adjust dynamically based on the input data.

The detailed code examples and explanations provided in this section illustrate how to implement these techniques effectively. With these tools at your disposal, you can design workflows that are both adaptive and maintainable, ensuring that your applications respond intelligently to changing conditions.

7.3 Performance Optimization and Scalability Strategies

As your LangGraph Python applications grow in complexity and handle larger datasets or higher throughput, performance optimization and scalability become critical. In this section, we will explore strategies to optimize performance and scale your graph-based workflows. We will discuss various techniques such as profiling and optimization, caching, parallel and asynchronous processing, and distributed computing. Detailed code examples, tables, and explanations are provided to help you implement these strategies effectively.

---

1. Profiling and Identifying Bottlenecks

Before optimizing, it's essential to identify where the performance bottlenecks occur. Profiling tools can help you measure execution time, memory usage, and identify inefficient code segments.

Techniques:

- **Python's `cProfile`:**
  Use the built-in profiler to capture performance metrics.
- **Timeit Module:**
  Measure execution time for small code snippets.
- **Logging and Monitoring:**
  Add logging statements to track the performance of critical nodes.

Example: Using cProfile

```python
import cProfile
import pstats

def run_workflow():
    # Assuming 'graph_manager' is already defined and set up
    graph_manager.run("input")

# Profile the workflow execution
profiler = cProfile.Profile()
profiler.enable()
```

```
run_workflow()
profiler.disable()

# Print profiling statistics
stats = pstats.Stats(profiler).sort_stats('cumtime')
stats.print_stats(10)
```

Explanation:

- The code uses `cProfile` to measure the cumulative time spent in each function, helping identify slow nodes or processes.

---

2. Caching and Memoization

Caching results of expensive computations can significantly improve performance. If a node performs a computation that is likely to be repeated with the same input, caching its output avoids redundant work.

Techniques:

- **In-Memory Caching:**
  Store results in a dictionary or use Python's `functools.lru_cache` decorator.
- **Persistent Caching:**
  Save results to disk if the computation is heavy and reused across multiple runs.

Example: Using `functools.lru_cache` in a Custom Node

```python
import functools

class CachedProcessingNode(Node):
    def __init__(self, name):
        super().__init__(name)

    @functools.lru_cache(maxsize=128)
    def expensive_operation(self, data):
        # Simulate an expensive operation, e.g., complex NLP task
        result = data.upper()  # Placeholder for an expensive computation
```

```
        return result

    def run(self, data):
        print(f"[{self.name}] Processing data: {data}")
        # Use cached result if available
        processed_data = self.expensive_operation(data)
        print(f"[{self.name}] Processed Data (Cached):
{processed_data}")
        for node in self.next_nodes:
            node.run(processed_data)

# Test the CachedProcessingNode
cached_node = CachedProcessingNode("CachedNode")
cached_node.run("Hello, LangGraph!")
cached_node.run("Hello, LangGraph!")  # This should use the
cached result
```

Explanation:

- **@lru_cache:**
  Caches the output of the `expensive_operation` method. If the same
  input is provided again, the function returns the cached result instead
  of recomputing it.

---

3. Parallel and Asynchronous Processing

For workflows that are CPU-bound or I/O-bound, parallel or asynchronous
execution can improve throughput and reduce latency.

Techniques:

- **Multithreading:**
  Useful for I/O-bound tasks. Python's `threading` module can run
  tasks concurrently.
- **Multiprocessing:**
  For CPU-bound tasks, use the `multiprocessing` module to run tasks
  in parallel across multiple CPU cores.
- **Asynchronous Programming:**
  Use `asyncio` for non-blocking I/O operations and high-concurrency
  workflows.

Example: Using Multiprocessing in a Node

python

```python
import multiprocessing
from time import sleep

class MultiprocessingNode(Node):
    def run(self, data):
        # Simulate a CPU-bound task that processes data in
parallel
        print(f"[{self.name}] Starting parallel processing
for data: {data}")

        def process_item(item):
            # Simulate processing time
            sleep(1)
            return item.upper()

        # Split data into items (for example, words in a
string)
        items = data.split()
        # Create a pool of workers
        with multiprocessing.Pool(processes=4) as pool:
            results = pool.map(process_item, items)

        processed_data = " ".join(results)
        print(f"[{self.name}] Processed Data (Parallel):
{processed_data}")
        for node in self.next_nodes:
            node.run(processed_data)

# Test the MultiprocessingNode
multiprocessing_node = MultiprocessingNode("MultiProcNode")
multiprocessing_node.run("Hello LangGraph Python")
```

Explanation:

- **Multiprocessing Pool:**
  The node splits the input into items and processes them in parallel
  using a pool of worker processes.
- **Performance Improvement:**
  Parallel processing reduces total execution time when processing
  large datasets.

Example: Using Asynchronous Processing with asyncio

python

```
import asyncio

class AsyncNode(Node):
    async def async_process(self, data):
        # Simulate an asynchronous I/O-bound task
        await asyncio.sleep(1)
        return data[::-1]  # Reverse the string as a simple
example

    def run(self, data):
        print(f"[{self.name}] Starting async processing for
data: {data}")
        loop = asyncio.get_event_loop()
        result =
loop.run_until_complete(self.async_process(data))
        print(f"[{self.name}] Processed Data (Async):
{result}")
        for node in self.next_nodes:
            node.run(result)

# Test the AsyncNode
async_node = AsyncNode("AsyncNode")
async_node.run("Hello, async LangGraph!")
```

Explanation:

- **Asyncio:**
  Uses asynchronous programming to perform non-blocking operations, ideal for I/O-bound tasks.

---

4. Distributed Computing Strategies

For large-scale applications, distributing the workload across multiple machines can further enhance scalability.

Techniques:

- **Message Queues:**
  Use message brokers like RabbitMQ or Kafka to distribute tasks between nodes.
- **Distributed Frameworks:**
  Integrate with frameworks like Apache Spark for distributed data processing.

- **Cloud Services:**
  Leverage cloud platforms (AWS, GCP, Azure) to deploy and scale your workflow horizontally.

Example: Conceptual Architecture Diagram for Distributed Workflow

lua

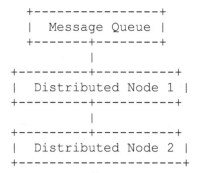

```
        +-----------------+
        |  Message Queue  |
        +-------+---------+
                |
     +----------+----------+
     |  Distributed Node 1  |
     +----------+----------+
                |
     +----------+----------+
     |  Distributed Node 2  |
     +---------------------+
```

Explanation:

- **Message Queue:**
  Acts as a buffer to distribute tasks among multiple processing nodes.
- **Distributed Nodes:**
  Multiple nodes process tasks in parallel across different machines, increasing throughput and resilience.

---

5. Summary Table: Optimization and Scalability Techniques

Technique	Description	Use Case	Example Tool/Module
Profiling	Identifying bottlenecks in code	Optimizing performance-critical nodes	cProfile, timeit
Caching/Memoization	Storing computed results to avoid redundancy	Repeatedly computing the same expensive operations	functools.lru_cache

Technique	Description	Use Case	Example Tool/Module
Multithreading	Concurrent execution for I/O-bound tasks	Handling multiple network requests simultaneously	threading module
Multiprocessing	Parallel execution for CPU-bound tasks	Data processing and heavy computations	multiprocessing module
Asynchronous Processing	Non-blocking I/O operations to handle concurrency	Real-time applications with many I/O operations	asyncio
Distributed Computing	Spreading workload across multiple machines	Large-scale data processing and high throughput systems	Apache Spark, RabbitMQ, Kafka, Cloud Services

Best Practices for Optimization and Scalability

- **Profile Early and Often:**
  Use profiling tools to identify bottlenecks before optimizing.
- **Cache Where Possible:**
  Cache intermediate results that are computationally expensive and frequently used.
- **Choose the Right Concurrency Model:**
  For I/O-bound tasks, consider asynchronous programming or multithreading; for CPU-bound tasks, use multiprocessing.
- **Plan for Scale:**
  Design your architecture to support distributed computing from the start if you expect significant growth.
- **Monitor and Iterate:**
  Continuously monitor the performance of your system in production and refine your strategies as needed.

Performance optimization and scalability are critical aspects of developing robust, real-world applications using LangGraph Python. By profiling your code, implementing caching strategies, leveraging parallel and asynchronous processing, and considering distributed computing options, you can ensure that your workflows are efficient and capable of handling increased load.

The code examples and strategies outlined in this section provide a foundation for optimizing individual nodes and scaling entire workflows. As you continue to develop your applications, remember that optimization is an iterative process—regular profiling, monitoring, and refinement will lead to a more responsive and scalable system.

7.4 Error Handling and Robust Debugging

Robust error handling and effective debugging are essential practices when building complex workflows with LangGraph Python. As your application grows in complexity, unexpected issues can arise due to invalid inputs, integration problems with external libraries, or unforeseen runtime conditions. In this section, we will explore strategies to manage errors gracefully and techniques to debug your workflows efficiently. We will cover best practices, provide detailed code examples, and include tables that summarize key error handling and debugging methods.

1. Importance of Error Handling and Debugging

Error Handling:
Proper error handling ensures that your application can manage and recover from unexpected conditions without crashing or producing incorrect results. It involves:

- **Detection:** Recognizing when an error occurs.
- **Reporting:** Logging detailed error information for later analysis.
- **Recovery:** Providing fallback logic or safe termination to maintain workflow stability.
- **Notification:** Alerting developers or users to critical issues that require attention.

Debugging:
Debugging is the process of identifying, isolating, and resolving issues within your code. Effective debugging techniques allow you to pinpoint problematic areas quickly and implement fixes with minimal disruption to the overall system.

---

2. Best Practices for Error Handling in LangGraph Python

When developing custom nodes and workflows, consider the following best practices:

- **Validate Input Data:**
  Always check that the data entering a node is in the expected format. Use explicit checks and raise descriptive errors if the data is invalid.
- **Use Try-Except Blocks:**
  Wrap code that may raise exceptions with try-except blocks to capture and handle errors gracefully. This prevents the entire workflow from crashing.
- **Log Detailed Error Messages:**
  Use Python's built-in `logging` module to record errors along with relevant contextual information (e.g., node name, input data). This information is invaluable when debugging issues.
- **Fallback Mechanisms:**
  Provide default behavior or fallback responses when a node fails. This can help maintain the workflow's overall operation even if one component encounters an issue.
- **Modular Design:**
  Keep node functionality focused and isolated. This makes it easier to identify which node is causing an issue.

Table: Best Practices for Error Handling

Best Practice	Description	Example
Input Validation	Check that inputs meet expected formats and constraints	Validate that a text input is non-empty
Try-Except Blocks	Use try-except to catch and handle exceptions	Wrap external API calls with try-except

Best Practice	Description	Example
Detailed Logging	Log errors with contextual details to aid in debugging	Use Python's `logging` module
Fallback Mechanisms	Provide alternative processing paths when errors occur	Default response for failed NLP analysis
Modular Design	Isolate node functionality to simplify identification of errors	Single-responsibility design for each custom node

3. Techniques for Robust Debugging

Effective debugging is critical for maintaining high-quality, reliable workflows. Some key debugging techniques include:

- **Print Debugging:**
  Inserting print statements at critical points in your node's code can help trace the flow of data and pinpoint where errors occur.
- **Logging:**
  Use logging instead of print statements for more controlled and configurable output. Logging levels (DEBUG, INFO, WARNING, ERROR, CRITICAL) help categorize messages.
- **Interactive Debuggers:**
  Use interactive debugging tools like Python's `pdb`, or integrated debuggers in IDEs like PyCharm or VS Code, to step through code and inspect variables.
- **Unit Testing:**
  Write unit tests for individual nodes and integration tests for entire workflows. Testing helps catch errors early and makes it easier to identify which component is failing.
- **Exception Tracebacks:**
  Always examine the full exception traceback to understand the context and root cause of an error.

Table: Debugging Techniques

Technique	Description	Use Case
Print Debugging	Inserting print statements to output variable values and flow info	Quick-and-dirty checks during development

Technique	Description	Use Case
Logging	Using Python's `logging` module for detailed, level-based messages	Production debugging and error monitoring
Interactive Debuggers	Tools like `pdb` for stepping through code and inspecting state	Complex issues that require step-by-step execution
Unit Testing	Automated tests for individual nodes and workflows	Preventing regressions and isolating faulty components
Exception Tracebacks	Reviewing detailed error messages provided by Python's interpreter	Diagnosing unexpected crashes or failures

4. Detailed Code Examples

Below are code examples that demonstrate robust error handling and debugging techniques in custom LangGraph Python nodes.

Example A: Input Validation and Try-Except Block

```python
class SafePreprocessingNode(Node):
    def run(self, data):
        try:
            # Validate input data
            if not isinstance(data, str) or not data.strip():
                raise ValueError(f"[{self.name}] Invalid input: Expected a non-empty string, got: {data}")

            # Preprocess the text (simple lowercasing)
            processed_text = data.lower().strip()
            print(f"[{self.name}] Processed Text: {processed_text}")
            for node in self.next_nodes:
                node.run(processed_text)
        except Exception as e:
            # Log the error and provide fallback logic
            print(f"[{self.name}] ERROR: {e}")
            # Fallback: Pass original data to next nodes
            for node in self.next_nodes:
                node.run(data)
```

```
# Testing SafePreprocessingNode with valid and invalid inputs
safe_node = SafePreprocessingNode("SafePreprocessor")
print("Testing with valid input:")
safe_node.run("Hello, LangGraph!")
print("\nTesting with invalid input:")
safe_node.run("")  # Should trigger error handling
```

Explanation:

- **Input Validation:**
  The node checks whether the input is a valid, non-empty string.
- **Try-Except:**
  The code is wrapped in a try-except block to catch exceptions.
- **Fallback Logic:**
  In case of an error, the node logs the error and passes the original
  data to subsequent nodes.

Example B: Using Logging for Debugging

python

```
import logging

# Configure logging settings
logging.basicConfig(level=logging.DEBUG,
format='[%(levelname)s] %(asctime)s - %(message)s')

class LoggingNode(Node):
    def run(self, data):
        logging.debug(f"[{self.name}] Received data: {data}")
        # Simulate processing
        try:
            # Example processing: reverse the string
            if not isinstance(data, str):
                raise TypeError("Input data must be a
string")
            result = data[::-1]
            logging.info(f"[{self.name}] Processed result:
{result}")
            for node in self.next_nodes:
                node.run(result)
        except Exception as e:
            logging.error(f"[{self.name}] Error during
processing: {e}")
```

```
# Test LoggingNode
logging_node = LoggingNode("Logger")
logging_node.run("LangGraph Debugging Example")
logging_node.run(123)  # Should log an error due to wrong
data type
```

Explanation:

- **Logging Configuration:**
  The `logging.basicConfig` function sets up the logging level and format.
- **Logging Statements:**
  Debug, info, and error messages are logged at various stages to trace execution and errors.
- **Error Handling:**
  If the input data is not a string, a `TypeError` is raised and caught, logging an error message.

Example C: Unit Testing a Custom Node

```python
python

import unittest

class ReverseNode(Node):
    def run(self, data):
        # Reverse the input string as a simple processing
step
        if not isinstance(data, str):
            raise ValueError("Input must be a string")
        return data[::-1]

class TestReverseNode(unittest.TestCase):
    def test_reverse_valid_input(self):
        node = ReverseNode("TestReverse")
        result = node.run("Hello")
        self.assertEqual(result, "olleH")

    def test_reverse_invalid_input(self):
        node = ReverseNode("TestReverse")
        with self.assertRaises(ValueError):
            node.run(123)

if __name__ == '__main__':
    unittest.main()
```

Explanation:

- **ReverseNode:**
  A simple node that reverses a string.
- **Unit Tests:**
  The tests validate both the correct functioning of the node with valid input and its ability to raise an error with invalid input.
- **Automated Testing:**
  Running the test suite ensures that modifications to the node do not introduce regressions.

5. Summary Table: Error Handling and Debugging Techniques

Technique	Purpose	Tool/Method	Example Outcome
Input Validation	Ensure inputs meet expected formats	if-else checks, ValueError	Prevents processing of invalid data
Try-Except Blocks	Catch and manage exceptions gracefully	try/except statements	Logs error and optionally provides fallback behavior
Logging	Record detailed debug and error messages	Python's `logging` module	Enables monitoring and post-mortem analysis
Interactive Debugging	Step through code execution	pdb, IDE debuggers	Helps isolate problematic code segments
Unit Testing	Automate validation of node functionality	unittest, pytest	Ensures that changes do not break existing functionality

Robust error handling and effective debugging are fundamental for developing reliable LangGraph Python applications. By validating inputs, catching exceptions with try-except blocks, using detailed logging, and incorporating unit tests, you can build workflows that gracefully handle errors and are easier to maintain and debug. Employing these techniques will lead to more resilient and robust applications, ensuring that your workflows continue to operate correctly even in the face of unexpected challenges.

Chapter 8: Extending LangGraph: APIs, Plugins, and Interoperability

8.1 Integrating External APIs and Services

Modern applications often rely on external APIs and services to augment their functionality—whether it's retrieving real-time data, performing specialized computations, or integrating with third-party platforms. LangGraph Python is designed to be flexible and extensible, allowing you to easily incorporate external APIs and services into your graph-based workflows. In this section, we will explore how to integrate these external resources, discuss best practices for ensuring smooth interoperability, and provide detailed code examples and supporting tables.

---

1. Why Integrate External APIs and Services?

Integrating external APIs and services into your LangGraph workflows can significantly enhance your application by:

- **Expanding Capabilities:**
  Leverage functionalities that are not built into LangGraph Python, such as geolocation, payment processing, or advanced analytics.
- **Real-Time Data Access:**
  Fetch live data (e.g., weather updates, stock prices, social media trends) that can dynamically influence your workflow.
- **Specialized Processing:**
  Utilize services that offer high-quality machine learning, natural language processing, or computer vision capabilities without having to develop these components in-house.
- **Interoperability:**
  Connect with other systems and platforms to create end-to-end solutions that span multiple services.

Table: Benefits of Integrating External APIs

Benefit	Description	Example
Expanded Capabilities	Add advanced features not built into your framework	Integrating sentiment analysis from an external NLP service
Real-Time Data Access	Retrieve up-to-date data for dynamic processing	Fetching live stock market data
Specialized Processing	Utilize highly specialized services for complex tasks	Using a cloud-based image recognition API
Interoperability	Connect with other systems and create integrated solutions	Integrating with CRM or ERP systems

2. Setting Up the Environment

Before integrating external APIs, ensure you have installed the necessary packages. Many APIs have dedicated Python SDKs or RESTful endpoints that you can access using libraries like `requests` or `httpx`.

For example, to install the `requests` library, run:

```bash
pip install requests
```

Additionally, if you plan to use a specific API with its own SDK, follow its installation instructions.

3. Creating Custom Nodes for External API Integration

In LangGraph Python, external API calls can be encapsulated within custom nodes. This approach keeps your workflow modular and makes it easier to handle API-specific logic (e.g., authentication, error handling, data parsing).

Example Scenario:
Imagine you want to integrate a weather API to fetch current weather data based on a city name. We will create a custom node called `WeatherAPINode`

that makes a REST API call to a weather service and passes the results to the next node in the workflow.

Step-by-Step Code Example:

1. **Define the Custom WeatherAPINode**

python

```python
import requests
from langgraph import Node

class WeatherAPINode(Node):
    def __init__(self, name, api_key):
        super().__init__(name)
        self.api_key = api_key
        self.base_url =
"http://api.openweathermap.org/data/2.5/weather"

    def run(self, data):
        """
        Fetches weather data for the specified city using an
external weather API.

        Parameters:
        - data (str): The city name for which to retrieve
weather information.
        """
        if not isinstance(data, str) or not data.strip():
            raise ValueError(f"[{self.name}] Invalid city
name provided: {data}")

        # Prepare parameters for the API call
        params = {
            "q": data,
            "appid": self.api_key,
            "units": "metric"  # Use metric units for
temperature
        }

        try:
            response = requests.get(self.base_url,
params=params)
            response.raise_for_status()  # Raise an exception
for HTTP errors
            weather_data = response.json()
            print(f"[{self.name}] Weather data for {data}:
{weather_data}")
        except requests.RequestException as e:
```

```
            print(f"[{self.name}] ERROR: Failed to fetch
weather data: {e}")
            # Fallback: Return an error message or default
data
            weather_data = {"error": str(e)}

        # Propagate the weather data to the next nodes
        for node in self.next_nodes:
            node.run(weather_data)
```

Explanation:

- **Initialization:**
  The node is initialized with a name and an API key. The base URL
  for the OpenWeatherMap API is stored as an attribute.
- **Input Validation:**
  The node checks that the input is a non-empty string (expected to be
  a city name).
- **API Request:**
  The node prepares the query parameters and uses the `requests`
  library to make an HTTP GET request. It handles HTTP errors using
  `raise_for_status()` and logs any exceptions that occur.
- **Data Propagation:**
  The weather data (or error message) is passed to the next nodes in the
  workflow.

2. **Create Supporting Nodes for a Complete Workflow**

To see the integration in context, we'll build a small workflow that:

- Captures a city name.
- Retrieves weather data using the `WeatherAPINode`.
- Outputs the final result.

Define Input and Output Nodes:

python

```python
class CityInputNode(Node):
    def run(self, data=None):
        # For demonstration, using a fixed city name
        city = "London"
        print(f"[{self.name}] City Input: {city}")
        for node in self.next_nodes:
            node.run(city)
```

```python
class OutputNode(Node):
    def run(self, data):
        print(f"[{self.name}] Final Output: {data}")
```

3. Build the Workflow with GraphManager

```python
python

from langgraph import GraphManager

# Create the Graph Manager instance
graph_manager = GraphManager()

# Replace 'YOUR_API_KEY_HERE' with your actual API key from
OpenWeatherMap
weather_api_key = "YOUR_API_KEY_HERE"

# Create node instances
city_input_node = CityInputNode("CityInput")
weather_node = WeatherAPINode("WeatherAPI",
api_key=weather_api_key)
output_node = OutputNode("Output")

# Register nodes with the Graph Manager
graph_manager.add_node("city_input", city_input_node)
graph_manager.add_node("weather", weather_node)
graph_manager.add_node("output", output_node)

# Connect nodes to form the workflow: CityInput -> WeatherAPI
-> Output
graph_manager.connect("city_input", "weather")
graph_manager.connect("weather", "output")

# Execute the workflow
print("Starting External API Integration Workflow...\n")
graph_manager.run("city_input")
```

Explanation:

- **CityInputNode:**
  Provides a fixed city name ("London") for demonstration purposes.
- **WeatherAPINode:**
  Fetches weather data using the OpenWeatherMap API.
- **OutputNode:**
  Displays the final weather data received from the API.

- **GraphManager:**
  Orchestrates the nodes and ensures that the city name flows to the WeatherAPINode and then to the OutputNode.

4. Best Practices for API Integration

- **API Key Management:**
  Securely store API keys (e.g., using environment variables or configuration files) rather than hardcoding them in your source code.
- **Rate Limiting and Retries:**
  Handle API rate limits gracefully by implementing retry logic with exponential backoff. Use libraries like `tenacity` for automated retries.
- **Error Handling:**
  Ensure that your nodes gracefully handle HTTP errors, network failures, or unexpected API responses.
- **Data Transformation:**
  Convert the API response into a format that can be easily consumed by subsequent nodes in the workflow.
- **Modular Design:**
  Encapsulate API calls within custom nodes so that the rest of your workflow remains agnostic of the external service details.

Table: Best Practices for API Integration

Practice	Description	Example/Tool
API Key Management	Securely manage API keys	Environment variables, config files
Rate Limiting & Retries	Implement logic to handle API rate limits and retry on failures	tenacity library, custom retry logic
Robust Error Handling	Catch and log errors from API calls	try-except blocks, logging
Data Transformation	Convert API responses to standard data formats	JSON parsing, custom data mapping functions
Modular Design	Encapsulate API logic within dedicated nodes	Custom node classes (e.g., WeatherAPINode)

5.

Integrating external APIs and services into LangGraph Python workflows significantly extends the capabilities of your applications. By encapsulating API calls within custom nodes, you maintain a modular architecture that is easier to manage, test, and extend. The detailed code examples provided in this section illustrate how to connect to an external weather API, handle errors gracefully, and integrate the response into a complete workflow.

As you build more complex systems, you can apply these principles to integrate various external services—whether for data retrieval, specialized processing, or inter-system communication—ensuring that your LangGraph Python applications are robust, secure, and scalable.

8.2 Building Plugins for Extended Functionality

Plugins provide a powerful way to extend the capabilities of LangGraph Python without modifying its core code. By designing your application to support plugins, you can add new features, integrate external services, or implement custom processing logic dynamically. This modular approach enables easier maintenance, flexibility in deployment, and faster adaptation to new requirements.

In this section, we will explore how to design a plugin system for LangGraph Python. We will cover the following topics:

1. **Concept of Plugins:** What are plugins and why they are useful.
2. **Designing a Plugin Interface:** Establishing a common contract for all plugins.
3. **Developing a Sample Plugin:** Creating a plugin that extends functionality.
4. **Integrating Plugins into Your Workflow:** How to load and use plugins within LangGraph Python.
5. **Best Practices for Plugin Development:** Guidelines for building robust, maintainable plugins.
6. **Summary Table:** A quick reference for key aspects of plugin design and integration.

1. Concept of Plugins

Definition:
A plugin is a software component that adds specific capabilities to an existing application. Plugins allow you to extend the functionality of your system without altering the core codebase. In the context of LangGraph Python, plugins can be used to add new node types, integrate external services, or modify data processing behavior.

Benefits:

- **Modularity:** Plugins encapsulate additional functionality in separate modules.
- **Extensibility:** New features can be added without changing the core framework.
- **Maintainability:** Core code remains clean and focused, while plugins can be updated or replaced independently.
- **Dynamic Loading:** Plugins can be discovered and loaded at runtime, allowing for flexible system configuration.

---

2. Designing a Plugin Interface

To build a robust plugin system, it is essential to define a clear plugin interface that all plugins must implement. This interface acts as a contract between the core system and the plugins.

Key Elements of a Plugin Interface:

- **Initialization:** A method to set up the plugin, often receiving configuration data.
- **Execution:** A method to perform the plugin's primary function.
- **Metadata:** Attributes that describe the plugin (e.g., name, version, description).

Example Plugin Interface:

```python
class PluginInterface:
    """
```

```
    Base class for all plugins. Every plugin must inherit
from this class
    and implement the required methods.
    """
    def __init__(self, config=None):
        self.config = config or {}
        self.name = self.config.get("name", "UnnamedPlugin")
        self.version = self.config.get("version", "1.0")
        self.description = self.config.get("description", "No
description provided.")

    def execute(self, data):
        """
        Execute the plugin's functionality on the given data.
        This method must be overridden by subclasses.

        Parameters:
        - data: The input data for processing.

        Returns:
        - Processed data.
        """
        raise NotImplementedError("Plugins must implement the
execute() method.")
```

Explanation:

- The `PluginInterface` class provides the basic structure that every plugin must follow.
- The `__init__` method accepts an optional configuration dictionary and sets common metadata.
- The `execute()` method is a placeholder that must be implemented by each plugin to perform its specific task.

---

3. Developing a Sample Plugin

Let's create a simple plugin that enhances text data by appending a custom message. This example will illustrate how to build a plugin that can be integrated into a LangGraph workflow.

Sample Plugin: TextEnhancerPlugin

```python
python

class TextEnhancerPlugin(PluginInterface):
```

```python
    def __init__(self, config=None):
        super().__init__(config)
        # Plugin-specific configuration can be loaded here
        self.append_text = self.config.get("append_text", " -
Enhanced by TextEnhancerPlugin")

    def execute(self, data):
        """
        Enhance the input text by appending a custom message.

        Parameters:
        - data (str): The input text.

        Returns:
        - str: The enhanced text.
        """
        if not isinstance(data, str):
            raise ValueError(f"{self.name} expected a string
as input, got {type(data)}")
        enhanced_text = data + self.append_text
        print(f"[{self.name}] Enhanced Text:
{enhanced_text}")
        return enhanced_text

# Example usage of the plugin independently
config = {
    "name": "TextEnhancer",
    "version": "1.0",
    "description": "Appends a custom message to input text.",
    "append_text": " - Powered by LangGraph Plugins"
}

plugin = TextEnhancerPlugin(config)
sample_input = "Hello, world!"
enhanced_output = plugin.execute(sample_input)
```

Explanation:

- **Initialization:**
  The `TextEnhancerPlugin` inherits from `PluginInterface` and reads a custom configuration (`append_text`) that defines the message to append.
- **Execution:**
  The `execute()` method validates the input, appends the custom message, and returns the enhanced text. It also prints the result for debugging purposes.

4. Integrating Plugins into Your Workflow

Once your plugins are developed, you need a mechanism to load and use them within your LangGraph workflows. This can be done by creating a custom node that serves as a plugin loader.

Example: PluginLoaderNode

```python
class PluginLoaderNode(Node):
    def __init__(self, name, plugin):
        """
        Initializes the node with a plugin instance.

        Parameters:
        - plugin: An instance of a class that implements
PluginInterface.
        """
        super().__init__(name)
        self.plugin = plugin

    def run(self, data):
        """
        Passes the data through the plugin's execute method
and forwards the result.

        Parameters:
        - data: The input data for the plugin.
        """
        print(f"[{self.name}] Loading plugin:
{self.plugin.name}")
        try:
            processed_data = self.plugin.execute(data)
            for node in self.next_nodes:
                node.run(processed_data)
        except Exception as e:
            print(f"[{self.name}] ERROR executing plugin
{self.plugin.name}: {e}")
            # Optionally, propagate the original data or
handle the error appropriately
            for node in self.next_nodes:
                node.run(data)

# Create a simple workflow that uses PluginLoaderNode
class SimpleInputNode(Node):
    def run(self, data=None):
        input_text = "Welcome to LangGraph!"
        print(f"[{self.name}] Input: {input_text}")
```

```
        for node in self.next_nodes:
            node.run(input_text)

class SimpleOutputNode(Node):
    def run(self, data):
        print(f"[{self.name}] Output: {data}")

# Setup the Graph Manager
graph_manager = GraphManager()

# Create node instances
input_node = SimpleInputNode("InputNode")
# Use the previously defined TextEnhancerPlugin
plugin_loader_node = PluginLoaderNode("PluginLoader", plugin)
output_node = SimpleOutputNode("OutputNode")

# Register nodes
graph_manager.add_node("input", input_node)
graph_manager.add_node("plugin_loader", plugin_loader_node)
graph_manager.add_node("output", output_node)

# Connect nodes: Input -> PluginLoader -> Output
graph_manager.connect("input", "plugin_loader")
graph_manager.connect("plugin_loader", "output")

# Execute the workflow
print("Starting Plugin Integration Workflow...\n")
graph_manager.run("input")
```

Explanation:

- **PluginLoaderNode:**
  This custom node encapsulates a plugin and calls its `execute()` method. It handles exceptions gracefully, logging errors and optionally propagating the original data.
- **Workflow Construction:**
  A simple workflow is constructed with an Input Node that provides a text message, the PluginLoaderNode that applies the plugin (TextEnhancerPlugin), and an Output Node that displays the final result.
- **Graph Manager:**
  The Graph Manager orchestrates the execution flow, ensuring that data flows from the input through the plugin loader and finally to the output.

5. Best Practices for Plugin Development

Best Practice	Description	Example/Tip
Define Clear Interfaces	Establish a plugin interface that all plugins must implement to ensure consistency.	Use a base class like `PluginInterface`.
Modular Design	Keep plugin functionality encapsulated and independent of core system logic.	Separate plugin code into distinct modules.
Robust Error Handling	Implement try-except blocks in plugins to handle exceptions and provide fallback behavior.	Catch and log errors within the `execute()` method.
Configuration Management	Use external configuration (e.g., JSON, environment variables) to manage plugin settings.	Pass a configuration dictionary to the plugin's initializer.
Documentation	Clearly document the expected inputs, outputs, and behavior of each plugin.	Include docstrings and usage examples in the plugin code.

Building plugins for extended functionality in LangGraph Python allows you to create a flexible, modular system that can adapt to changing requirements. By defining a clear plugin interface, developing custom plugins to encapsulate additional features, and integrating these plugins into your workflows using nodes like PluginLoaderNode, you can significantly enhance your application's capabilities without altering the core framework.

The detailed code examples and best practices provided in this section offer a solid foundation for developing your own plugins. As you extend your application, consider how plugins can help you achieve modularity, reusability, and ease of maintenance.

8.3 Interoperability with Other Graph and Data Processing Tools

In modern data-driven applications, it is common to combine multiple specialized tools to achieve a comprehensive solution. LangGraph Python is designed with interoperability in mind, allowing you to integrate its graph-based workflows with other graph processing libraries and data processing tools. This interoperability enables you to leverage the strengths of different technologies—such as advanced graph analytics, high-quality visualizations, and scalable data processing—within a single application.

---

1. What is Interoperability?

Interoperability refers to the ability of different software systems and tools to work together seamlessly. For LangGraph Python, this means that you can:

- **Export or import graph structures:** For example, converting your LangGraph workflow into a NetworkX graph for further analysis or visualization.
- **Integrate with data processing frameworks:** Use tools like Pandas for data manipulation or Apache Spark for distributed processing alongside your LangGraph workflow.
- **Communicate with external databases:** Interface with graph databases like Neo4j to store and query complex relationships.

The goal is to create a cohesive ecosystem where LangGraph Python acts as one component among many, each contributing its specialized functionality.

---

2. Common Tools and Their Use Cases

Below is an overview of some popular graph and data processing tools and how they can complement LangGraph Python:

Tool/Library	Use Case	Integration Method
NetworkX	Graph analysis, algorithm implementation, and visualization	Export/import graph structures, leverage NetworkX functions for analysis and visualization.
Graphviz	Creating publication-quality graph visualizations	Export workflow diagrams for static visualization.
Neo4j	Storing and querying complex graph data	Use Neo4j drivers to push or pull graph data from LangGraph workflows.
Pandas	Data manipulation and analysis	Convert DataFrames to/from data used in LangGraph nodes.
Apache Spark	Distributed data processing and analytics	Integrate with Spark for handling large-scale data before feeding into the workflow.

3. Integrating with NetworkX

One common interoperability scenario is to export your LangGraph workflow into a NetworkX graph. This allows you to perform additional graph analytics or use advanced visualization techniques provided by NetworkX and Matplotlib.

Example: Converting a LangGraph Workflow to a NetworkX Graph

```python
python

import networkx as nx
import matplotlib.pyplot as plt

def langgraph_to_networkx(graph_manager):
    """
    Converts the LangGraph workflow managed by GraphManager
into a NetworkX DiGraph.

    Parameters:
    - graph_manager (GraphManager): The manager that contains
LangGraph nodes and their connections.

    Returns:
    - nx.DiGraph: A directed graph representing the workflow.
    """
```

```
G = nx.DiGraph()
# Add nodes from the Graph Manager
for node_name in graph_manager.nodes:
    G.add_node(node_name)

# Add edges based on next_nodes connections
for node_name, node in graph_manager.nodes.items():
    for next_node in node.next_nodes:
        # Find the name of the next node by searching the
graph manager
        for key, value in graph_manager.nodes.items():
            if value == next_node:
                G.add_edge(node_name, key)
                break
    return G

# Example usage with an existing GraphManager (from previous
sections)
# Assume `graph_manager` is already populated with nodes and
connections.
G = langgraph_to_networkx(graph_manager)
pos = nx.spring_layout(G, seed=42)
plt.figure(figsize=(8, 6))
nx.draw(G, pos, with_labels=True, node_size=1500,
node_color="lightgreen", arrowstyle="->", arrowsize=20)
plt.title("LangGraph Workflow Visualization using NetworkX")
plt.show()
```

Explanation:

- **Function Definition:**
  The `langgraph_to_networkx` function iterates over nodes in the
  Graph Manager and adds them to a NetworkX directed graph
  (`DiGraph`).
- **Edge Creation:**
  For each node, it checks its `next_nodes` list and adds an edge from
  the current node to each connected node.
- **Visualization:**
  The resulting graph is visualized using Matplotlib with a spring
  layout, making it easier to analyze the workflow structure.

---

4. Integrating with Pandas for Data Processing

Sometimes, nodes in your workflow may need to process tabular data.
Pandas is a powerful library for data manipulation and analysis. You can

convert Pandas DataFrames to lists or dictionaries and pass them to LangGraph nodes for further processing.

Example: Processing Data from a Pandas DataFrame in a Custom Node

python

```python
import pandas as pd
from langgraph import Node

# Sample DataFrame
data = {
    "id": [1, 2, 3],
    "text": ["LangGraph is powerful", "Interoperability is key", "Data processing made easy"]
}
df = pd.DataFrame(data)

class DataProcessingNode(Node):
    def run(self, data):
        """
        Processes a list of dictionaries representing rows from a DataFrame.

        Parameters:
        - data (list): List of dictionaries from DataFrame records.
        """
        # Process each record (e.g., convert text to uppercase)
        processed_records = []
        for record in data:
            processed_text = record["text"].upper()
            processed_records.append({"id": record["id"], "processed_text": processed_text})
        print(f"[{self.name}] Processed Records: {processed_records}")
        for node in self.next_nodes:
            node.run(processed_records)

# Convert DataFrame to dictionary records and test the node
records = df.to_dict(orient="records")
data_processing_node = DataProcessingNode("DataProcessor")
data_processing_node.run(records)
```

Explanation:

- **DataFrame Conversion:**
  The DataFrame is converted to a list of dictionaries using `to_dict(orient="records")`.
- **Custom Node Processing:**
  The `DataProcessingNode` processes each record by converting the text to uppercase and prints the processed records.
- **Integration:**
  This node can be integrated into a larger workflow where data flows from a DataFrame to processing nodes.

---

5. Integrating with Apache Spark

For large-scale data processing, Apache Spark can be used in conjunction with LangGraph Python. Spark can process huge datasets in a distributed manner, and its results can be fed into LangGraph nodes for further analysis.

Conceptual Example:

1. **Process Data in Spark:**
   Use Spark to perform heavy data transformations.
2. **Export Processed Data:**
   Collect the results into a Pandas DataFrame or a list.
3. **Feed into LangGraph:**
   Pass the processed data into a LangGraph node for further processing.

Note: Detailed Spark integration code would require a Spark environment setup and is beyond the scope of this simple example.

---

6. Summary Table: Interoperability Tools and Integration Methods

Tool/Library	Primary Use Case	Integration Method	Example
NetworkX	Graph analysis and	Convert LangGraph workflow to	`langgraph_to_networkx()` function

Tool/Library	Primary Use Case	Integration Method	Example
	visualization	a NetworkX DiGraph	
Graphviz	High-quality static graph diagrams	Export workflow diagrams as DOT files	Use Python Graphviz interface to render DOT files
Pandas	Data manipulation and analysis	Convert DataFrames to lists/dictionaries for node processing	Using `df.to_dict(orient="records")` in a custom node
Apache Spark	Distributed processing for large-scale data	Process data in Spark, export results to Pandas, then feed into nodes	Collect Spark DataFrame and convert to Pandas DataFrame
Neo4j	Graph database for storing and querying complex relationships	Use Neo4j Python driver to import/export graph data	Connect LangGraph output to a Neo4j database using `neo4j-driver`

7. Best Practices for Interoperability

- **Standardize Data Formats:**
  Use common data formats (e.g., JSON, dictionaries, DataFrame records) to ensure smooth data exchange between LangGraph and external tools.

- **Modular Integration:**
  Encapsulate interoperability logic within custom nodes. This keeps your core workflow clean and allows easy swapping of external tools.
- **Error Handling:**
  Implement robust error handling when interacting with external systems to manage network issues, data conversion errors, and API failures.
- **Documentation and Testing:**
  Document the data contracts and integration points, and write tests to ensure that data is correctly passed between systems.

Interoperability with other graph and data processing tools significantly enhances the capabilities of your LangGraph Python workflows. By integrating with libraries like NetworkX, Pandas, Apache Spark, and even graph databases such as Neo4j, you can build comprehensive systems that leverage the strengths of multiple technologies. The examples provided in this section demonstrate practical methods for converting workflow data into formats compatible with these external tools, allowing you to perform advanced analysis, visualization, and distributed processing.

With a well-designed interoperability strategy, your LangGraph Python applications can easily scale and adapt to evolving data processing needs, creating a powerful ecosystem of interconnected tools.

8.4 Security Considerations and Best Practices

When extending LangGraph Python with external integrations and custom functionality, security becomes a paramount concern. Ensuring the integrity, confidentiality, and availability of your application and its data is essential. This section provides detailed guidance on security considerations and best practices for developing and deploying LangGraph Python applications. We will cover secure coding practices, API key management, input validation, error handling, and logging, along with code examples and summary tables.

1. Secure Coding Practices

Adhering to secure coding practices helps prevent vulnerabilities that could be exploited by attackers. Some key principles include:

- **Input Validation and Sanitization:**
  Always validate and sanitize any data received from external sources or users to prevent injection attacks, cross-site scripting (XSS), and other malicious activities.
- **Least Privilege:**
  Limit the access rights for users, processes, and API keys to only what is necessary for their function.
- **Separation of Duties:**
  Isolate critical functionalities into separate nodes or modules, reducing the risk that a compromise in one area will impact others.
- **Regular Updates:**
  Keep all dependencies and libraries updated to incorporate the latest security patches.

Example: Input Validation in a Custom Node

python

```
class SecurePreprocessingNode(Node):
    def run(self, data):
        # Validate that data is a non-empty string to prevent
injection or malformed data.
        if not isinstance(data, str) or not data.strip():
            raise ValueError(f"[{self.name}] Invalid input
data: Expected non-empty string, got {data}")

        # Sanitize input: For demonstration, we remove any
suspicious characters.
        # In production, consider using libraries like Bleach
for HTML sanitization.
        safe_data = ''.join(c for c in data if c.isalnum() or
c.isspace() or c in {'.', ',', '!', '?'})
        processed_data = safe_data.lower().strip()

        print(f"[{self.name}] Processed and sanitized data:
{processed_data}")
        for node in self.next_nodes:
            node.run(processed_data)
```

Explanation:

- The node validates the input ensuring it is a non-empty string.

- It sanitizes the input by filtering out unwanted characters, ensuring that malicious scripts or commands are not processed further.

---

2. API Key Management and Authentication

When integrating with external APIs or services, secure management of API keys and credentials is critical. Best practices include:

- **Environment Variables:**
  Store API keys and secrets in environment variables instead of hardcoding them into your source code.
- **Configuration Files:**
  Use configuration files that are excluded from version control (e.g., using .gitignore) to store sensitive information securely.
- **Secure Vaults:**
  For enterprise applications, consider using secret management tools like HashiCorp Vault, AWS Secrets Manager, or Azure Key Vault.

Example: Using Environment Variables for API Key Management

```python
python

import os
from langgraph import Node

class SecureWeatherAPINode(Node):
    def __init__(self, name):
        super().__init__(name)
        # Retrieve the API key from environment variables
        self.api_key = os.getenv("OPENWEATHER_API_KEY")
        if not self.api_key:
            raise EnvironmentError(f"[{self.name}]
OPENWEATHER_API_KEY not set in environment variables.")
        self.base_url =
"http://api.openweathermap.org/data/2.5/weather"

    def run(self, data):
        if not isinstance(data, str) or not data.strip():
            raise ValueError(f"[{self.name}] Invalid city
name provided: {data}")

        params = {
            "q": data,
            "appid": self.api_key,
```

```
            "units": "metric"
        }

        try:
            import requests
            response = requests.get(self.base_url,
params=params)
            response.raise_for_status()
            weather_data = response.json()
            print(f"[{self.name}] Weather data for {data}:
{weather_data}")
        except Exception as e:
            print(f"[{self.name}] ERROR: Failed to fetch
weather data: {e}")
            weather_data = {"error": str(e)}

        for node in self.next_nodes:
            node.run(weather_data)
```

Explanation:

- The node retrieves the API key from an environment variable, ensuring sensitive data is not exposed in the code.
- It raises an error if the API key is not set, enforcing a secure configuration.

---

3. Robust Error Handling and Logging

Implementing robust error handling and logging mechanisms helps in detecting, diagnosing, and mitigating security issues.

- **Error Handling:**
  Use try-except blocks to catch exceptions and handle them gracefully. Ensure that error messages do not leak sensitive information.
- **Logging:**
  Log errors and security-related events using Python's `logging` module. Ensure logs are stored securely and contain sufficient context for debugging.

Example: Enhanced Logging and Error Handling

python

```python
import logging

# Configure logging settings for security and error tracking
logging.basicConfig(level=logging.DEBUG,
format='[%(levelname)s] %(asctime)s - %(message)s')

class SecureAPICallNode(Node):
    def run(self, data):
        logging.debug(f"[{self.name}] Received input data:
{data}")
        try:
            # Simulate an API call that could fail
            if data == "fail":
                raise ConnectionError("Simulated API
connection error")
            result = data.upper()   # Dummy processing
            logging.info(f"[{self.name}] Processed result:
{result}")
        except Exception as e:
            logging.error(f"[{self.name}] Error during API
call: {e}")
            # Optionally, set a default result or halt
execution
            result = "default result"
        for node in self.next_nodes:
            node.run(result)

# Test the node with both valid and error-inducing inputs
secure_api_node = SecureAPICallNode("SecureAPICall")
secure_api_node.run("test data")
secure_api_node.run("fail")
```

Explanation:

- The node logs detailed debug information about received data.
- It uses try-except to catch exceptions, logging errors at the ERROR level.
- Default behavior is provided in case of failure, ensuring the workflow can continue in a controlled manner.

4. Summary Table: Security Best Practices

Best Practice	Description	Example/Tool
Input Validation & Sanitization	Ensure that all external and user inputs are validated and sanitized to prevent injection attacks.	Custom validation in nodes, using libraries like Bleach for HTML sanitation.
Secure API Key Management	Store API keys and secrets in secure, external locations rather than hardcoding them in source code.	Environment variables, secret management tools (e.g., AWS Secrets Manager).
Error Handling & Logging	Use try-except blocks to handle exceptions gracefully and log errors without exposing sensitive data.	Python's logging module, structured error messages.
Least Privilege Principle	Limit access rights and permissions to only what is necessary for each component.	Role-based access control (RBAC) for systems and APIs.
Regular Updates and Patching	Keep dependencies and libraries updated to protect against known vulnerabilities.	Use tools like pip-tools and Dependabot to manage updates.

Security is a critical aspect of any application, especially when building complex workflows that integrate multiple external systems. By incorporating robust input validation, secure API key management, comprehensive error handling, and detailed logging, you can significantly reduce the risk of vulnerabilities in your LangGraph Python applications.

The examples and best practices outlined in this section provide a strong foundation for developing secure, resilient workflows. As you continue to extend your applications, remember that security is an ongoing process—regularly review and update your practices to adapt to new threats and challenges.

Chapter 6: Integrating Language Models and NLP Pipelines

9.1 Automated Testing Strategies for Graph Workflows

Automated testing is an essential part of developing reliable and maintainable applications. For graph-based workflows in LangGraph Python, automated testing helps ensure that individual nodes and the entire workflow function as expected even as the system grows more complex. In this section, we will explore strategies for automating tests for your graph workflows. We will cover unit tests for individual nodes, integration tests for entire workflows, and best practices for structuring tests using popular testing frameworks such as `unittest` and `pytest`.

---

1. Why Automated Testing Matters

Automated testing for graph workflows offers several benefits:

- **Reliability:**
  Automated tests catch regressions and unexpected behavior early, ensuring that updates or new features do not break existing functionality.
- **Maintainability:**
  With a robust test suite, you can refactor and extend your workflow confidently.
- **Documentation:**
  Tests serve as live documentation of how nodes are expected to behave, making it easier for new developers to understand the system.
- **Efficiency:**
  Running tests automatically (e.g., in a continuous integration pipeline) saves time compared to manual testing.

Table: Benefits of Automated Testing

Benefit	Description	Outcome
Reliability	Detects issues and regressions quickly	Consistent, bug-free behavior
Maintainability	Facilitates safe refactoring and feature additions	Easier code evolution and updates
Documentation	Provides examples of expected input/output behavior	Clear understanding of node functionalities
Efficiency	Automates repetitive testing tasks	Saves time and reduces manual errors

2. Unit Testing Individual Nodes

Unit tests focus on verifying that each node in your workflow performs its specific task correctly. Testing nodes in isolation makes it easier to identify issues.

Example: Unit Testing a Custom Node Using `unittest`

Let's consider a custom node that reverses the input string. We will create a unit test to verify its functionality.

python

```python
# custom_nodes.py

class ReverseNode(Node):
    def run(self, data):
        """
        Reverses the input string.
        Parameters:
        - data (str): The input text.
        Returns:
        - str: The reversed string.
        """
        if not isinstance(data, str) or not data:
            raise ValueError("Input must be a non-empty
string.")
        return data[::-1]
```

python

```python
# test_custom_nodes.py
```

```
import unittest
from custom_nodes import ReverseNode

class TestReverseNode(unittest.TestCase):
    def setUp(self):
        self.node = ReverseNode("ReverseNode")

    def test_reverse_valid_input(self):
        input_text = "LangGraph"
        expected_output = "hparGgnaL"
        result = self.node.run(input_text)
        self.assertEqual(result, expected_output)

    def test_reverse_empty_input(self):
        with self.assertRaises(ValueError):
            self.node.run("")

    def test_reverse_non_string_input(self):
        with self.assertRaises(ValueError):
            self.node.run(123)

if __name__ == '__main__':
    unittest.main()
```

Explanation:

- **ReverseNode:**
  Implements a simple string reversal with input validation.
- **Unit Tests:**
  The tests cover valid input, empty string input, and non-string input, ensuring that the node behaves as expected under different conditions.
- **setUp Method:**
  Initializes the node instance for reuse in each test case.

---

3. Integration Testing for Complete Workflows

Integration tests validate that multiple nodes work together seamlessly. In a graph-based workflow, this means verifying that data flows correctly between nodes and that the final output is as expected.

Example: Integration Test of a Simple Workflow

Consider a workflow that consists of:

1. An Input Node that provides a string.
2. A Reverse Node (from the previous example) that reverses the string.
3. An Output Node that collects the final output.

python

```python
# workflow_nodes.py

class SimpleInputNode(Node):
    def run(self, data=None):
        input_text = "LangGraph"
        print(f"[{self.name}] Input: {input_text}")
        for node in self.next_nodes:
            node.run(input_text)

class SimpleOutputNode(Node):
    def __init__(self, name):
        super().__init__(name)
        self.received_output = None

    def run(self, data):
        self.received_output = data
        print(f"[{self.name}] Output: {data}")

# Build a simple workflow using GraphManager
from langgraph import GraphManager

def build_simple_workflow():
    graph_manager = GraphManager()

    input_node = SimpleInputNode("InputNode")
    reverse_node = ReverseNode("ReverseNode")
    output_node = SimpleOutputNode("OutputNode")

    graph_manager.add_node("input", input_node)
    graph_manager.add_node("reverse", reverse_node)
    graph_manager.add_node("output", output_node)

    graph_manager.connect("input", "reverse")
    graph_manager.connect("reverse", "output")

    return graph_manager, output_node
```
python

```python
# test_workflow_integration.py
import unittest
from workflow_nodes import build_simple_workflow

class TestWorkflowIntegration(unittest.TestCase):
    def test_workflow_output(self):
```

```
        graph_manager, output_node = build_simple_workflow()
        graph_manager.run("input")
        expected_output = "hparGgnaL"
        self.assertEqual(output_node.received_output,
expected_output)

if __name__ == '__main__':
    unittest.main()
```

Explanation:

- **SimpleInputNode and SimpleOutputNode:**
  These nodes simulate input capture and output collection.
- **Workflow Construction:**
  The `build_simple_workflow()` function sets up a simple workflow where the Reverse Node is placed between the Input and Output Nodes.
- **Integration Test:**
  The test runs the workflow and verifies that the output of the workflow matches the expected reversed string.

---

4. Using Pytest for More Flexible Testing

While `unittest` is built into Python, `pytest` is a powerful alternative that offers a more concise syntax and additional features. Below is an example of using `pytest` for testing the ReverseNode.

Example: Pytest Test for ReverseNode

python

```
# test_reverse_node.py
import pytest
from custom_nodes import ReverseNode

@pytest.fixture
def reverse_node():
    return ReverseNode("ReverseNode")

def test_reverse_valid_input(reverse_node):
    assert reverse_node.run("LangGraph") == "hparGgnaL"

def test_reverse_empty_input(reverse_node):
    with pytest.raises(ValueError):
```

```
        reverse_node.run("")

def test_reverse_non_string_input(reverse_node):
    with pytest.raises(ValueError):
        reverse_node.run(123)
```

Explanation:

- **Pytest Fixture:**
  The `reverse_node` fixture creates an instance of ReverseNode for each test.
- **Tests:**
  Similar tests as before, but with a more concise syntax.
- **Execution:**
  Running `pytest` will automatically discover and run these tests, providing detailed output.

5. Best Practices for Testing Graph Workflows

Best Practice	Description	Example/Tip
Isolate Unit Tests	Test each node individually to ensure they perform as expected.	Use `unittest` or `pytest` to write tests for each custom node.
Test Data Contracts	Define and document the expected input/output formats for each node.	Write tests that verify the correct data types and structures.
Integration Tests	Validate that nodes work together correctly by testing complete workflows.	Build workflows in tests and assert the final output.
Mock External Dependencies	When nodes rely on external APIs or services, use mocks to simulate responses.	Use libraries like `unittest.mock` to simulate API calls.
Automate Test Runs	Integrate tests into a continuous integration (CI) pipeline for automatic execution.	Use tools like GitHub Actions, Jenkins, or Travis CI.

Automated testing is a cornerstone of developing robust graph-based workflows in LangGraph Python. By implementing unit tests for individual nodes and integration tests for entire workflows, you can ensure that your application behaves as expected, even as it evolves and scales. The strategies and examples provided in this section offer a comprehensive approach to testing—helping you catch errors early, document functionality, and maintain high code quality.

9.2 Deployment Best Practices

Deploying your LangGraph Python workflows into production requires careful planning to ensure that your applications are reliable, scalable, and secure. In this section, we will explore deployment best practices that cover environment preparation, containerization, configuration management, scaling strategies, and monitoring. These practices will help ensure that your workflows run smoothly and efficiently in a production environment.

---

1. Environment Preparation

Before deployment, it's essential to ensure that your production environment closely mirrors your development and testing environments. This consistency helps prevent unexpected issues when your workflow goes live.

Key Steps:

- **Environment Isolation:**
  Use virtual environments or containerization to isolate dependencies.
- **Dependency Management:**
  Use tools like `pip freeze` or `requirements.txt` to document and install exact versions of dependencies.
- **Configuration Management:**
  Store configuration details (e.g., API keys, database URIs) outside your code, using environment variables or configuration files.

Example: requirements.txt File

```plaintext
```

```
langgraph==1.0.0
transformers==4.30.0
spacy==3.5.0
requests==2.28.1
```

Table: Environment Preparation Checklist

Step	Action	Tool/Method
Environment Isolation	Use virtual environments or containers	venv, Docker
Dependency Management	Freeze and document dependencies	pip freeze, requirements.txt
Configuration Management	Store sensitive configs externally	Environment variables, config files

2. Containerization with Docker

Containerization packages your application with all its dependencies, ensuring consistency across environments. Docker is the most popular tool for containerization.

Example: Dockerfile for a LangGraph Python Application

```dockerfile
dockerfile

# Use an official Python runtime as a parent image
FROM python:3.9-slim

# Set environment variables to ensure that Python output is
sent straight to terminal
ENV PYTHONUNBUFFERED 1

# Set a working directory in the container
WORKDIR /app

# Copy the requirements file into the container
COPY requirements.txt /app/

# Install any needed packages specified in requirements.txt
RUN pip install --upgrade pip && \
    pip install -r requirements.txt

# Copy the rest of the application code into the container
COPY . /app/
```

```
# Expose the port on which the application will run (if
applicable)
EXPOSE 8000

# Define environment variable for configuration (example)
ENV APP_CONFIG="production"

# Run the application
CMD ["python", "main.py"]
```

Explanation:

- **Base Image:**
  Using a lightweight Python image reduces overhead.
- **Working Directory:**
  Sets `/app` as the working directory.
- **Dependency Installation:**
  Copies and installs dependencies from `requirements.txt`.
- **Application Code:**
  Copies the application into the container.
- **Environment Variables:**
  Set environment variables for configuration.
- **Command:**
  Defines the command to run the application.

---

3. Configuration and Secret Management

Managing configuration and secrets securely is critical during deployment.

- **Use Environment Variables:**
  Inject configuration values at runtime rather than hardcoding them.
  For example, API keys, database URIs, and other sensitive
  information should be managed via environment variables.
- **Secret Management Tools:**
  For enterprise-level deployments, use secret management solutions
  such as HashiCorp Vault, AWS Secrets Manager, or Azure Key
  Vault.

Example: Loading Environment Variables in Python

```python
```

```python
import os

def load_config():
    config = {
        "api_key": os.getenv("OPENWEATHER_API_KEY"),
        "db_uri": os.getenv("DATABASE_URI",
"sqlite:///default.db"),
        "debug_mode": os.getenv("DEBUG_MODE",
"False").lower() == "true"
    }
    return config

config = load_config()
print(f"API Key: {config['api_key']}")
print(f"Database URI: {config['db_uri']}")
print(f"Debug Mode: {config['debug_mode']}")
```

4. Scaling and Load Balancing

As your workflow handles more data or traffic, you may need to scale your application.

Scaling Strategies:

- **Horizontal Scaling:**
  Deploy multiple instances of your application behind a load balancer. This approach distributes incoming requests evenly among instances.
- **Vertical Scaling:**
  Increase resources (CPU, memory) on your existing machines. This may be simpler but has limits.
- **Container Orchestration:**
  Use orchestration tools like Kubernetes or Docker Swarm to manage multiple containers, scaling them automatically based on demand.

Table: Scaling Strategies

Strategy	Description	Pros	Cons
Horizontal Scaling	Add more instances of your application	High availability, easier load distribution	More complex orchestration, potential synchronization issues

Strategy	Description	Pros	Cons
Vertical Scaling	Increase resources on a single instance	Simpler management	Limited by hardware capacity
Container Orchestration	Use Kubernetes/Docker Swarm for managing containerized apps	Automated scaling and management	Higher operational complexity

5. Monitoring and Logging

Monitoring and logging are essential to ensure your deployed application is running correctly and to detect issues early.

Key Considerations:

- **Centralized Logging:**
  Use centralized logging solutions (e.g., ELK Stack, Splunk) to collect and analyze logs from all instances.
- **Health Checks:**
  Implement health check endpoints that your orchestration platform (e.g., Kubernetes) can use to monitor the application's status.
- **Performance Metrics:**
  Use monitoring tools like Prometheus and Grafana to track key metrics (CPU, memory, response time).

Example: Health Check Endpoint in Flask

```python
from flask import Flask, jsonify

app = Flask(__name__)

@app.route('/health', methods=['GET'])
def health_check():
    # Implement logic to check application health
    return jsonify(status="OK", message="Service is
running"), 200

if __name__ == "__main__":
    app.run(host="0.0.0.0", port=8000)
```

Explanation:

- **Health Check Endpoint:**
  A simple Flask application defines a `/health` endpoint that returns the status of the application.
- **Integration with Orchestration Tools:**
  This endpoint can be used by Kubernetes or another orchestration tool to monitor the health of your application instances.

---

6. Deployment Automation and CI/CD

Automate your deployment process using CI/CD pipelines. Tools like GitHub Actions, Jenkins, or GitLab CI can automate testing, building, and deploying your containers to your chosen environment.

Example: Simple GitHub Actions Workflow

```yaml
yaml

name: Deploy LangGraph App

on:
  push:
    branches: [ main ]

jobs:
  build-and-deploy:
    runs-on: ubuntu-latest

    steps:
      - uses: actions/checkout@v2

      - name: Set up Python
        uses: actions/setup-python@v2
        with:
          python-version: 3.9

      - name: Install dependencies
        run: |
          python -m pip install --upgrade pip
          pip install -r requirements.txt

      - name: Run tests
        run: |
          pytest --maxfail=1 --disable-warnings -q
```

```
- name: Build Docker image
  run: |
    docker build -t langgraph-app .

- name: Deploy (simulate deployment)
  run: echo "Deployment steps go here"
```

Explanation:

- **CI/CD Pipeline:**
  The workflow is triggered on pushes to the main branch.
- **Steps:**
  The pipeline checks out the code, sets up Python, installs
  dependencies, runs tests, builds a Docker image, and simulates
  deployment.

7. Summary Table: Deployment Best Practices

Aspect	Best Practice	Example/Tool
Environment Preparation	Use virtual environments/containers, document dependencies	venv, Docker, requirements.txt
Containerization	Package the app with Docker for consistent deployment	Dockerfile
Configuration Management	Externalize sensitive configuration using environment variables	os.getenv(), configuration files
Scaling	Use horizontal scaling and orchestration tools for high availability	Kubernetes, Docker Swarm
Monitoring and Logging	Implement centralized logging and health checks	ELK Stack, Prometheus, Grafana, Flask health endpoint
Deployment Automation	Automate testing and deployment using CI/CD pipelines	GitHub Actions, Jenkins, GitLab CI

Deploying LangGraph Python workflows effectively requires a comprehensive approach that addresses environment setup, containerization, configuration, scalability, and monitoring. By following these best practices, you can ensure that your applications are robust, secure, and capable of handling production workloads.

Adopting automated deployment pipelines and centralized monitoring systems not only minimizes downtime but also enables proactive issue detection and resolution. As you continue to build and deploy more complex workflows, these best practices will help you maintain high reliability and performance across your applications.

9.3 Continuous Integration/Continuous Deployment (CI/CD)

Continuous Integration (CI) and Continuous Deployment (CD) are critical practices in modern software development. They ensure that your code is automatically built, tested, and deployed with minimal manual intervention. For LangGraph Python workflows, CI/CD pipelines provide a systematic way to maintain code quality, catch bugs early, and accelerate the release of new features. This section provides an in-depth explanation of CI/CD concepts, outlines common tools and strategies, and includes detailed code examples and tables to help you set up your automated pipeline.

1. Overview of CI/CD

Continuous Integration (CI):

- **Definition:**
  Continuous Integration is the practice of merging all developers' working copies to a shared repository several times a day. Automated builds and tests run on every change, ensuring that the integrated code is always in a working state.
- **Benefits:**
  - Early detection of integration issues.
  - Faster development cycles.
  - Improved code quality due to frequent testing.

Continuous Deployment (CD):

- **Definition:**
  Continuous Deployment is an extension of CI that automates the release of code changes to production. Once the code passes all automated tests, it is automatically deployed to the production environment.
- **Benefits:**
  - Accelerated time-to-market.
  - Reduced manual deployment errors.
  - Consistent, repeatable, and reliable deployments.

Table: CI/CD Key Concepts

Concept	Definition	Key Benefit
Continuous Integration	Automated merging and testing of code changes in a shared repo	Early detection of bugs and smoother integration
Continuous Deployment	Automated release of code changes to production	Faster, reliable, and repeatable deployments

2. CI/CD Tools and Technologies

There are several tools available to implement CI/CD pipelines. Some popular choices include:

- **GitHub Actions:**
  Provides integrated CI/CD workflows directly within GitHub. It allows you to define your pipeline in YAML files and trigger actions on various events (e.g., push, pull request).
- **Jenkins:**
  An open-source automation server that can build, test, and deploy your code using a wide range of plugins.
- **GitLab CI/CD:**
  Integrated with GitLab repositories, enabling seamless CI/CD processes.
- **Travis CI and CircleCI:**
  Cloud-based CI/CD services that integrate with GitHub and other version control systems.

For this example, we will focus on GitHub Actions due to its ease of use and tight integration with GitHub.

3. Setting Up a CI/CD Pipeline for LangGraph Python

A typical CI/CD pipeline for a LangGraph Python application involves several stages:

1. **Code Checkout:**
   Retrieve the latest code from the repository.
2. **Dependency Installation:**
   Install the required Python packages as defined in your `requirements.txt`.
3. **Automated Testing:**
   Run unit and integration tests using frameworks such as `unittest` or `pytest`.
4. **Building and Packaging:**
   Build your application or Docker image if your deployment process requires containerization.
5. **Deployment:**
   Deploy your application to a staging or production environment.
6. **Notification:**
   Inform your team about the build status via email, Slack, or other notification tools.

4. Example: GitHub Actions Workflow

Below is an example of a GitHub Actions workflow configuration file (`.github/workflows/ci-cd.yml`) for a LangGraph Python project.

```yaml
name: CI/CD Pipeline for LangGraph Python

on:
  push:
    branches: [ main ]
  pull_request:
    branches: [ main ]

jobs:
  build:
    runs-on: ubuntu-latest
```

```
steps:
  # Step 1: Checkout code from repository
  - name: Checkout Code
    uses: actions/checkout@v2

  # Step 2: Set up Python environment
  - name: Set up Python 3.9
    uses: actions/setup-python@v2
    with:
      python-version: 3.9

  # Step 3: Install Dependencies
  - name: Install Dependencies
    run: |
      python -m pip install --upgrade pip
      pip install -r requirements.txt

  # Step 4: Run Automated Tests
  - name: Run Tests
    run: |
      pytest --maxfail=1 --disable-warnings -q

  # Step 5: Build Docker Image (if containerization is
used)
  - name: Build Docker Image
    run: |
      docker build -t langgraph-app .

  # Step 6: Deploy to Staging (Simulated deployment for
demonstration)
  - name: Deploy to Staging
    if: github.ref == 'refs/heads/main'
    run: |
      echo "Deploying application to staging
environment..."
      # Here, add your actual deployment commands, e.g.,
SSH into server or use cloud CLI commands

  # Step 7: Notify Team
  - name: Notify Team
    uses: dawidd6/action-send-mail@v3
    with:
      server_address: smtp.example.com
      server_port: 587
      username: ${{ secrets.EMAIL_USERNAME }}
      password: ${{ secrets.EMAIL_PASSWORD }}
      subject: "LangGraph Python CI/CD Pipeline - Build
${{ github.run_number }}"
      to: team@example.com
```

```
      body: "The latest build and deployment of the
LangGraph Python application have completed successfully."
```

Explanation:

- **Triggers:**
  The workflow is triggered on pushes and pull requests to the `main` branch.
- **Checkout Code:**
  Uses `actions/checkout@v2` to pull the latest code.
- **Setup Python:**
  Sets up Python 3.9 using `actions/setup-python@v2`.
- **Install Dependencies:**
  Upgrades pip and installs dependencies from `requirements.txt`.
- **Run Tests:**
  Executes tests using `pytest`, which is critical to ensure that the code works as expected.
- **Docker Build:**
  (Optional) Builds a Docker image if you are deploying containerized applications.
- **Deployment:**
  Executes deployment steps if the push is on the `main` branch. In a real-world scenario, you would replace the placeholder with actual deployment commands.
- **Notification:**
  Sends an email notification to the team using an email action, with credentials securely stored as GitHub Secrets.

---

5. Best Practices for CI/CD

Implementing a robust CI/CD pipeline requires adherence to best practices:

- **Automate the Entire Process:**
  Ensure every step, from testing to deployment, is automated to reduce human error and speed up the release cycle.
- **Keep Environments Consistent:**
  Use containerization (e.g., Docker) to ensure that development, testing, and production environments are identical.

- **Manage Dependencies:**
  Freeze dependencies using `requirements.txt` and regularly update them to incorporate security patches and new features.
- **Implement Comprehensive Testing:**
  Automate unit tests, integration tests, and end-to-end tests. This ensures that any changes do not break existing functionality.
- **Securely Manage Secrets:**
  Use environment variables or secret management tools to handle sensitive information like API keys and passwords.
- **Monitor and Rollback:**
  Set up monitoring to detect issues post-deployment and have rollback strategies in place to revert to previous stable versions if necessary.

Table: CI/CD Best Practices

Best Practice	Description	Implementation Tool/Method
Automate Everything	Automate build, test, and deployment processes to reduce errors.	GitHub Actions, Jenkins, GitLab CI/CD
Environment Consistency	Ensure development, testing, and production environments are identical.	Docker, Kubernetes
Dependency Management	Freeze and regularly update dependencies.	requirements.txt, pip-tools
Comprehensive Testing	Use unit, integration, and end-to-end tests to catch issues early.	pytest, unittest
Secure Secrets Management	Store and manage sensitive data outside the source code.	GitHub Secrets, AWS Secrets Manager
Monitoring and Rollback	Monitor deployments and implement rollback strategies for failed builds.	Prometheus, Grafana, CI/CD rollback scripts

Implementing CI/CD for LangGraph Python workflows is not just about automating the build and deployment process—it's about creating a reliable, scalable, and maintainable development ecosystem. By integrating continuous integration and continuous deployment into your workflow, you can catch issues early, streamline your release cycle, and ensure that your applications are always in a deployable state.

The GitHub Actions example provided illustrates a complete pipeline that includes code checkout, dependency installation, automated testing, Docker image building, deployment, and notifications. Adopting these practices will help you maintain high-quality code, reduce manual errors, and accelerate the development process.

9.4 Monitoring and Logging in Production Environments

Effective monitoring and logging are critical to ensuring that your LangGraph Python applications remain healthy, performant, and secure in production. Monitoring provides real-time insights into the state of your application, while logging captures detailed information about events and errors that occur during execution. Together, they enable proactive issue detection, quick troubleshooting, and informed decision-making.

In this section, we will cover:

- **The Importance of Monitoring and Logging:**
  Understand why monitoring and logging are essential in production environments.
- **Tools and Techniques:**
  Explore popular tools and methodologies for monitoring and logging, including Python's logging module, centralized logging systems, and monitoring frameworks.
- **Best Practices:**
  Learn strategies to ensure your logs are useful and your monitoring setup is comprehensive.
- **Code Examples:**
  Detailed code examples that demonstrate setting up logging, creating health check endpoints, and integrating with external monitoring services.
- **Summary Table:**
  A quick reference for key concepts, tools, and best practices.

---

1. The Importance of Monitoring and Logging

Monitoring provides continuous visibility into the performance, availability, and resource utilization of your application. It helps in:

- **Detecting Anomalies:**
  Quickly identifying performance degradation, unusual patterns, or outages.
- **Capacity Planning:**
  Assessing resource usage trends to plan for scaling.
- **Ensuring Reliability:**
  Confirming that your application remains healthy through automated health checks and alerts.

Logging captures detailed records of application events, which are invaluable for:

- **Troubleshooting Errors:**
  Pinpointing the source of issues by reviewing error logs and tracebacks.
- **Auditing and Compliance:**
  Maintaining records for security audits and compliance requirements.
- **Performance Analysis:**
  Understanding the application's behavior under load and identifying bottlenecks.

Table: Benefits of Monitoring and Logging

Aspect	Monitoring	Logging
Purpose	Real-time system status and performance metrics	Detailed event and error records
Key Benefits	Early anomaly detection, capacity planning, uptime tracking	Troubleshooting, auditing, root cause analysis
Tools	Prometheus, Grafana, ELK Stack, health check endpoints	Python logging module, centralized logging systems

2. Tools and Techniques for Monitoring and Logging

A. Logging with Python's Logging Module

The built-in `logging` module in Python provides a flexible framework for emitting log messages from your applications. It allows you to configure log levels, output formats, and log destinations (console, file, remote servers).

Example: Setting Up Basic Logging

```python
python

import logging

# Configure the logging system
logging.basicConfig(
    level=logging.DEBUG,
    format='[%(levelname)s] %(asctime)s - %(name)s - %(message)s',
    datefmt='%Y-%m-%d %H:%M:%S',
    handlers=[
        logging.FileHandler("langgraph_app.log"),
        logging.StreamHandler()
    ]
)

logger = logging.getLogger("LangGraphApp")

def process_data(data):
    logger.info("Starting data processing")
    try:
        # Simulate data processing
        processed = data.upper()
        logger.debug(f"Processed data: {processed}")
        return processed
    except Exception as e:
        logger.error("Error during processing", exc_info=True)
        raise

# Example usage
if __name__ == "__main__":
    sample_data = "Hello, LangGraph!"
    result = process_data(sample_data)
    logger.info(f"Final result: {result}")
```

Explanation:

- **Configuration:**
  The `logging.basicConfig()` function sets up logging to output both to a file (`langgraph_app.log`) and the console.

- **Logger Usage:**
  The `logger` instance is used to log messages at various levels (INFO, DEBUG, ERROR). The `exc_info=True` flag in `logger.error` logs the stack trace.
- **Output:**
  Log messages are formatted with timestamps, log level, logger name, and message content.

B. Centralized Logging Systems

For production environments, it's best practice to centralize logs from multiple instances or services. Tools such as the ELK (Elasticsearch, Logstash, Kibana) Stack or Splunk allow you to collect, index, and visualize logs.

- **Elasticsearch:** Stores and indexes log data.
- **Logstash:** Processes and transports log data.
- **Kibana:** Visualizes log data through dashboards.

C. Monitoring with Health Checks and External Tools

Implement health check endpoints in your application to allow monitoring tools to verify system status. For example, a simple Flask application can expose a `/health` endpoint.

Example: Health Check Endpoint in Flask

```python
from flask import Flask, jsonify

app = Flask(__name__)

@app.route('/health', methods=['GET'])
def health_check():
    # Perform necessary checks (e.g., database connectivity,
service availability)
    status = "OK"
    message = "Service is running smoothly."
    return jsonify(status=status, message=message), 200

if __name__ == "__main__":
    app.run(host="0.0.0.0", port=8000)
```

Explanation:

- **Endpoint:**
  The `/health` endpoint returns a JSON response with the status and message.
- **Integration:**
  Monitoring systems like Prometheus or Kubernetes can periodically query this endpoint to ensure the application is healthy.

D. External Monitoring Tools

- **Prometheus & Grafana:**
  Prometheus collects and stores metrics, while Grafana visualizes them through dashboards.
- **Cloud Monitoring Solutions:**
  Services such as AWS CloudWatch, Google Cloud Monitoring, or Azure Monitor can be integrated to track metrics, logs, and set up alerts.

---

3. Best Practices for Monitoring and Logging

A. Log Management

- **Log Levels:**
  Use appropriate log levels (DEBUG, INFO, WARNING, ERROR, CRITICAL) to differentiate between normal operational messages and issues.
- **Log Rotation:**
  Configure log rotation to prevent log files from consuming excessive disk space.
- **Structured Logging:**
  Use structured logs (e.g., JSON format) to make it easier to parse and analyze log data with centralized logging tools.

B. Monitoring Strategy

- **Define Key Metrics:**
  Identify and track metrics critical to your application's performance (e.g., response time, error rate, CPU/memory usage).
- **Set Up Alerts:**
  Configure alerts for abnormal conditions so that you can respond quickly to issues.

- **Regular Reviews:**
  Periodically review logs and monitoring dashboards to identify trends and potential problems before they escalate.

Table: Best Practices for Monitoring and Logging

Aspect	Best Practice	Implementation
Log Levels	Use DEBUG, INFO, WARNING, ERROR, CRITICAL consistently	Configure logging.basicConfig with level and format
Log Rotation	Prevent log files from growing indefinitely	Use logging.handlers.RotatingFileHandler
Structured Logging	Log data in JSON format for easier parsing	Use python-json-logger or similar libraries
Health Checks	Expose endpoints for monitoring system health	Create /health endpoints in your web framework
Alerting	Set up automated alerts for critical metrics	Use Prometheus alert rules, cloud monitoring alerts
Centralized Logging	Aggregate logs from multiple sources for analysis	Use ELK Stack, Splunk, or cloud-based logging solutions

Monitoring and logging are the lifeblood of production environments, providing insights into application performance and alerting you to potential issues. For LangGraph Python workflows, a robust monitoring and logging strategy involves:

- **Implementing comprehensive logging** using Python's logging module and centralizing logs for analysis.
- **Exposing health check endpoints** to enable real-time monitoring of system status.
- **Leveraging external tools** like Prometheus, Grafana, and cloud monitoring services to gather metrics and visualize data.

- **Adhering to best practices** for log management, structured logging, and proactive alerting.

By incorporating these strategies, you can ensure that your LangGraph Python applications remain reliable, performant, and secure in production environments. Regularly reviewing logs and monitoring dashboards, combined with automated alerts, will empower you to address issues before they impact users.

Part IV: Real-World Applications and Future Trends

Chapter 10: Practical Applications and Case Studies

10.1 Building a Scalable Chatbot System

In this chapter, we explore how to design and implement a scalable chatbot system using LangGraph Python. A scalable chatbot must handle an increasing volume of user interactions without degradation in performance or responsiveness. This requires careful design of the underlying workflow, integration of robust NLP components, and the adoption of scalable infrastructure practices. We will cover the architecture, key components, integration techniques, and strategies for scaling, along with complete code examples and tables to illustrate each concept.

---

1. Architectural Overview

A scalable chatbot system typically involves multiple layers:

- **Input Layer:**
  Captures user queries from various channels (web, mobile, messaging apps).
- **Processing Layer:**
  Uses LangGraph Python to orchestrate various NLP tasks such as preprocessing, intent detection, entity recognition, dialogue management, and response generation. This layer leverages modular nodes to allow independent scaling and optimization.
- **Integration Layer:**
  Connects to external NLP services (e.g., Hugging Face Transformers for intent detection and response generation) and databases (e.g., for storing user sessions or conversation history).
- **Output Layer:**
  Delivers responses back to the user and may integrate with front-end systems or messaging platforms.
- **Scaling & Infrastructure:**
  Uses containerization, load balancing, and orchestration (e.g.,

Docker, Kubernetes) to ensure that the system can scale horizontally as demand increases.

Architecture Diagram:

pgsql

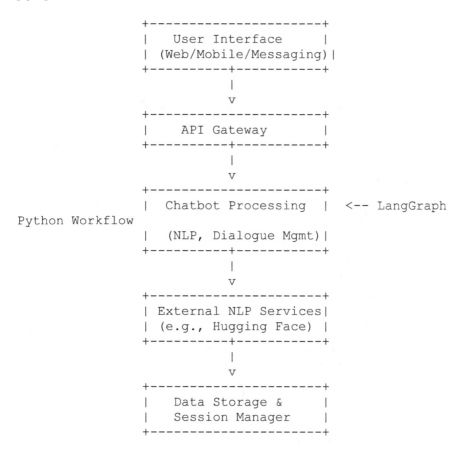

Explanation:

- **User Interface and API Gateway:**
  Provide a unified entry point for user requests.
- **Chatbot Processing Layer:**
  Implements the core logic using LangGraph Python to manage workflow nodes.
- **External NLP Services:**
  Enhance the system with state-of-the-art NLP models.

- **Data Storage:**
  Maintain conversation state and user context, essential for personalized experiences.
- **Scalability:**
  The processing layer is designed to run on multiple instances using container orchestration for horizontal scaling.

---

2. Key Components and Workflow Design

A scalable chatbot workflow can be broken down into modular nodes:

- **Input Node:**
  Receives the user query and performs initial logging or validation.
- **Preprocessing Node:**
  Cleans and tokenizes the query, handling language normalization.
- **Intent & Entity Recognition Node:**
  Utilizes external NLP libraries (e.g., Hugging Face Transformers) to classify the query and extract key entities.
- **Dialogue Management Node:**
  Determines the appropriate response or routing based on intent, user context, and conversation history.
- **Response Generation Node:**
  Generates or retrieves the final response using text generation models or predefined templates.
- **Output Node:**
  Delivers the final response back to the user.

Table: Key Workflow Components

Component	Function	Example Technology/Method
Input Node	Captures and validates user input	LangGraph custom node
Preprocessing Node	Cleans, tokenizes, and normalizes text	Custom node, spaCy
Intent & Entity Recognition	Classifies query and extracts entities	Hugging Face Transformers, Zero-shot classification

Component	Function	Example Technology/Method
Dialogue Management	Manages conversation flow and determines routing	Custom logic, rule-based systems
Response Generation	Generates response using templates or generative models	GPT-2, GPT-3, or custom response retrieval
Output Node	Sends the response to the user	Custom node integrated with messaging APIs

3. Sample Code Example: Scalable Chatbot Workflow

Below is a simplified, end-to-end example using LangGraph Python that illustrates the workflow for a scalable chatbot system. This example integrates key NLP components and demonstrates how the system can be extended for scalability.

```python
python

# Import necessary libraries and modules
from langgraph import Node, GraphManager
from transformers import pipeline
import spacy

# Load spaCy model for preprocessing (NER can also be done
with spaCy if needed)
nlp_spacy = spacy.load("en_core_web_sm")

# 1. Input Node: Captures user query
class ChatInputNode(Node):
    def run(self, data=None):
        # Simulate receiving a user query (in production,
this might be from an API gateway)
        user_query = "I need help booking a flight to New
York."
        print(f"[{self.name}] Received Query: {user_query}")
        for node in self.next_nodes:
            node.run(user_query)

# 2. Preprocessing Node: Normalizes and tokenizes text
class ChatPreprocessingNode(Node):
    def run(self, data):
        processed_query = data.lower().strip()
```

```python
        print(f"[{self.name}] Processed Query:
{processed_query}")
        for node in self.next_nodes:
            node.run(processed_query)


# 3. Intent & Entity Recognition Node: Uses Hugging Face for
intent detection
class ChatIntentNode(Node):
    def __init__(self, name):
        super().__init__(name)
        # Initialize a zero-shot classification pipeline for
intent detection
        self.classifier = pipeline("zero-shot-
classification", model="facebook/bart-large-mnli")
        # Define candidate intents
        self.intents = ["booking", "inquiry", "complaint",
"greeting"]

    def run(self, data):
        print(f"[{self.name}] Detecting intent for:
'{data}'")
        result = self.classifier(data,
candidate_labels=self.intents)
        detected_intent = result["labels"][0]
        print(f"[{self.name}] Detected Intent:
{detected_intent}")
        # Forward both the processed query and detected
intent
        for node in self.next_nodes:
            node.run((data, detected_intent))


# 4. Dialogue Management Node: Determines response based on
intent
class ChatDialogueManagerNode(Node):
    def run(self, data):
        query, intent = data
        # Simple dialogue management logic based on intent
        if intent == "booking":
            response_template = "Sure, I can help you with
booking a flight. What is your preferred travel date?"
        elif intent == "inquiry":
            response_template = "Could you please clarify
your inquiry?"
        elif intent == "complaint":
            response_template = "I'm sorry to hear that.
Could you provide more details so we can help resolve the
issue?"
        else:
            response_template = "Hello! How can I assist you
today?"
```

```python
        print(f"[{self.name}] Selected Response Template:
{response_template}")
        for node in self.next_nodes:
            node.run(response_template)

# 5. Response Generation Node: Generates final response using
GPT-2
class ChatResponseGenerationNode(Node):
    def __init__(self, name):
        super().__init__(name)
        self.generator = pipeline("text-generation",
model="gpt2")

    def run(self, data):
        prompt = f"User Query Processed: {data}\nFinal
Response:"
        print(f"[{self.name}] Generating response with
prompt: {prompt}")
        result = self.generator(prompt, max_length=60,
num_return_sequences=1)
        generated_response = result[0]['generated_text']
        print(f"[{self.name}] Generated Response:
{generated_response}")
        for node in self.next_nodes:
            node.run(generated_response)

# 6. Output Node: Sends final response back to user
class ChatOutputNode(Node):
    def run(self, data):
        print(f"[{self.name}] Final Chatbot Response:
{data}")
        # In production, this might involve sending the
response via an API gateway or messaging service.

# Build the Chatbot Workflow using GraphManager
graph_manager = GraphManager()

# Create node instances
input_node = ChatInputNode("ChatInput")
preprocessing_node =
ChatPreprocessingNode("ChatPreprocessing")
intent_node = ChatIntentNode("ChatIntent")
dialogue_manager_node =
ChatDialogueManagerNode("DialogueManager")
response_node =
ChatResponseGenerationNode("ResponseGeneration")
output_node = ChatOutputNode("ChatOutput")

# Register nodes with the Graph Manager
graph_manager.add_node("input", input_node)
graph_manager.add_node("preprocess", preprocessing_node)
```

```
graph_manager.add_node("intent", intent_node)
graph_manager.add_node("dialogue", dialogue_manager_node)
graph_manager.add_node("response", response_node)
graph_manager.add_node("output", output_node)

# Connect nodes to form the complete workflow:
graph_manager.connect("input", "preprocess")
graph_manager.connect("preprocess", "intent")
graph_manager.connect("intent", "dialogue")
graph_manager.connect("dialogue", "response")
graph_manager.connect("response", "output")

# Execute the scalable chatbot workflow
print("Starting Scalable Chatbot Workflow...\n")
graph_manager.run("input")
```

Explanation:

1. **ChatInputNode:**
   Simulates capturing a user query. In a production environment, this node could interface with a messaging API or web service.
2. **ChatPreprocessingNode:**
   Normalizes the query text (lowercasing, trimming whitespace) to prepare it for NLP analysis.
3. **ChatIntentNode:**
   Uses a Hugging Face zero-shot classification pipeline to detect the user's intent from the query. It forwards the query and detected intent to the next node.
4. **ChatDialogueManagerNode:**
   Implements simple rule-based logic to choose a response template based on the detected intent.
5. **ChatResponseGenerationNode:**
   Uses GPT-2 to generate a refined, context-aware response based on the template provided by the dialogue manager.
6. **ChatOutputNode:**
   Outputs the final response. In a live system, this might push the response to a chat interface or messaging system.
7. **Graph Manager:**
   Orchestrates the workflow by registering nodes and ensuring that data flows sequentially through the workflow.

---

4. Scaling Strategies for the Chatbot System

To ensure that your chatbot system can handle increased load, consider the following strategies:

- **Horizontal Scaling:**
  Deploy multiple instances of the chatbot workflow behind a load balancer. This can be achieved using container orchestration platforms like Kubernetes.
- **Caching:**
  Cache frequently requested responses or intermediate NLP results to reduce processing time.
- **Asynchronous Processing:**
  Use asynchronous frameworks (e.g., `asyncio`) to handle high concurrency and improve responsiveness for I/O-bound tasks.
- **Stateless Design:**
  Design nodes to be stateless where possible so that they can be easily scaled horizontally without dependency on local state.
- **Monitoring and Logging:**
  Continuously monitor system performance and use logs to diagnose and address bottlenecks in real time.

Table: Scaling Strategies for Chatbot Systems

Strategy	Description	Benefits
Horizontal Scaling	Deploy multiple instances behind a load balancer	Improves availability and load distribution
Caching	Store common responses or intermediate results	Reduces processing time and resource usage
Asynchronous Processing	Use non-blocking I/O to handle concurrent requests	Enhances responsiveness for I/O-bound tasks
Stateless Design	Ensure nodes do not maintain session-specific state	Simplifies scaling and load balancing
Monitoring and Logging	Track performance and errors in real time	Facilitates proactive maintenance and troubleshooting

Building a scalable chatbot system with LangGraph Python involves designing a modular workflow that integrates advanced NLP components and accommodates future growth. By decomposing the system into discrete nodes—each responsible for a specific task—you can easily optimize, test, and scale your chatbot. Incorporating external services (such as Hugging Face Transformers for intent detection and text generation) further enhances the capability and flexibility of the system.

Adopting best practices in workflow design, horizontal scaling, caching, and asynchronous processing will ensure that your chatbot remains responsive and reliable even under high demand. The provided code examples and tables offer a comprehensive guide to constructing and scaling a robust chatbot system.

10.2 Graph-Driven Recommendation Engines

Graph-driven recommendation engines leverage the power of graph theory to capture and analyze complex relationships among users, items, and their interactions. By representing users, items, and their interconnections as nodes and edges in a graph, these systems can uncover hidden patterns, identify similar items, and generate personalized recommendations. This chapter explains the principles behind graph-driven recommendation systems, their architectural components, and provides complete code examples and tables to help you build and understand such systems using LangGraph Python.

---

1. Overview of Recommendation Systems

Recommendation systems aim to suggest relevant items to users based on their preferences, historical behavior, or the behavior of similar users. Traditional recommendation approaches include:

- **Content-Based Filtering:**
  Recommends items similar to those the user has liked based on item features.
- **Collaborative Filtering:**
  Recommends items based on the preferences of similar users.
- **Hybrid Approaches:**
  Combine both content-based and collaborative filtering.

Graph-driven recommendation engines extend these approaches by representing the recommendation problem as a graph. In this graph:

- **User nodes** represent individual users.
- **Item nodes** represent products, movies, articles, etc.
- **Edges** represent interactions such as ratings, clicks, or purchases.

This structure allows the recommendation engine to perform complex queries, such as finding items that are indirectly connected through similar user preferences, and supports advanced algorithms like random walks or graph embeddings.

---

2. Benefits of Graph-Driven Recommendations

Using graph structures for recommendations offers several advantages:

- **Capturing Complex Relationships:**
  Graphs can model multi-hop relationships (e.g., a user's friend's preferences) and various types of interactions simultaneously.
- **Enhanced Flexibility:**
  Graph-based models can easily incorporate additional data, such as item categories, social connections, and contextual information.
- **Scalability:**
  Graph databases and libraries are optimized to handle large datasets with complex interconnections, enabling efficient processing even with millions of nodes and edges.
- **Improved Personalization:**
  Advanced algorithms such as Personalized PageRank or Graph Neural Networks (GNNs) can generate more tailored recommendations by learning intricate patterns in user-item interactions.

---

3. Architectural Components of Graph-Driven Recommendation Engines

A typical graph-driven recommendation engine built with LangGraph Python may consist of the following components:

1. **Data Ingestion Node:**
   Loads user-item interaction data, such as ratings or clicks, and constructs the initial graph.
2. **Preprocessing Node:**
   Cleans and normalizes data, transforming raw interactions into a graph format (e.g., building an adjacency list).
3. **Graph Construction Node:**
   Creates a graph where nodes represent users and items, and edges represent interactions. Weighting on edges can capture the strength or frequency of interactions.
4. **Similarity/Ranking Node:**
   Implements algorithms to calculate similarities between items or users. Techniques include collaborative filtering, random walks, or graph-based ranking (e.g., PageRank).
5. **Recommendation Generation Node:**
   Uses the computed similarities to generate a ranked list of recommendations for a given user.
6. **Output Node:**
   Delivers the final list of recommendations to the user or to an external system.

Diagram: Graph-Driven Recommendation Workflow

lua

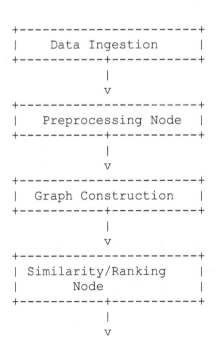

```
+----------------------+
| Recommendation       |
| Generation Node      |
+----------+-----------+
           |
           v
+----------------------+
|     Output Node      |
+----------------------+
```

4. Implementation: A Code Example

Below is a complete code example demonstrating how to build a simple graph-driven recommendation engine using LangGraph Python and NetworkX for graph processing. In this example, we simulate a scenario where we have user-item interactions, construct a graph, and generate recommendations based on item similarity.

Step 1: Define Custom Nodes for Each Component

python

```python
import networkx as nx
from langgraph import Node, GraphManager

# Data Ingestion Node: Loads user-item interactions
class DataIngestionNode(Node):
    def run(self, data=None):
        # Simulated interaction data: (user, item, rating)
        interactions = [
            ("User1", "ItemA", 5),
            ("User1", "ItemB", 3),
            ("User2", "ItemA", 4),
            ("User2", "ItemC", 2),
            ("User3", "ItemB", 4),
            ("User3", "ItemC", 5),
        ]
        print(f"[{self.name}] Loaded interactions: {interactions}")
        for node in self.next_nodes:
            node.run(interactions)

# Graph Construction Node: Builds a bipartite graph of users
and items
class GraphConstructionNode(Node):
    def run(self, data):
        interactions = data
```

```python
        G = nx.Graph()
        # Add user and item nodes, using a bipartite
attribute
        for user, item, rating in interactions:
            G.add_node(user, bipartite="users")
            G.add_node(item, bipartite="items")
            # Add an edge with weight equal to rating
            G.add_edge(user, item, weight=rating)
        print(f"[{self.name}] Constructed graph with nodes:
{G.nodes(data=True)} and edges: {list(G.edges(data=True))}")
        for node in self.next_nodes:
            node.run(G)


# Similarity/Ranking Node: Calculates item similarity based
on common users
class SimilarityRankingNode(Node):
    def run(self, data):
        G = data
        # Extract item nodes (bipartite attribute "items")
        items = [n for n, attr in G.nodes(data=True) if
attr.get("bipartite") == "items"]
        item_similarity = {}
        # Calculate similarity as the number of common users
        for i in items:
            for j in items:
                if i != j:
                    # Find common neighbors (users)
                    common_users = set(G.neighbors(i)) &
set(G.neighbors(j))
                    similarity = len(common_users)
                    item_similarity[(i, j)] = similarity
        print(f"[{self.name}] Calculated item similarities:
{item_similarity}")
        for node in self.next_nodes:
            node.run((G, item_similarity))


# Recommendation Generation Node: Recommends items for a
given user based on similarity
class RecommendationNode(Node):
    def __init__(self, name, target_user):
        super().__init__(name)
        self.target_user = target_user

    def run(self, data):
        G, item_similarity = data
        # Get items already rated by the user
        rated_items = set(G.neighbors(self.target_user))
        recommendations = {}
        # For each item the user hasn't rated, accumulate
similarity scores from rated items
        for (i, j), similarity in item_similarity.items():
```

```
            if i in rated_items and j not in rated_items:
                recommendations[j] = recommendations.get(j,
0) + similarity
            elif j in rated_items and i not in rated_items:
                recommendations[i] = recommendations.get(i,
0) + similarity
        # Sort recommendations by accumulated similarity
score
        sorted_recommendations =
sorted(recommendations.items(), key=lambda x: x[1],
reverse=True)
        print(f"[{self.name}] Recommendations for
{self.target_user}: {sorted_recommendations}")
        for node in self.next_nodes:
            node.run(sorted_recommendations)

# Output Node: Displays the final recommendations
class OutputNode(Node):
    def run(self, data):
        print(f"[{self.name}] Final Recommendations: {data}")
```

Step 2: Build and Execute the Workflow

```python
python

# Create a Graph Manager instance
graph_manager = GraphManager()

# Create node instances
data_ingestion_node = DataIngestionNode("DataIngestion")
graph_construction_node =
GraphConstructionNode("GraphConstruction")
similarity_node = SimilarityRankingNode("SimilarityRanking")
# Target user for recommendations
recommendation_node = RecommendationNode("Recommendation",
target_user="User1")
output_node = OutputNode("Output")

# Register nodes with the Graph Manager
graph_manager.add_node("ingestion", data_ingestion_node)
graph_manager.add_node("construction",
graph_construction_node)
graph_manager.add_node("similarity", similarity_node)
graph_manager.add_node("recommendation", recommendation_node)
graph_manager.add_node("output", output_node)

# Connect nodes to form the workflow:
# DataIngestion -> GraphConstruction -> SimilarityRanking ->
Recommendation -> Output
graph_manager.connect("ingestion", "construction")
```

```
graph_manager.connect("construction", "similarity")
graph_manager.connect("similarity", "recommendation")
graph_manager.connect("recommendation", "output")

# Execute the workflow
print("Starting Graph-Driven Recommendation Workflow...\n")
graph_manager.run("ingestion")
```

Explanation:

- **DataIngestionNode:**
  Loads simulated user-item interaction data.
- **GraphConstructionNode:**
  Constructs a bipartite graph where users and items are nodes, and edges are weighted by user ratings.
- **SimilarityRankingNode:**
  Calculates similarity between items based on the number of common users. This simple approach exemplifies collaborative filtering.
- **RecommendationNode:**
  For a target user (e.g., "User1"), it identifies items not yet rated by the user and recommends them based on accumulated similarity scores from the items the user has rated.
- **OutputNode:**
  Displays the final list of recommendations.
- **Graph Manager:**
  Orchestrates the execution flow of the nodes in the defined order.

---

5. Best Practices for Graph-Driven Recommendation Engines

- **Data Quality:**
  Ensure that user-item interaction data is accurate and complete to improve recommendation quality.
- **Graph Construction:**
  Use efficient data structures and algorithms for constructing and traversing large graphs.
- **Algorithm Selection:**
  Choose similarity and ranking algorithms that best match your domain and data characteristics.
- **Scalability:**
  Design your system to handle large-scale data by leveraging distributed graph databases or parallel processing techniques.

- **Personalization:**
  Continuously refine your models using feedback and updated interaction data to improve personalization.

Table: Best Practices for Recommendation Engines

Best Practice	Description	Implementation Tip
Data Quality	Ensure accurate and complete interaction data	Regular data cleaning and validation
Efficient Graph Construction	Use optimized libraries and algorithms for building graphs	Leverage NetworkX or graph databases
Algorithm Selection	Choose methods that suit your data and domain	Experiment with collaborative filtering and graph-based ranking
Scalability	Design for handling large volumes of data and interactions	Consider distributed processing and caching
Personalization	Incorporate user feedback and behavioral data to refine recommendations	Implement user-specific weighting in similarity calculations

Graph-driven recommendation engines offer a powerful, flexible approach to generating personalized recommendations by leveraging the inherent structure and relationships in your data. By modeling user-item interactions as a graph, you can uncover nuanced patterns and deliver highly relevant recommendations.

This chapter demonstrated how to construct a recommendation workflow using LangGraph Python, including data ingestion, graph construction, similarity computation, and recommendation generation. The modular design enables easy extension and integration with other systems, while best practices ensure scalability, performance, and high-quality recommendations.

10.3 Dynamic Data Analysis Pipelines

Dynamic data analysis pipelines are designed to adapt in real time to changing datasets, analytical requirements, and environmental conditions.

Unlike static pipelines—which follow a fixed sequence of steps—dynamic pipelines adjust their behavior based on the data they receive and the outcomes of intermediate processing stages. This adaptability is essential for modern data analysis applications where the volume, velocity, and variety of data can vary widely over time.

In this section, we will explore the principles behind dynamic data analysis pipelines, discuss their key components and strategies for dynamic adaptation, and provide detailed code examples and tables to illustrate how to build such pipelines using LangGraph Python.

---

1. Overview of Dynamic Data Analysis Pipelines

Dynamic data analysis pipelines are characterized by their ability to:

- **Adapt to Variable Data:**
  Automatically adjust processing steps based on input characteristics (e.g., data quality, format, or volume).
- **Make Real-Time Decisions:**
  Incorporate conditional branching, iterative loops, or parallel processing to handle diverse scenarios.
- **Scale and Optimize on the Fly:**
  Utilize techniques such as caching, asynchronous processing, or distributed computing to maintain performance under changing workloads.

These pipelines are particularly useful in scenarios like real-time analytics, streaming data processing, and adaptive reporting systems, where static workflows might fail to deliver timely or accurate insights.

---

2. Key Components of a Dynamic Pipeline

A dynamic data analysis pipeline in LangGraph Python typically consists of several modular nodes, each performing a specific function while allowing for flexibility and conditional behavior:

- **Input Node:**
  Captures raw data from various sources (databases, streams, files, etc.).
- **Preprocessing Node:**
  Cleans and transforms the data, and may apply different processing strategies based on data characteristics.
- **Conditional Branching Node:**
  Evaluates conditions (e.g., data quality thresholds, volume checks) and routes data to different processing paths accordingly.
- **Iterative Processing Node:**
  Handles tasks that require repeated refinement (e.g., convergence algorithms, iterative data cleaning).
- **Aggregation and Analysis Node:**
  Aggregates data from multiple sources or paths and performs complex analysis (e.g., statistical computations, machine learning inference).
- **Output Node:**
  Delivers final results to downstream systems, dashboards, or storage solutions.

Diagram: Dynamic Data Analysis Pipeline

pgsql

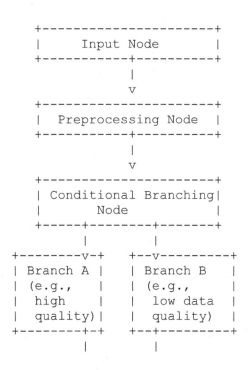

```
        +---------------------+
        |     Input Node      |
        +----------+----------+
                   |
                   v
        +---------------------+
        |  Preprocessing Node |
        +----------+----------+
                   |
                   v
        +---------------------+
        | Conditional Branching|
        |        Node         |
        +-----+--------+------+
              |        |
    +--------v-+   +--v---------+
    | Branch A |   | Branch B   |
    | (e.g.,   |   | (e.g.,     |
    |  high    |   |  low data  |
    |  quality)|   |  quality)  |
    +--------+-+   +--+---------+
             |        |
```

263

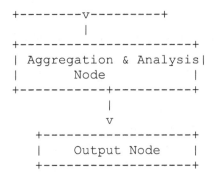

```
+---------v---------+
          |
+-----------------------+
| Aggregation & Analysis|
|         Node          |
+-----------+-----------+
            |
            v
  +-------------------+
  |    Output Node    |
  +-------------------+
```

---

3. Strategies for Dynamic Adaptation

To build a truly dynamic pipeline, consider the following strategies:

- **Conditional Execution:**
  Use conditional branching nodes to determine which path to take based on criteria such as data quality or volume. For example, if data quality is poor, the pipeline might route data through additional cleaning stages.
- **Iterative Refinement:**
  Implement nodes that perform iterative processing, where the node re-executes until a convergence criterion is met. This is useful in machine learning model tuning or data normalization tasks.
- **Parallel Processing:**
  Exploit parallel processing to handle different branches or multiple data streams concurrently, improving throughput and responsiveness.
- **Dynamic Scaling:**
  Integrate with orchestration tools (e.g., Kubernetes) to dynamically allocate resources based on the workload. Although this typically involves infrastructure-level adjustments, your pipeline design should support stateless operations to facilitate scaling.

---

4. Detailed Code Example: Building a Dynamic Pipeline

Below is an end-to-end example of a dynamic data analysis pipeline using LangGraph Python. This example simulates processing a dataset where the pipeline adjusts its behavior based on the quality of the data. For demonstration, we assume "data quality" is determined by the length of the input string.

264

Step 1: Define Custom Nodes

python

```python
from langgraph import Node, GraphManager

# Input Node: Simulates capturing raw data
class DynamicInputNode(Node):
    def run(self, data=None):
        # Simulated input data; in a real scenario, this may
come from an API, file, or stream.
        raw_data = "This is a sample dataset for dynamic
analysis."
        print(f"[{self.name}] Raw Data: {raw_data}")
        for node in self.next_nodes:
            node.run(raw_data)

# Preprocessing Node: Cleans and normalizes data
class DynamicPreprocessingNode(Node):
    def run(self, data):
        # Simple preprocessing: lowercasing and trimming
whitespace
        processed_data = data.lower().strip()
        print(f"[{self.name}] Processed Data:
{processed_data}")
        for node in self.next_nodes:
            node.run(processed_data)

# Conditional Branching Node: Evaluates data quality and
routes accordingly
class DataQualityDecisionNode(Node):
    def run(self, data):
        # Determine "quality" based on the length of the data
(for demonstration)
        if len(data) < 30:
            quality = "low"
            print(f"[{self.name}] Data quality is LOW")
        else:
            quality = "high"
            print(f"[{self.name}] Data quality is HIGH")

        # Pass the data along with the quality assessment
        for node in self.next_nodes:
            node.run((data, quality))

# Branch Node A: For high-quality data, proceed with standard
analysis
class HighQualityBranchNode(Node):
    def run(self, data):
        text, quality = data
```

```python
        response = f"High-quality analysis performed on:
{text}"
        print(f"[{self.name}] {response}")
        for node in self.next_nodes:
            node.run(response)

# Branch Node B: For low-quality data, apply additional
processing
class LowQualityBranchNode(Node):
    def run(self, data):
        text, quality = data
        # Simulate additional cleaning for low-quality data
        cleaned_text = text.replace("sample", "improved
sample")
        response = f"Additional processing applied:
{cleaned_text}"
        print(f"[{self.name}] {response}")
        for node in self.next_nodes:
            node.run(response)

# Aggregation Node: Combines results from different branches
(if needed)
class AggregationNode(Node):
    def run(self, data):
        # For simplicity, just forward the data as-is
        print(f"[{self.name}] Aggregating results: {data}")
        for node in self.next_nodes:
            node.run(data)

# Output Node: Final node that outputs the processed result
class DynamicOutputNode(Node):
    def run(self, data):
        print(f"[{self.name}] Final Output: {data}")
```

Step 2: Build the Workflow Using GraphManager

```python
python

# Create an instance of GraphManager
graph_manager = GraphManager()

# Create node instances
input_node = DynamicInputNode("DynamicInput")
preprocessing_node =
DynamicPreprocessingNode("DynamicPreprocessing")
decision_node =
DataQualityDecisionNode("DataQualityDecision")
high_quality_node =
HighQualityBranchNode("HighQualityBranch")
low_quality_node = LowQualityBranchNode("LowQualityBranch")
```

```
aggregation_node = AggregationNode("Aggregation")
output_node = DynamicOutputNode("DynamicOutput")

# Register nodes with the Graph Manager
graph_manager.add_node("input", input_node)
graph_manager.add_node("preprocessing", preprocessing_node)
graph_manager.add_node("decision", decision_node)
graph_manager.add_node("high", high_quality_node)
graph_manager.add_node("low", low_quality_node)
graph_manager.add_node("aggregation", aggregation_node)
graph_manager.add_node("output", output_node)

# Connect nodes to form the dynamic pipeline:
# Input -> Preprocessing -> Decision -> [HighQualityBranch,
LowQualityBranch] -> Aggregation -> Output
graph_manager.connect("input", "preprocessing")
graph_manager.connect("preprocessing", "decision")

# Decision node connects to both branches
decision_node.add_next(high_quality_node)
decision_node.add_next(low_quality_node)

# Both branches connect to the Aggregation node
high_quality_node.add_next(aggregation_node)
low_quality_node.add_next(aggregation_node)

# Aggregation node connects to the Output node
graph_manager.connect("aggregation", "output")

# Execute the dynamic data analysis pipeline
print("Starting Dynamic Data Analysis Pipeline...\n")
graph_manager.run("input")
```

Explanation:

- **Input and Preprocessing Nodes:**
  The DynamicInputNode simulates receiving raw data, and the DynamicPreprocessingNode cleans and normalizes it.
- **Conditional Branching:**
  The DataQualityDecisionNode evaluates the data quality based on the length of the processed text and routes it to the appropriate branch:
    o **HighQualityBranchNode:** Processes data deemed to be of high quality.
    o **LowQualityBranchNode:** Applies additional processing for low-quality data.

- **Aggregation and Output:**
  Both branches forward their outputs to the `AggregationNode`, which can combine results (if needed) before passing the final data to the `DynamicOutputNode`.
- **Graph Manager:**
  The Graph Manager registers and connects nodes to create the complete dynamic pipeline and initiates its execution.

---

5. Best Practices for Dynamic Data Analysis Pipelines

- **Modular Node Design:**
  Ensure each node has a single responsibility, making it easier to update or replace individual components.
- **Clear Data Contracts:**
  Document the input and output formats of each node to ensure seamless integration and correct routing in conditional branches.
- **Efficient Conditional Branching:**
  Use decision nodes to dynamically route data based on real-time criteria. Optimize these checks for performance, especially when handling large volumes of data.
- **Robust Error Handling:**
  Incorporate error handling within each node to prevent failures from cascading through the pipeline. Log errors and, if necessary, implement fallback strategies.
- **Scalability:**
  Design your pipeline to be stateless wherever possible so that it can be easily scaled horizontally. Consider integrating caching and parallel processing techniques to handle high throughput.

Table: Best Practices for Dynamic Data Analysis Pipelines

Practice	Description	Implementation Tip
Modular Node Design	Each node should perform one distinct task	Use separate classes for input, processing, decision, and output
Clear Data Contracts	Document and enforce expected input/output formats	Use type hints and docstrings in your node methods

Practice	Description	Implementation Tip
Efficient Conditional Branching	Implement conditions to dynamically route data without delay	Optimize conditional checks and avoid heavy computations in decision nodes
Robust Error Handling	Catch errors within nodes and log them for troubleshooting	Use try-except blocks and centralized logging
Scalability	Design for horizontal scaling by keeping nodes stateless	Use caching and asynchronous processing where applicable

Dynamic data analysis pipelines enable your applications to respond to changing data conditions and varying processing requirements in real time. By incorporating conditional branching and iterative processing, you can create flexible workflows that adapt on the fly, ensuring that your analyses remain accurate and efficient under diverse scenarios.

The example provided in this section demonstrates how to build a dynamic pipeline using LangGraph Python, with nodes that capture input, preprocess data, evaluate quality, route processing conditionally, and finally aggregate and output the results. By following these principles and best practices, you can design pipelines that are not only robust and scalable but also capable of delivering real-time insights from dynamic datasets.

10.4 Lessons Learned and Industry Insights

Over the course of developing and deploying graph-driven applications with LangGraph Python, we have gathered a wealth of practical experience and insights that are invaluable for both new and seasoned developers. In this chapter, we share these lessons learned and industry insights to guide you in building robust, scalable, and efficient applications. We will discuss key technical challenges, best practices, and emerging trends that have shaped the field of graph-based systems and NLP integrations.

1. Key Lessons Learned

1.1 Modularity is Essential

Breaking down workflows into discrete, well-defined nodes makes the system easier to develop, test, and maintain. Each node should have a single responsibility—whether it's data ingestion, processing, or output—which not only simplifies debugging but also allows for easy replacement or upgrading of individual components.

1.2 Robust Error Handling and Logging

In production environments, unexpected issues are inevitable. Implementing comprehensive error handling, logging, and fallback mechanisms within each node prevents a single failure from cascading and affecting the entire workflow. Structured logs and centralized logging systems (like ELK Stack) have proven to be critical in diagnosing issues quickly.

1.3 Dynamic and Adaptive Workflows

Data environments and user requirements are not static. Implementing conditional branching and iterative processing in your workflows allows the system to adapt dynamically to changing inputs, ensuring that the processing logic remains optimal regardless of the data quality or volume. Flexibility in design is key to future-proofing your application.

1.4 Performance Optimization is an Ongoing Process

Performance bottlenecks can arise in any complex system. Regular profiling using tools like `cProfile` and continuous performance testing are essential. Caching, parallel processing, and even distributed computing should be considered as the workload grows. Optimization isn't a one-time task—it requires ongoing attention as the system evolves.

1.5 Security Cannot Be an Afterthought

Integrating external APIs and handling sensitive user data necessitates robust security measures. Secure API key management, input validation, and adherence to the principle of least privilege are all best practices that must be integrated into every part of your workflow.

1.6 Interoperability Enhances Value

Graph-driven systems are often one part of a larger ecosystem. Interoperability with tools like NetworkX for advanced analytics, Pandas for data processing, and even graph databases like Neo4j greatly enhances the overall capability of your system. Standardizing data formats and using modular integration techniques ensures that your workflow can communicate effectively with other systems.

2. Industry Insights

2.1 Growing Importance of Graph Technologies
In recent years, graph databases and graph analytics have seen rapid adoption across industries—from social networks and recommendation engines to fraud detection and supply chain management. Companies are leveraging graphs to model complex relationships that traditional relational databases cannot efficiently capture. This trend underscores the value of graph-based architectures, and tools like LangGraph Python provide a framework for leveraging these advantages in application development.

2.2 AI and NLP Convergence
The integration of advanced NLP models, particularly those built on transformer architectures, with graph-driven workflows is becoming increasingly common. This convergence allows for richer contextual analysis and personalized interactions. Industries such as finance, healthcare, and e-commerce are harnessing these combined capabilities to improve customer service, automate processes, and drive business insights.

2.3 Scalability and Cloud Adoption
Scalable systems are a critical requirement for modern applications, and the ability to horizontally scale workflows using container orchestration platforms like Kubernetes is now mainstream. Industry leaders are moving toward cloud-native architectures that support dynamic scaling, robust monitoring, and automated deployment pipelines (CI/CD), which are essential for handling fluctuating workloads and ensuring high availability.

2.4 Emphasis on Continuous Delivery
Organizations are placing a strong emphasis on continuous integration and continuous deployment to rapidly iterate and deliver new features. The implementation of automated CI/CD pipelines not only speeds up development cycles but also minimizes the risk of errors in production. This approach has become a standard best practice, driving improvements in reliability and user satisfaction.

2.5 Data-Driven Decision Making
As businesses increasingly rely on data analytics for decision making, the ability to quickly process, analyze, and visualize large datasets is crucial.

Graph-driven data analysis pipelines are particularly well-suited for these tasks, as they can capture complex relationships and provide actionable insights in real time. This capability is becoming a cornerstone in industries ranging from marketing to logistics.

3. Summary Table: Lessons Learned and Industry Insights

Aspect	Lessons Learned	Industry Insights
Modularity	Build workflows using discrete, single-responsibility nodes for easier maintenance and testing.	Modular architectures are essential in modern software development to handle complex systems.
Error Handling & Logging	Implement robust error handling and logging to prevent system-wide failures and facilitate debugging.	Centralized logging and monitoring are critical for rapid issue detection and resolution in production.
Dynamic Adaptation	Use conditional branching and iterative processing to create adaptive workflows that adjust to data variability.	Flexibility in data processing is vital as data environments continue to evolve and become more complex.
Performance Optimization	Regularly profile and optimize workflows using caching, parallel processing, and distributed computing strategies.	Scalability and performance are key drivers behind the adoption of cloud-native and distributed systems.
Security	Ensure secure API key management, input validation, and adherence to best practices to safeguard data and integrations.	Security remains a top priority, especially with the increased integration of external APIs and cloud services.
Interoperability	Standardize data formats and modularize integrations with external tools to extend functionality.	Seamless interoperability between systems enhances overall application

Aspect	Lessons Learned	Industry Insights
		capability and data-driven insights.

The journey of building graph-driven applications with LangGraph Python has provided invaluable insights into best practices and the evolving industry landscape. From modular design and robust error handling to dynamic workflow adaptation and seamless integration with external tools, every aspect plays a crucial role in developing scalable, efficient, and secure systems.

By incorporating these lessons and industry insights into your development practices, you can build systems that not only meet today's demands but are also resilient and adaptable to future challenges. Embrace continuous learning and refinement to ensure that your workflows remain at the forefront of technological innovation.

Chapter 11: Emerging Trends and Future Directions

11.1 Advances in Graph Neural Networks and Their Impact

Graph Neural Networks (GNNs) have emerged as a transformative technology in the field of graph-based data analysis. By extending deep learning techniques to graph-structured data, GNNs enable models to learn from both node features and the complex interrelationships represented by edges. This chapter section explores the latest advances in GNN architectures, their applications, and the profound impact they have on diverse domains such as natural language processing (NLP), social network analysis, recommendation systems, and more.

---

1. Introduction to Graph Neural Networks

Graph Neural Networks are designed to operate on graph-structured data by learning node representations that capture both local features and global graph structure. Unlike traditional neural networks, GNNs aggregate information from a node's neighbors and, in some cases, even from multiple hops away. This capability makes GNNs particularly effective in modeling relational data.

Key Concepts:

- **Node Embeddings:**
  GNNs generate low-dimensional vector representations for nodes, encapsulating their features and the structure of their neighborhood.
- **Message Passing:**
  Nodes exchange "messages" with their neighbors. In each layer of a GNN, these messages are aggregated and used to update node representations.
- **Graph Convolutions:**
  Similar to convolutional neural networks (CNNs) in image

processing, GNNs apply convolution-like operations on graphs, effectively capturing spatial relationships.

- **Pooling and Readout:**
  After several layers of message passing, pooling operations can be used to aggregate node representations into a graph-level representation for tasks like graph classification.

---

2. Advances in GNN Architectures

Recent advances in GNNs have focused on improving their ability to capture complex graph structures and scaling them to large graphs. Here are some notable developments:

- **Graph Convolutional Networks (GCN):**
  Introduced a layer-wise propagation rule to aggregate neighborhood information. GCNs laid the groundwork for many subsequent models.
- **Graph Attention Networks (GAT):**
  Introduce attention mechanisms to weigh the importance of different neighbors, allowing the model to focus on the most relevant parts of the graph.
- **GraphSAGE:**
  Enables inductive learning by sampling and aggregating features from a fixed-size neighborhood, making it scalable to large graphs.
- **Graph Isomorphism Networks (GIN):**
  Aim to achieve maximum discriminative power in graph representation by mimicking the Weisfeiler-Lehman graph isomorphism test.
- **Dynamic GNNs:**
  Adapt to evolving graphs by updating node embeddings in real time, which is critical for applications such as social network analysis where the graph structure changes over time.

Table: Summary of Key GNN Architectures

GNN Architecture	Key Innovation	Primary Use Case
Graph Convolutional Networks (GCN)	Layer-wise aggregation of neighbor features	Semi-supervised node classification, link prediction
Graph Attention Networks (GAT)	Attention mechanism for neighbor weighting	Social network analysis, recommendation systems
GraphSAGE	Inductive learning via sampling of fixed-size neighborhoods	Large-scale graph data processing
Graph Isomorphism Networks (GIN)	High discriminative power mimicking graph isomorphism tests	Graph classification, chemical molecule analysis
Dynamic GNNs	Real-time update of node embeddings in evolving graphs	Social networks, dynamic recommendation systems

3. Impact of GNNs on Industry and Applications

Enhanced Personalization and Recommendations:
GNNs significantly improve recommendation systems by leveraging user-item interaction graphs. They capture complex patterns like multi-hop relationships and community structures, which traditional collaborative filtering methods might miss.

Improved Natural Language Processing:
In NLP, GNNs are used to model relationships between words or sentences. For instance, in document classification, a graph can represent the relationships between words (or phrases), and GNNs can generate more nuanced representations that improve classification performance.

Social Network Analysis:
GNNs excel in analyzing social networks, where they can identify influential users, detect communities, and predict trends by learning from both node features and the structure of the network.

Bioinformatics and Chemical Molecule Analysis:
In drug discovery, molecules can be modeled as graphs where atoms are

nodes and bonds are edges. GNNs have shown promising results in predicting molecular properties, which accelerates the identification of potential drug candidates.

---

4. Code Example: A Simple GCN with PyTorch Geometric

Below is a complete code example demonstrating a simple Graph Convolutional Network (GCN) using PyTorch Geometric. This example illustrates how to build a GNN that performs node classification on a small graph.

Step 1: Installation Requirements

Make sure you have installed PyTorch and PyTorch Geometric. You can install them via:

bash

```
pip install torch torchvision torchaudio
pip install torch-geometric
```

Step 2: GCN Code Example

python

```python
import torch
import torch.nn.functional as F
from torch_geometric.nn import GCNConv
from torch_geometric.data import Data

# Define a simple GCN model
class SimpleGCN(torch.nn.Module):
    def __init__(self, num_features, hidden_channels,
num_classes):
        super(SimpleGCN, self).__init__()
        self.conv1 = GCNConv(num_features, hidden_channels)
        self.conv2 = GCNConv(hidden_channels, num_classes)

    def forward(self, data):
        x, edge_index = data.x, data.edge_index
        # First GCN layer with ReLU activation
        x = self.conv1(x, edge_index)
        x = F.relu(x)
        # Second GCN layer for final classification
```

```
        x = self.conv2(x, edge_index)
        return F.log_softmax(x, dim=1)

# Create a simple graph
# Node features: 3 nodes with 2 features each
x = torch.tensor([[1, 2], [2, 3], [3, 4]], dtype=torch.float)
# Edge indices: define a graph structure (directed edges)
edge_index = torch.tensor([[0, 1, 1, 2],
                           [1, 0, 2, 1]], dtype=torch.long)

# Create a data object
data = Data(x=x, edge_index=edge_index)

# Define the model, loss function, and optimizer
model = SimpleGCN(num_features=2, hidden_channels=4,
num_classes=2)
optimizer = torch.optim.Adam(model.parameters(), lr=0.01)
criterion = torch.nn.NLLLoss()

# Dummy labels for nodes
labels = torch.tensor([0, 1, 0], dtype=torch.long)

# Training loop (for demonstration purposes, a simple 50-
epoch run)
model.train()
for epoch in range(50):
    optimizer.zero_grad()
    out = model(data)
    loss = criterion(out, labels)
    loss.backward()
    optimizer.step()
    print(f"Epoch {epoch+1}, Loss: {loss.item():.4f}")

# Evaluation
model.eval()
_, pred = model(data).max(dim=1)
print("Predicted classes:", pred.tolist())
```

Explanation:

- **Model Definition:**
  The SimpleGCN model consists of two graph convolutional layers.
  The first layer applies a ReLU activation, and the second outputs log
  probabilities for classification.
- **Graph Data:**
  A small graph with three nodes and a set of directed edges is created
  using PyTorch Geometric's Data class.

- **Training:**
  A simple training loop demonstrates how the model learns to classify nodes using a dummy label tensor.
- **Evaluation:**
  The predicted classes for the nodes are printed after training.

---

5. Industry Impact and Future Directions

The advances in GNNs are reshaping how industries process and analyze complex data. Key impacts include:

- **Enhanced Predictive Capabilities:**
  GNNs enable more accurate predictions by leveraging relational information in data. This is particularly valuable in fraud detection, recommendation systems, and social network analysis.
- **Interdisciplinary Applications:**
  From bioinformatics to transportation logistics, GNNs are applied to problems that involve intricate relationships, offering insights that were previously unattainable.
- **Scalability and Efficiency:**
  With ongoing research, GNN architectures are becoming more scalable and efficient, making them suitable for real-world applications with massive datasets.
- **Future Trends:**
  Research is focused on dynamic and temporal GNNs, which can model time-evolving graphs, and on integrating GNNs with other deep learning models to enhance multimodal data processing.

Table: Impact of GNN Advances

Impact Area	Description	Examples
Predictive Analytics	Improved accuracy by considering relational data	Fraud detection, recommendation systems
Multimodal Integration	Combining graph data with images, text, and other modalities	Social media analysis, healthcare diagnostics

Impact Area	Description	Examples
Scalability	Handling large and dynamic datasets effectively	Large-scale social networks, transportation systems
Research and Innovation	Continuous advancements in model architectures and efficiency	Dynamic GNNs, temporal graph networks

Advances in Graph Neural Networks are having a transformative impact on how we model and analyze complex data. Their ability to learn from both node features and graph structure is enabling a new generation of applications that are more accurate, scalable, and insightful. As research progresses, GNNs will continue to evolve, further enhancing their capabilities and expanding their range of applications across industries.

By integrating GNNs with frameworks like LangGraph Python, developers can harness these advanced techniques to build robust, intelligent systems that leverage the full potential of graph-based learning. As you explore these emerging trends, you are well-positioned to drive innovation in your own projects and contribute to the evolving landscape of graph-based machine learning.

11.2 The Future of NLP and Graph-Based AI

The fields of Natural Language Processing (NLP) and Graph-Based Artificial Intelligence (AI) are evolving rapidly, driven by advances in machine learning, increased computational power, and the availability of large-scale datasets. As these domains converge, they are opening up new possibilities for understanding and processing complex data in ways that were previously unimaginable. In this section, we explore the future directions of NLP and graph-based AI, discuss emerging trends, and outline the implications these advancements may have on industry and research.

1. Emerging Trends in NLP

1.1 Transformer Models and Beyond
Transformer architectures such as BERT, GPT-3, and T5 have

revolutionized NLP by enabling models to understand context more effectively and generate human-like text. The future will likely see:

- **Larger and More Efficient Models:**
  Continued growth in model size is accompanied by innovations in efficiency (e.g., sparse transformers, model distillation) to reduce resource consumption.
- **Multilingual and Cross-Lingual Models:**
  Models that understand and generate text across multiple languages, facilitating global applications.
- **Task-Agnostic and Zero-Shot Learning:**
  NLP systems will become increasingly capable of generalizing to new tasks with little to no task-specific training, reducing the need for large annotated datasets.

1.2 Integration of Multimodal Data
The future of NLP is not limited to text alone. There is a growing trend towards multimodal models that integrate text, images, video, and audio. This will enhance applications like:

- **Contextual Search:**
  Combining textual and visual information to provide more accurate search results.
- **Enhanced Virtual Assistants:**
  Virtual assistants that understand and respond to visual cues along with spoken language.
- **Richer Content Summarization:**
  Systems that summarize both written and visual content, offering comprehensive insights.

1.3 Ethical and Explainable AI
As NLP models become more pervasive, ethical considerations such as bias, fairness, and transparency are paramount. Future advancements will focus on:

- **Explainable NLP:**
  Developing models that not only provide predictions but also offer explanations for their decisions.
- **Bias Mitigation:**
  Creating techniques to identify, quantify, and reduce bias in language models.

- **Regulatory Compliance:**
  Ensuring that NLP systems comply with emerging data privacy and ethical guidelines globally.

---

2. Advances in Graph-Based AI

2.1 Graph Neural Networks (GNNs)
Graph Neural Networks have already transformed many applications by effectively capturing relationships in complex data. Future directions include:

- **Dynamic and Temporal GNNs:**
  These models will better handle evolving graphs, capturing time-dependent changes and adapting in real time to dynamic data environments.
- **Scalable GNNs:**
  With growing data sizes, the focus will be on making GNNs more scalable—through innovations in parallel processing and distributed computing.
- **Integration with Other Modalities:**
  GNNs will increasingly integrate with other deep learning models to process multimodal data (e.g., combining graph data with images or text).

2.2 Graph-Based Reasoning and Knowledge Graphs
Knowledge graphs are becoming central to many AI systems due to their ability to represent complex relationships. Future developments will likely include:

- **Automated Knowledge Graph Construction:**
  Using NLP to automatically extract entities and relationships from unstructured data and build comprehensive knowledge graphs.
- **Real-Time Graph Updates:**
  Systems that continuously update knowledge graphs with real-time data from various sources, enhancing the accuracy and relevance of information.
- **Advanced Graph Querying:**
  Improved graph querying languages and tools to perform more complex analyses, enabling better decision-making and insights.

2.3 Hybrid Models

One of the most exciting trends is the convergence of NLP and graph-based AI. Hybrid models will:

- **Combine Language Models with Graph Structures:**
  Leverage the strengths of transformers for language understanding along with GNNs for relational reasoning. For example, using a transformer to generate contextual embeddings that are then refined by a GNN to incorporate relationship information.
- **Improve Recommendation and Search:**
  Hybrid systems can provide more nuanced recommendations and search results by combining content-based and graph-based insights.
- **Enhance Interpretability:**
  Graph structures can provide a visual and logical explanation for the decisions made by NLP systems, improving transparency and trust.

---

3. Practical Implications and Future Directions

3.1 Industry Applications

The advancements in NLP and graph-based AI are expected to have a transformative impact across various sectors:

- **Healthcare:**
  Enhanced diagnostic systems that integrate patient records, research literature, and clinical guidelines using knowledge graphs and advanced NLP.
- **Finance:**
  Fraud detection, risk assessment, and personalized financial services will benefit from the rich relational insights provided by graph-based models.
- **E-commerce:**
  More accurate recommendation systems and customer support chatbots that leverage multimodal data and complex user-item relationships.
- **Social Media:**
  Improved sentiment analysis, content moderation, and trend prediction by understanding both the content and the social network structure.

3.2 Research Directions

Academic and industry research will continue to push the boundaries of what is possible with these technologies:

- **Efficiency and Sustainability:**
  Research will focus on making large models more efficient, reducing their environmental impact, and enabling their deployment on edge devices.
- **Interdisciplinary Applications:**
  Combining insights from NLP, graph theory, and other domains (e.g., computer vision, reinforcement learning) to create comprehensive AI systems.
- **Standardization and Benchmarks:**
  The development of standardized benchmarks for evaluating the performance of hybrid NLP and graph-based models, facilitating broader adoption and comparison of techniques.

---

4. Code Example: A Simple Hybrid Model

Below is an illustrative example that combines basic NLP processing with graph analysis using NetworkX. This example is simplified but demonstrates the idea of combining text data with graph-based reasoning.

```python
python

import networkx as nx
from transformers import pipeline

# Step 1: Use a Hugging Face transformer to get text
embeddings (simulated here with a dummy function)
def get_text_embedding(text):
    # In a real application, this function would use a model
like BERT to generate embeddings.
    # Here, we simulate an embedding as a vector of length 3.
    return [len(text) % 5, len(text) % 7, len(text) % 3]

# Step 2: Create a simple graph where nodes represent
sentences in a document
sentences = [
    "Graph neural networks are powerful.",
    "Natural language processing is evolving rapidly.",
    "Hybrid models integrate graphs and NLP for better
insights."
]
```

```
# Create a directed graph
G = nx.DiGraph()
for idx, sentence in enumerate(sentences):
    embedding = get_text_embedding(sentence)
    G.add_node(idx, text=sentence, embedding=embedding)

# Connect nodes based on similarity (for demonstration,
connect sequentially)
for idx in range(len(sentences) - 1):
    G.add_edge(idx, idx + 1, weight=1.0)

# Step 3: Use a transformer pipeline to generate a summary
(dummy simulation)
text_generator = pipeline("text-generation", model="gpt2")
prompt = "Summarize the key insights: " + " ".join(sentences)
summary_result = text_generator(prompt, max_length=50,
num_return_sequences=1)
summary = summary_result[0]['generated_text']

# Output the graph and summary
print("Constructed Graph Nodes:")
for node, attr in G.nodes(data=True):
    print(f"Node {node}: {attr}")

print("\nConstructed Graph Edges:")
for u, v, attr in G.edges(data=True):
    print(f"Edge from Node {u} to Node {v}: {attr}")

print("\nGenerated Summary:")
print(summary)
```

Explanation:

- **Text Embedding Simulation:**
  A dummy function `get_text_embedding` simulates generating embeddings for sentences.
- **Graph Construction:**
  A directed graph is built with nodes representing sentences and edges connecting them sequentially.
- **Hybrid Model:**
  A transformer pipeline is used to generate a summary of the document, demonstrating how NLP outputs can be combined with graph structures.
- **Output:**
  The constructed graph and generated summary are printed, illustrating a simple hybrid approach.

5. Summary Table: Future of NLP and Graph-Based AI

Area	Emerging Trend	Impact/Benefit
Transformer Models	Larger, more efficient, multilingual models	Improved contextual understanding and task generalization
Multimodal Integration	Combining text, images, audio, and graph data	Richer, more comprehensive AI systems
Graph Neural Networks	Dynamic, scalable, and efficient GNN architectures	Enhanced relational reasoning and predictive capabilities
Hybrid Models	Integration of NLP and GNN for complex tasks	Better personalization, explainability, and performance
Ethical and Explainable AI	Bias mitigation, transparency, and compliance	Increased trust and adoption in critical applications
Scalability and Cloud	Cloud-native, containerized, and distributed systems	Robust, high-availability applications that scale with demand

The future of NLP and graph-based AI is marked by exciting advancements that promise to unlock new levels of intelligence and efficiency in data processing. The integration of transformer models with graph neural networks, the rise of hybrid models, and a stronger emphasis on ethical and explainable AI are poised to reshape industries ranging from healthcare to finance.

As these technologies evolve, practitioners must stay informed of emerging trends and continuously refine their approaches. By leveraging the strengths of both NLP and graph-based AI, you can build systems that are not only more accurate and personalized but also more robust and scalable. Embrace these innovations to drive impactful solutions and remain at the forefront of AI development.

11.3 Integrating LangGraph with Emerging Technologies

As technology rapidly evolves, integrating graph-driven workflows with emerging technologies can unlock new dimensions of functionality and security. LangGraph Python's modular design and flexibility make it well-suited for integration with cutting-edge systems such as blockchain and the Internet of Things (IoT). In this section, we explore how to extend LangGraph workflows to interact with blockchain networks and IoT devices. We'll discuss the benefits, challenges, and strategies for integration, and provide detailed code examples and supporting tables to illustrate each concept.

---

1. Overview of Integration with Emerging Technologies

Emerging technologies like blockchain and IoT are transforming various industries:

- **Blockchain:**
  Provides a decentralized and secure method for data storage, transaction processing, and smart contract execution. Integrating blockchain with LangGraph workflows can enhance data integrity, traceability, and security in applications such as supply chain management, digital identity verification, and secure data sharing.
- **IoT (Internet of Things):**
  Connects physical devices, sensors, and actuators to the internet, enabling real-time data collection and control. When combined with LangGraph, IoT integration allows you to process and analyze sensor data dynamically, driving smart decision-making in domains like smart cities, industrial automation, and healthcare monitoring.

---

2. Integrating LangGraph with Blockchain

2.1 Rationale and Benefits

- **Data Integrity and Immutability:**
  Blockchain technology ensures that data, once recorded, cannot be

tampered with. This feature is particularly useful for logging critical workflow events or securely storing transaction records.

- **Decentralization and Trust:**
  In environments where trust is paramount, blockchain provides a decentralized ledger that can verify and authenticate actions performed within your LangGraph workflows.
- **Smart Contracts:**
  By interfacing with blockchain smart contracts, you can automate contractual agreements, enforce rules, and trigger events based on predefined conditions.

2.2 Example: Recording Workflow Output on a Blockchain

Below is a simplified example that demonstrates how to create a custom LangGraph node to record a workflow's output on a blockchain using the `web3.py` library.

Step 1: Installation

Ensure you have the necessary package installed:

```bash
pip install web3
```

Step 2: Custom Blockchain Node

```python
from langgraph import Node
from web3 import Web3
import os

class BlockchainLoggingNode(Node):
    def __init__(self, name, contract_address, abi):
        super().__init__(name)
        # Connect to an Ethereum node (e.g., Infura or a
local Ganache instance)
        self.web3 =
Web3(Web3.HTTPProvider(os.getenv("ETH_NODE_URL",
"http://127.0.0.1:8545")))
        if not self.web3.isConnected():
            raise ConnectionError("Failed to connect to the
Ethereum node.")
        # Set up contract instance
```

```python
        self.contract_address =
Web3.toChecksumAddress(contract_address)
        self.contract =
self.web3.eth.contract(address=self.contract_address,
abi=abi)
        # Assume the default account is set
        self.account = self.web3.eth.accounts[0]

    def run(self, data):
        # Record the workflow output on the blockchain using
a smart contract function
        print(f"[{self.name}] Recording data on blockchain:
{data}")
        try:
            # For demonstration, we assume the contract has a
function `logData(string message)`
            txn =
self.contract.functions.logData(data).buildTransaction({
                'from': self.account,
                'nonce':
self.web3.eth.getTransactionCount(self.account),
                'gas': 200000,
                'gasPrice': self.web3.toWei('50', 'gwei')
            })
            signed_txn =
self.web3.eth.account.sign_transaction(txn,
private_key=os.getenv("PRIVATE_KEY"))
            tx_hash =
self.web3.eth.sendRawTransaction(signed_txn.rawTransaction)
            print(f"[{self.name}] Transaction sent. TX Hash:
{tx_hash.hex()}")
        except Exception as e:
            print(f"[{self.name}] ERROR recording data on
blockchain: {e}")

        # Propagate data to the next nodes
        for node in self.next_nodes:
            node.run(data)
```

Explanation:

- **Connection Setup:**
  The node connects to an Ethereum node using a provider URL (e.g., Infura or Ganache).
- **Contract Interaction:**
  The node sets up a smart contract instance using its address and ABI. It then builds, signs, and sends a transaction to call a smart contract function (e.g., logData) with the workflow data.

- **Security:**
  API keys and private keys are retrieved from environment variables, ensuring sensitive information is not hardcoded.

---

3. Integrating LangGraph with IoT

3.1 Rationale and Benefits

- **Real-Time Data Processing:**
  IoT devices generate continuous streams of data. Integrating IoT data into your LangGraph workflows enables real-time analysis and decision-making.
- **Automation and Control:**
  With IoT integration, workflows can trigger actions based on sensor data, such as adjusting environmental controls, sending alerts, or updating dashboards.
- **Scalability:**
  IoT ecosystems often involve large-scale data ingestion. LangGraph's modular nodes can be scaled horizontally to handle high-throughput data streams.

3.2 Example: Ingesting IoT Sensor Data

Below is an example of a custom node that simulates receiving data from an IoT sensor.

Step 1: Simulate IoT Sensor Data

```python
import random
import time

class IoTSensorNode(Node):
    def run(self, data=None):
        # Simulate sensor data: e.g., temperature readings in
Celsius
        sensor_data = {"timestamp": time.time(),
"temperature": round(random.uniform(20.0, 30.0), 2)}
        print(f"[{self.name}] Sensor Data: {sensor_data}")
        for node in self.next_nodes:
            node.run(sensor_data)
```

Explanation:

- **Simulated Data:**
  The node simulates IoT sensor data by generating a random temperature value and a timestamp.
- **Data Propagation:**
  The sensor data is then passed to the next nodes for further processing, such as analysis or storage.

---

4. Best Practices for Integrating Emerging Technologies

A. Security and Authentication:

- Use environment variables or secure vaults to manage API keys, private keys, and sensitive configuration details.
- Implement robust authentication mechanisms when interfacing with external services.

B. Data Consistency and Format Standardization:

- Define clear data contracts for your nodes so that IoT data or blockchain responses are consistently formatted.
- Use serialization formats like JSON for data exchange between systems.

C. Scalability and Resilience:

- Design nodes to be stateless when possible, facilitating horizontal scaling.
- Implement error handling and retries, especially for network requests to external services.

D. Monitoring and Logging:

- Integrate comprehensive logging within nodes to monitor interactions with external APIs or IoT devices.
- Use centralized logging and monitoring tools to track the performance and health of your integrations.

Table: Best Practices for Integration

Practice	Description	Implementation Tip
Secure API Key Management	Store sensitive keys in environment variables or vaults	Use os.getenv() and secret management tools
Data Format Standardization	Define clear data contracts and use standardized formats	Use JSON for data serialization
Stateless Design	Ensure nodes do not rely on internal state for easier scaling	Design nodes to process each input independently
Robust Error Handling	Implement retries and graceful degradation in case of failures	Use try-except blocks and retry libraries like tenacity
Comprehensive Logging	Log all interactions with external systems for troubleshooting	Integrate Python's logging module with a centralized log management system

Integrating LangGraph Python with emerging technologies such as blockchain and IoT opens up new opportunities for building advanced, secure, and real-time applications. By developing custom nodes tailored to interact with blockchain networks and IoT devices, you can extend the capabilities of your workflows to include data integrity, decentralized record-keeping, and real-time sensor data processing.

The examples provided in this section demonstrate how to construct custom nodes for both blockchain logging and IoT sensor data ingestion. They also illustrate the importance of secure key management, standardized data formats, and robust error handling in ensuring smooth integration.

As you explore these emerging technologies, remember to follow best practices and continually adapt your integration strategies to new challenges and opportunities. This proactive approach will help you build versatile, scalable, and secure systems that harness the power of both graph-based workflows and cutting-edge technologies.

11.4 Preparing for the Next Generation of AI Workflows

As AI continues to evolve, so too must the workflows that support its development, deployment, and continuous improvement. Preparing for the next generation of AI workflows means building systems that are not only robust and scalable today but also adaptable and future-proof. In this section, we explore the key considerations and strategies for designing AI workflows that can seamlessly incorporate emerging technologies, advanced automation, and continuous learning.

1. Embracing Flexibility and Adaptability

Next-generation AI workflows need to be flexible. With rapidly evolving algorithms, diverse data sources, and changing business requirements, static workflows quickly become obsolete. To prepare:

- **Modular Architecture:**
  Design your workflows as a collection of loosely-coupled modules or nodes. This modularity allows you to update or swap individual components without rearchitecting the entire system.
- **Dynamic Routing and Conditional Logic:**
  Incorporate conditional branching and iterative loops in your pipelines. This enables workflows to adjust in real time based on the data being processed or feedback from deployed models.
- **Continuous Learning and Adaptation:**
  Integrate mechanisms for model retraining, performance monitoring, and automated feedback loops. This way, your system can learn from new data and adapt to changes over time.

2. Leveraging Emerging Technologies

To stay ahead of the curve, next-generation workflows will integrate emerging technologies that enhance AI capabilities:

- **Edge Computing:**
  With the proliferation of IoT and edge devices, processing data closer to the source reduces latency and conserves bandwidth. AI workflows can leverage edge computing to perform preliminary analysis and filtering before sending data to centralized systems.
- **Federated Learning:**
  Privacy and data security are becoming increasingly important. Federated learning allows models to be trained on decentralized data (e.g., data on user devices) while preserving privacy. This approach can be integrated into AI workflows to continuously improve models without centralizing sensitive data.
- **Quantum Computing (Emerging):**
  Though still in its early stages, quantum computing promises to revolutionize certain types of optimization and search problems. Keeping an eye on these developments may lead to integrating quantum-inspired algorithms into your workflows.
- **Hybrid AI Models:**
  The convergence of NLP, computer vision, and graph-based models is creating more holistic AI systems. Next-generation workflows will need to support the integration of multimodal data and the orchestration of multiple AI models working in tandem.

---

3. Automation and Orchestration

Automation remains the backbone of efficient AI workflows:

- **Advanced CI/CD Pipelines:**
  Incorporate continuous integration and deployment pipelines that are designed for AI applications. These pipelines should support automated testing, model validation, and rollback mechanisms to ensure reliability during updates.
- **Orchestration Platforms:**
  Tools like Kubernetes, Apache Airflow, or Prefect can help manage complex workflows, allowing for scheduling, monitoring, and dynamic resource allocation. These platforms enable you to run workflows at scale and adapt to varying loads.
- **Dynamic Resource Allocation:**
  Use cloud-native features to automatically scale resources (compute, storage) based on workload. This not only improves performance but also optimizes costs.

Example: Pseudocode for a Dynamic Orchestration Task

python

```python
# This pseudocode demonstrates how you might dynamically
adjust a workflow task
def dynamic_task_scheduler(current_load, threshold,
task_queue):
    if current_load > threshold:
        # Scale up: add more tasks to handle load
        additional_tasks =
create_additional_tasks(current_load, threshold)
        task_queue.extend(additional_tasks)
        print("Scaling up: Added additional tasks to the
queue.")
    else:
        print("Current load is within limits. No scaling
needed.")
    return task_queue

# Example usage:
current_load = 85   # e.g., CPU usage percentage
threshold = 75
task_queue = ["task1", "task2"]
updated_queue = dynamic_task_scheduler(current_load,
threshold, task_queue)
print("Updated Task Queue:", updated_queue)
```

Explanation:

- **Dynamic Scheduling:**
  The pseudocode shows a function that adjusts the task queue based
  on current system load, a concept that can be applied to scheduling
  workflow tasks.
- **Scalability:**
  Similar logic can be implemented within an orchestration platform to
  scale AI tasks dynamically.

---

4. Security, Privacy, and Compliance

As AI workflows become more integrated and data-driven, maintaining
security and privacy becomes paramount:

- **Data Protection:**
  Implement strong encryption and access controls to protect sensitive data throughout the workflow.
- **Compliance:**
  Ensure that your workflows adhere to relevant data protection regulations (e.g., GDPR, HIPAA). This may involve anonymizing data or implementing audit trails.
- **Robust Access Controls:**
  Apply the principle of least privilege for all components in your workflow, and regularly review and update security policies.

5. Best Practices for Preparing Next-Generation AI Workflows

Best Practice	Description	Implementation Tip
Modular Design	Break down workflows into independent, reusable modules or nodes.	Use clear APIs between nodes and enforce single responsibility.
Dynamic Adaptation	Incorporate conditional branching and iterative loops to adjust workflows in real time.	Implement decision nodes that assess data quality and adapt processing paths.
Integration of Emerging Tech	Leverage edge computing, federated learning, and multimodal AI to enhance workflows.	Stay updated with industry trends and integrate APIs for new technologies.
Automation and Orchestration	Utilize CI/CD pipelines and orchestration platforms for scalable, automated deployments.	Use tools like Kubernetes and Apache Airflow for dynamic resource allocation.
Security and Compliance	Ensure data protection, privacy, and regulatory compliance across the workflow.	Use encryption, secure API key management, and audit logs.
Continuous Monitoring and Feedback	Implement robust monitoring and feedback loops to continuously optimize workflows.	Integrate Prometheus, Grafana, and centralized logging for real-time insights.

6.

Preparing for the next generation of AI workflows is about building systems that are flexible, scalable, secure, and capable of integrating cutting-edge technologies. As AI models grow more sophisticated and data environments become more dynamic, your workflows must adapt accordingly. Emphasizing modular design, dynamic adaptation, and robust orchestration will enable you to create resilient AI systems that can evolve with emerging trends.

By adopting these best practices and continuously refining your approach, you ensure that your AI workflows remain at the forefront of technological innovation, ready to tackle future challenges and opportunities.

Appendix

Appendix A: Installation Guides and Environment Setup Scripts

This appendix provides comprehensive installation guides and environment setup scripts for LangGraph Python. Whether you're setting up your development environment on a local machine or preparing a production server, these step-by-step instructions and scripts will help you configure your system consistently and securely. The following sections cover prerequisites, creating virtual environments, installing dependencies, and optionally containerizing your application with Docker.

---

1. Prerequisites

Before installing LangGraph Python, ensure your system meets the following prerequisites:

- **Python Version:**
  LangGraph Python requires Python 3.7 or higher. Verify your Python version by running:

  bash

  ```
  python --version
  ```

  Expected Output:

  plaintext

  ```
  Python 3.9.12
  ```

- **Package Manager (pip):**
  Make sure pip is installed and updated. You can upgrade pip with:

  bash

  ```
  python -m pip install --upgrade pip
  ```

- **Optional Tools:**

- o **Virtual Environment Manager:** Using `venv` (built-in) or `conda` is recommended to isolate project dependencies.
- o **Docker:** For containerized deployments, install Docker from Docker's official website.

2. Creating a Virtual Environment

Using a virtual environment isolates your project dependencies from system-wide packages. Below are instructions for creating and activating a virtual environment using Python's built-in `venv` module.

Step 1: Create a Virtual Environment

Open your terminal and navigate to your project directory, then run:

```bash
python -m venv langgraph-env
```

This command creates a new directory called `langgraph-env` containing a complete Python environment.

Step 2: Activate the Virtual Environment

- **On Windows:**

  ```bash
  langgraph-env\Scripts\activate
  ```

- **On macOS and Linux:**

  ```bash
  source langgraph-env/bin/activate
  ```

Verification:
After activation, your terminal prompt should change to show the virtual environment name (e.g., `(langgraph-env)`).

3. Installing Dependencies

Once the virtual environment is activated, install LangGraph Python and its dependencies.

Step 1: Create a `requirements.txt` File

Create a file named `requirements.txt` in your project root with the following contents:

```plaintext
langgraph==1.0.0
transformers==4.30.0
spacy==3.5.0
requests==2.28.1
networkx==2.8.8
matplotlib==3.6.2
```

Note: Adjust the versions as needed based on your project requirements.

Step 2: Install Dependencies

Run the following command in your terminal:

```bash
pip install -r requirements.txt
```

This command installs all necessary packages. If you are integrating additional tools (e.g., Docker), ensure you install their required packages separately.

Step 3: Download Additional Resources (e.g., spaCy Language Model)

For spaCy, download the required language model:

```bash
python -m spacy download en_core_web_sm
```

---

4. Environment Setup Scripts

Below are sample scripts that automate the environment setup process. Save these scripts as `setup.sh` for Unix-based systems and `setup.bat` for Windows.

Unix-Based Setup Script (`setup.sh`):

```bash
#!/bin/bash

# Exit immediately if a command exits with a non-zero status.
set -e

echo "Checking Python version..."
python --version

echo "Creating virtual environment 'langgraph-env'..."
python -m venv langgraph-env

echo "Activating virtual environment..."
source langgraph-env/bin/activate

echo "Upgrading pip..."
python -m pip install --upgrade pip

echo "Installing dependencies from requirements.txt..."
pip install -r requirements.txt

echo "Downloading spaCy English model..."
python -m spacy download en_core_web_sm

echo "Environment setup complete. To activate the virtual environment, run:"
echo "source langgraph-env/bin/activate"
```

Windows Setup Script (`setup.bat`):

```batch
@echo off
REM Exit if any command fails
SETLOCAL ENABLEDELAYEDEXPANSION

echo Checking Python version...
python --version

echo Creating virtual environment "langgraph-env"...
python -m venv langgraph-env
```

```
echo Activating virtual environment...
call langgraph-env\Scripts\activate

echo Upgrading pip...
python -m pip install --upgrade pip

echo Installing dependencies from requirements.txt...
pip install -r requirements.txt

echo Downloading spaCy English model...
python -m spacy download en_core_web_sm

echo Environment setup complete.
echo To activate the virtual environment, run:
echo langgraph-env\Scripts\activate
pause
```

Explanation:

- The **Unix-based script** uses bash commands to create, activate, and set up the virtual environment.
- The **Windows script** uses batch commands and `call` to run the activation script.
- Both scripts upgrade pip, install dependencies from `requirements.txt`, and download the spaCy model.

---

5. Optional: Containerizing with Docker

Containerization provides consistency across different environments. Below is a sample `Dockerfile` for a LangGraph Python application.

Dockerfile:

```dockerfile
dockerfile

# Use an official Python runtime as a parent image
FROM python:3.9-slim

# Prevent Python from buffering stdout and stderr
ENV PYTHONUNBUFFERED=1

# Set the working directory to /app
WORKDIR /app

# Copy the requirements file into the container at /app
```

```
COPY requirements.txt /app/

# Install any needed packages specified in requirements.txt
RUN pip install --upgrade pip && \
    pip install -r requirements.txt

# Download spaCy English model (optional)
RUN python -m spacy download en_core_web_sm

# Copy the rest of the application code into the container at
/app
COPY . /app/

# Expose port 8000 if your app uses it (optional)
EXPOSE 8000

# Run the application
CMD ["python", "main.py"]
```

Explanation:

- **Base Image:**
  Uses a lightweight Python 3.9 image.
- **Environment Variable:**
  `PYTHONUNBUFFERED=1` ensures that output is not buffered.
- **Working Directory:**
  Sets `/app` as the working directory.
- **Dependencies:**
  Installs dependencies from `requirements.txt` and downloads the spaCy model.
- **Code Copy and Execution:**
  Copies application code and sets the default command to run your application (e.g., `main.py`).

---

6. Summary Table: Environment Setup Checklist

Step	Action	Tool/Command
Check Python Version	Verify Python 3.7+ is installed	`python --version`
Create Virtual Environment	Isolate project dependencies	`python -m venv langgraph-env`

Step	Action	Tool/Command
Activate Virtual Environment	Enable the isolated environment	`source langgraph-env/bin/activate` (Unix) or `langgraph-env\Scripts\activate` (Windows)
Upgrade Pip	Ensure latest package installer	`python -m pip install --upgrade pip`
Install Dependencies	Install packages from requirements file	`pip install -r requirements.txt`
Download Additional Resources	Install language models or other resources	`python -m spacy download en_core_web_sm`
(Optional) Containerization	Build Docker image for deployment	Use provided Dockerfile commands

A well-prepared environment is the foundation of a successful LangGraph Python project. This appendix has provided detailed installation guides and environment setup scripts that ensure your development and production environments are consistent, secure, and efficient. Whether you are working locally, on a remote server, or deploying containers with Docker, these instructions and scripts will help you get started quickly and reliably.

Appendix B: Glossary of Terms and Acronyms

This glossary provides definitions for key terms and acronyms frequently used throughout this book. It is designed to serve as a quick reference guide for readers, ensuring that technical concepts are clearly understood and consistently applied. Each entry includes a concise definition, relevant context, and, where applicable, examples that illustrate the term's usage in the context of LangGraph Python, NLP, and graph-based workflows.

Glossary Table

Term / Acronym	Definition	Example / Context
API (Application Programming Interface)	A set of rules and protocols for building and interacting with software applications. APIs allow different software systems to communicate.	Integrating external services (e.g., a weather API) into a LangGraph Python workflow.
CI/CD (Continuous Integration/Continuous Deployment)	Practices that automate the integration, testing, and deployment of code changes. CI ensures code quality while CD automates delivery to production.	Using GitHub Actions to run tests and deploy updates automatically.
Edge	In graph theory, an edge is a connection between two nodes, representing a relationship or data flow between them.	In a social network graph, an edge may represent a friendship between two users.
Graph	A data structure consisting of nodes (vertices) and edges that connect them, used to model pairwise relationships between entities.	A recommendation engine might use a graph to represent user-item interactions.
GNN (Graph Neural Network)	A type of neural network designed to operate on graph-structured data, learning from both node features and the connections between nodes.	Used in applications like social network analysis and molecule property prediction.
LangGraph Python	A Python framework for building graph-based	Provides a modular approach to designing

Term / Acronym	Definition	Example / Context
	workflows that integrates graph theory with natural language processing (NLP) and other data-driven applications.	complex systems with interconnected nodes.
Node	The fundamental processing unit in a graph-based workflow. Each node encapsulates a specific function or task, receiving inputs, processing data, and producing outputs.	A node might perform text preprocessing, sentiment analysis, or API calls in a chatbot workflow.
Pipeline	A sequence of processing steps arranged in a specific order to transform input data into a final output. In LangGraph, a pipeline is composed of interconnected nodes.	A data analysis pipeline might include steps for data ingestion, preprocessing, analysis, and output generation.
NLP (Natural Language Processing)	A field of artificial intelligence that focuses on the interaction between computers and human language, including text analysis, language generation, and translation.	Applications include chatbots, sentiment analysis, and machine translation.
Transformer	A neural network architecture that uses self-attention mechanisms to process sequential data, revolutionizing tasks in NLP by enabling parallel processing and improved context understanding.	Models like BERT, GPT-3, and T5 are based on transformer architectures.

Term / Acronym	Definition	Example / Context
Zero-shot Classification	A technique that allows a model to classify data into categories that it has not seen during training, using a descriptive prompt and candidate labels.	Used in intent detection in chatbots to determine the most relevant intent without specialized training on every category.
Graph Convolutional Network (GCN)	A type of GNN that applies convolutional operations to graph data, aggregating feature information from neighboring nodes in a layer-wise manner.	Commonly used for node classification tasks in semi-supervised learning.
Graph Attention Network (GAT)	A GNN that incorporates attention mechanisms to weight the importance of neighboring nodes, thereby refining node embeddings based on contextual relevance.	Enhances performance in social network analysis by focusing on influential relationships.
Federated Learning	A machine learning approach where models are trained across multiple decentralized devices holding local data samples, without exchanging them.	Enhances privacy by allowing devices to collaboratively learn a shared prediction model while keeping data local.
Docker	A platform for developing, shipping, and running applications in isolated containers. It ensures consistency across development, testing, and production environments.	Containerizing LangGraph Python workflows for deployment.
Kubernetes	An orchestration system for automating deployment, scaling, and	Used for horizontal scaling of applications and

Term / Acronym	Definition	Example / Context
	management of containerized applications.	managing multiple instances of LangGraph workflows in production.
Monitoring	The process of continuously tracking application performance, system health, and resource usage in real time.	Using Prometheus and Grafana to monitor a chatbot's performance and uptime.
Logging	The systematic recording of events, errors, and operational details in an application, which assists in debugging and performance analysis.	Python's logging module is used to track workflow events and errors in LangGraph applications.
Graph Database	A type of database optimized for storing and querying graph-structured data, allowing efficient operations on complex relationships.	Neo4j is a popular graph database used in recommendation systems and social network analysis.
Message Passing	A process in GNNs where nodes exchange information with their neighbors, aggregating and updating node representations.	Fundamental to the operation of GNNs, enabling nodes to learn contextual representations.
Pooling	A technique in neural networks, including GNNs, to aggregate node features into a graph-level representation, often used in graph classification tasks.	Global pooling methods such as max pooling or average pooling are used to summarize node features.

Term / Acronym	Definition	Example / Context
CI/CD Pipeline	A set of automated processes that integrate code changes, run tests, and deploy applications continuously, ensuring code quality and rapid delivery.	Implemented using tools like GitHub Actions, Jenkins, or GitLab CI/CD.

---

3. Detailed Explanations

Below are detailed explanations for a few key terms to further clarify their significance in the context of LangGraph Python and graph-based AI workflows.

LangGraph Python:
A framework designed to facilitate the creation of graph-based workflows by treating each processing step as a node in a graph. LangGraph Python allows developers to build, visualize, and manage complex workflows that can integrate NLP, data processing, and external services. Its modular design promotes reusability and scalability.

Graph Neural Networks (GNNs):
GNNs are a class of neural networks that extend traditional deep learning to handle graph-structured data. They learn node representations by aggregating information from neighboring nodes through message passing. GNNs have broad applications, from predicting user behavior in social networks to analyzing molecular structures in drug discovery.

CI/CD (Continuous Integration/Continuous Deployment):
CI/CD pipelines automate the building, testing, and deployment processes of an application. By integrating CI/CD, developers ensure that code changes are continuously merged, tested, and deployed, reducing the risk of integration issues and accelerating the development cycle.

This glossary is an essential resource for understanding the technical terminology and acronyms encountered throughout this book. It is designed to provide clarity and consistency, ensuring that both newcomers and experienced practitioners have a common understanding of key concepts in LangGraph Python, NLP, and graph-based AI workflows.

Keep this glossary handy as you progress through the book, and refer back to it whenever you encounter unfamiliar terms. Continuous learning and clear communication are critical to mastering the evolving fields of AI and data analysis.

Appendix C: Additional Resources and Further Reading

This appendix provides a curated list of additional resources and further reading materials to deepen your understanding of LangGraph Python, graph theory, NLP, and related advanced AI technologies. Whether you are looking to expand your technical knowledge, explore cutting-edge research, or connect with the broader community, the following resources have been carefully selected to help guide your journey. Each section includes descriptions, recommended resources, and, where applicable, tables summarizing key tools and references.

---

1. Books and Textbooks

Books offer a comprehensive foundation and detailed explanations of theoretical concepts and practical applications. Consider adding these titles to your reading list:

- **"Graph Theory" by Reinhard Diestel**
  An excellent introduction to the fundamentals of graph theory with rigorous proofs and a wealth of examples.
- **"Networks, Crowds, and Markets: Reasoning About a Highly Connected World" by David Easley and Jon Kleinberg**
  Explores the interdisciplinary aspects of networks and graph theory, including applications in economics and social sciences.
- **"Natural Language Processing with Python" by Steven Bird, Ewan Klein, and Edward Loper (the NLTK Book)**
  A practical guide to NLP using Python, covering core concepts and hands-on projects.
- **"Deep Learning" by Ian Goodfellow, Yoshua Bengio, and Aaron Courville**

Provides a deep dive into neural network architectures, including discussions relevant to GNNs and transformers.
- **"Graph Representation Learning" by William L. Hamilton**
Focuses on modern techniques for learning representations on graphs, including GNNs, and covers recent research trends and applications.

Table: Recommended Books

Title	Author(s)	Key Topics
Graph Theory	Reinhard Diestel	Fundamentals, proofs, and applications
Networks, Crowds, and Markets	Easley & Kleinberg	Interdisciplinary graph theory and applications
Natural Language Processing with Python (NLTK Book)	Bird, Klein, & Loper	NLP fundamentals and practical projects
Deep Learning	Goodfellow, Bengio, & Courville	Neural networks, deep learning architectures
Graph Representation Learning	William L. Hamilton	Graph embeddings, GNNs, modern graph techniques

2. Research Papers and Academic Journals

Keeping up with the latest research is crucial for staying at the forefront of AI and graph-based methodologies. Some key papers and journals include:

- **Key Research Papers:**
  - *"Semi-Supervised Classification with Graph Convolutional Networks"* by Kipf and Welling (2017): Introduces GCNs and has become a seminal work in the field.
  - *"Graph Attention Networks"* by Veličković et al. (2018): Describes the use of attention mechanisms in graph neural networks.
  - *"Inductive Representation Learning on Large Graphs"* by Hamilton et al. (2017): Introduces GraphSAGE, a scalable approach to graph representation learning.
- **Academic Journals:**
  - **Journal of Machine Learning Research (JMLR)**

- o **IEEE Transactions on Neural Networks and Learning Systems**
- o **ACM Transactions on Knowledge Discovery from Data (TKDD)**
- **Conferences and Workshops:**
  - o **NeurIPS (Conference on Neural Information Processing Systems)**
  - o **ICLR (International Conference on Learning Representations)**
  - o **KDD (Knowledge Discovery and Data Mining)**

Table: Key Research Papers

Paper Title	Authors	Significance
Semi-Supervised Classification with Graph Convolutional Networks	Kipf & Welling	Foundational work on GCNs
Graph Attention Networks	Veličković et al.	Introduced attention mechanisms in GNNs
Inductive Representation Learning on Large Graphs	Hamilton et al.	Proposed scalable GraphSAGE method

3. Online Courses and Tutorials

Online courses offer interactive learning experiences and practical exercises. Some recommended platforms and courses include:

- **Coursera:**
  - o *"Deep Learning Specialization"* by Andrew Ng: Covers deep learning fundamentals and includes modules relevant to NLP and GNNs.
  - o *"Graph Analytics for Big Data"* by University of California, San Diego: Focuses on graph theory and analytics, providing practical insights.
- **edX:**
  - o *"Natural Language Processing with Deep Learning"* by Stanford University: Explores modern NLP techniques using deep learning frameworks.
- **Udacity:**

- o *"AI Programming with Python"* and *"Deep Learning Nanodegree"*: Both courses cover essential topics in AI and include practical projects.
- **YouTube Channels and Blogs:**
  - o **Two Minute Papers:** Provides short, engaging summaries of recent research breakthroughs.
  - o **Distill.pub:** Known for its clear, interactive explanations of complex AI concepts.

Table: Recommended Online Courses

Platform	Course Title	Key Focus
Coursera	Deep Learning Specialization (Andrew Ng)	Neural networks, deep learning fundamentals
Coursera	Graph Analytics for Big Data	Graph theory and analytics
edX	Natural Language Processing with Deep Learning	NLP using deep learning
Udacity	Deep Learning Nanodegree	Advanced deep learning techniques

4. Websites, Blogs, and Community Forums

Engaging with the community and following industry blogs can keep you updated on the latest trends and practical advice:

- **KDnuggets:**
  A popular website for data science, machine learning, and AI news.
- **Medium (Towards Data Science):**
  Hosts numerous articles and tutorials on NLP, graph neural networks, and AI.
- **Stack Overflow and GitHub:**
  Participate in forums and repositories to get help, share projects, and collaborate with other developers.
- **Reddit (r/MachineLearning, r/DataScience):**
  Active communities discussing the latest research, tools, and best practices in AI and data analysis.

Table: Online Communities and Blogs

Platform/Website	Focus Area	Benefits
KDnuggets	Data Science and AI News	Regular updates, tutorials, and industry insights
Medium (Towards Data Science)	AI, Machine Learning, NLP, and Graph Neural Networks	In-depth articles and practical guides
Stack Overflow	Programming Q&A	Community support and troubleshooting help
GitHub	Open-source projects and code collaboration	Discover and contribute to relevant projects
Reddit (r/MachineLearning)	Discussion on AI and ML	Insights, news, and community discussions

5. Tools and Libraries

Familiarize yourself with tools and libraries that are essential for graph-based workflows and NLP. The following resources can provide additional support and capabilities:

- **LangGraph Python Documentation:**
  The official documentation provides detailed guides, API references, and usage examples.
- **PyTorch Geometric:**
  A library for building graph neural networks in PyTorch.
- **TensorFlow and Keras:**
  Widely used for building and training deep learning models, including those for NLP.
- **NLTK, spaCy, and Transformers:**
  Key libraries for natural language processing, each offering unique functionalities for text analysis, language modeling, and more.
- **Docker and Kubernetes:**
  Essential for containerizing and orchestrating scalable applications.

This appendix is designed to serve as a comprehensive resource for further exploration into LangGraph Python, graph theory, NLP, and advanced AI technologies. Whether you are a beginner seeking foundational knowledge or an experienced professional looking to stay updated with the latest trends, the resources listed above will support your journey.

Keep this appendix as a handy reference, and continuously explore new materials and community discussions to enhance your skills and stay ahead in the rapidly evolving fields of AI and data analysis.

Appendix D: Sample Code Repository and Project Templates

This appendix provides a comprehensive overview of the sample code repository and project templates designed for LangGraph Python applications. These resources serve as practical starting points and references, helping you quickly set up your projects, understand best practices, and explore advanced features. Whether you're a beginner or an experienced developer, these templates and sample projects can accelerate your development process and ensure consistency across your work.

---

1. Overview

The sample code repository is a curated collection of example projects and reusable templates that demonstrate how to build graph-based workflows with LangGraph Python. These examples cover various aspects, including:

- **Basic Workflow Implementation:**
  Simple projects that illustrate fundamental concepts such as node creation, edge connections, and data flow management.
- **Advanced Use Cases:**
  Projects incorporating NLP integrations, API interactions, dynamic data processing, and scalable deployment strategies.
- **Best Practices:**
  Code organization, error handling, logging, testing, and deployment strategies are exemplified in these projects.

The project templates provide a ready-to-use structure that includes essential files and directories, ensuring that you follow a standardized approach when starting new projects.

---

2. Sample Code Repository Structure

A well-organized code repository is key to maintaining readability and scalability. Below is an example of a typical project structure for a LangGraph Python application:

bash

```
langgraph-project/
├── README.md
├── requirements.txt
├── setup.sh                  # Unix-based environment setup
script
├── setup.bat                 # Windows environment setup script
├── Dockerfile                # For containerized deployments
├── src/
│   ├── __init__.py
│   ├── main.py               # Entry point for the application
│   ├── nodes/                # Custom node implementations
│   │   ├── __init__.py
│   │   ├── input_node.py
│   │   ├── processing_node.py
│   │   └── output_node.py
│   ├── workflows/            # Predefined workflow examples
│   │   ├── __init__.py
│   │   ├── chatbot_workflow.py
│   │   └── recommendation_workflow.py
│   └── utils/                # Utility functions and helpers
│       ├── __init__.py
│       └── logger.py
├── tests/                    # Unit and integration tests
│   ├── __init__.py
│   ├── test_nodes.py
│   └── test_workflows.py
└── docs/                     # Documentation and further reading
    └── installation_guide.md
```

Table: Repository Structure

Directory/File	Description
`README.md`	Overview of the project, usage instructions, and key details.
`requirements.txt`	List of project dependencies and versions.
`setup.sh/setup.bat`	Environment setup scripts for Unix-based and Windows systems.
`Dockerfile`	Instructions for containerizing the application using Docker.
`src/`	Source code for the application.
`src/main.py`	The main entry point for running the application.
`src/nodes/`	Custom node implementations for LangGraph Python workflows.
`src/workflows/`	Predefined workflow examples (e.g., chatbot, recommendation systems).
`src/utils/`	Utility functions, including custom logging setups.
`tests/`	Automated tests for unit and integration testing.
`docs/`	Documentation, guides, and further reading materials.

3. Project Templates

Project templates are designed to provide a standardized starting point for your LangGraph Python projects. They include all necessary configurations, directory structures, and sample code to jumpstart your development. Here's an example of a simple project template:

Example: `src/main.py`

```python
from langgraph import GraphManager
from nodes.input_node import InputNode
from nodes.processing_node import ProcessingNode
from nodes.output_node import OutputNode

def main():
    # Create a Graph Manager instance
    graph_manager = GraphManager()
```

```python
    # Initialize nodes
    input_node = InputNode("InputNode")
    processing_node = ProcessingNode("ProcessingNode")
    output_node = OutputNode("OutputNode")

    # Register nodes
    graph_manager.add_node("input", input_node)
    graph_manager.add_node("process", processing_node)
    graph_manager.add_node("output", output_node)

    # Connect nodes: Input -> Processing -> Output
    graph_manager.connect("input", "process")
    graph_manager.connect("process", "output")

    # Run the workflow starting from the Input Node
    graph_manager.run("input")

if __name__ == "__main__":
    main()
```

Explanation:

- **GraphManager Initialization:**
  Sets up the workflow orchestrator.
- **Node Creation and Registration:**
  Creates instances of custom nodes (e.g., InputNode, ProcessingNode, OutputNode) and registers them.
- **Connecting Nodes:**
  Defines the flow of data by connecting the nodes in a linear sequence.
- **Workflow Execution:**
  Initiates the workflow by running the GraphManager from the input node.

Example: `src/nodes/input_node.py`

python

```python
from langgraph import Node

class InputNode(Node):
    def run(self, data=None):
        # For demonstration, use a fixed input value.
        input_data = "Welcome to LangGraph Python!"
        print(f"[{self.name}] Input: {input_data}")
        for node in self.next_nodes:
            node.run(input_data)
```

Example: src/nodes/processing_node.py

```python
from langgraph import Node

class ProcessingNode(Node):
    def run(self, data):
        # Example processing: convert input text to
uppercase.
        processed_data = data.upper()
        print(f"[{self.name}] Processed Data:
{processed_data}")
        for node in self.next_nodes:
            node.run(processed_data)
```

Example: src/nodes/output_node.py

```python
from langgraph import Node

class OutputNode(Node):
    def run(self, data):
        print(f"[{self.name}] Final Output: {data}")
```

---

4. Testing and Documentation

Your project templates should include a `tests/` directory with sample unit and integration tests, ensuring that each component functions as expected. Additionally, comprehensive documentation in the `docs/` directory helps onboard new developers and maintain consistency.

Example: tests/test_nodes.py

```python
import unittest
from nodes.input_node import InputNode

class TestInputNode(unittest.TestCase):
    def test_input_node(self):
        node = InputNode("TestInput")
        # Capture output by redirecting stdout if needed
        # Here, we simply ensure no exceptions occur during
execution.
```

```
    try:
        node.run()
    except Exception as e:
        self.fail(f"InputNode.run() raised an exception:
{e}")

if __name__ == "__main__":
    unittest.main()
```

Explanation:

- **Unit Test:**
  The test verifies that the `InputNode` executes without errors. Similar tests should be written for other nodes and workflows.
- **Documentation:**
  Detailed guides in `docs/installation_guide.md` provide step-by-step instructions on setting up the environment and deploying the application.

---

5. How to Use the Repository and Templates

1. **Clone the Repository:**

   bash

   ```
   git clone https://github.com/yourusername/langgraph-
   sample.git
   cd langgraph-sample
   ```

2. **Set Up the Environment:**
   - Run the setup script (e.g., `setup.sh` for Unix or `setup.bat` for Windows) to create a virtual environment and install dependencies.
   - Alternatively, use Docker to build the container:

     bash

     ```
     docker build -t langgraph-app .
     ```

3. **Explore Sample Projects:**
   - Navigate to the `src/workflows/` directory to review example workflows.

- o Examine custom node implementations in `src/nodes/`.
4. **Run Tests:**

   ```bash
   bash

   pytest --maxfail=1 --disable-warnings -q
   ```

5. **Deploy Your Application:**
   - o Follow instructions in `docs/installation_guide.md` for deploying locally or on a production server.

Table: Quick Start Checklist

Step	Command/Action	Description
Clone Repository	`git clone https://github.com/yourusername/langgraph-sample.git`	Clone the sample code repository to your local machine.
Environment Setup	`./setup.sh` (Unix) or `setup.bat` (Windows)	Create a virtual environment and install dependencies.
Run Tests	`pytest --maxfail=1 --disable-warnings -q`	Execute unit and integration tests to verify functionality.
Build Docker Image	`docker build -t langgraph-app .`	(Optional) Containerize the application for consistent deployment.

Step	Command/Action	Description
Deploy Application	Follow instructions in `docs/installation_guide.md`	Deploy the application in your chosen environment.

The sample code repository and project templates provided in this appendix are designed to serve as a practical foundation for your LangGraph Python projects. By following these templates, you can ensure that your code is organized, maintainable, and scalable from the very beginning. Use these resources as a guide, and feel free to modify and extend them to suit the specific needs of your projects.

With a well-structured repository and robust project templates, you'll be able to focus on building innovative graph-based workflows and advanced AI applications, confident that your development environment is set up for success.

Appendix E: Troubleshooting and FAQs

This appendix serves as a comprehensive resource to help you troubleshoot common issues and answer frequently asked questions (FAQs) related to LangGraph Python. Whether you're facing installation problems, runtime errors, or unexpected behavior in your graph workflows, this guide provides detailed explanations, step-by-step solutions, and practical examples to get you back on track. We also cover frequently asked questions to clarify common doubts and provide best practices for maintaining and debugging your applications.

1. Troubleshooting Common Issues

Below is a list of common issues encountered when working with LangGraph Python, along with potential causes and solutions.

Table: Common Issues and Solutions

Issue	Possible Cause	Solution
Installation Errors	- Incorrect Python version - Missing dependencies - Virtual environment not activated	- Verify Python version (>= 3.7) - Check and install dependencies from `requirements.txt` - Activate virtual environment (e.g., `source langgraph-env/bin/activate`)
Module Not Found Error	- Package not installed - Wrong import paths	- Ensure `pip install langgraph` has been run - Verify module paths and correct capitalization
Runtime Exceptions in Node Execution	- Invalid input data - Unhandled exceptions in custom node code	- Implement input validation and error handling (try-except blocks) - Review node logs for detailed error messages
Graph Not Connecting Properly	- Nodes not added to the Graph Manager - Incorrect node names used in connections	- Ensure all nodes are registered using `add_node()` - Verify node names in `connect()` calls are accurate and consistent
Data Not Propagating Through Nodes	- Missing calls to propagate data (e.g., not iterating over `next_nodes`)	- Confirm that each node's `run()` method calls `for node in self.next_nodes: node.run(processed_data)`
Performance Issues	- Inefficient algorithms in nodes - Lack of caching or parallel processing	- Profile code using `cProfile` - Consider using caching (e.g., `functools.lru_cache`) or parallel processing methods

2. Troubleshooting Techniques

A. Debugging with Print Statements and Logging

Often, the first step in troubleshooting is to insert print statements or use logging to track the flow of data and monitor the execution of nodes.

Example: Adding Debugging Output to a Node

python

```python
import logging
from langgraph import Node

# Configure logging for debugging
logging.basicConfig(level=logging.DEBUG,
format='[%(levelname)s] %(asctime)s - %(message)s')

class DebugNode(Node):
    def run(self, data):
        logging.debug(f"[{self.name}] Received data: {data}")
        try:
            # Simulate a processing step (for example,
converting text to uppercase)
            if not isinstance(data, str):
                raise ValueError("Input must be a string")
            processed_data = data.upper()
            logging.info(f"[{self.name}] Processed data:
{processed_data}")
            for node in self.next_nodes:
                node.run(processed_data)
        except Exception as e:
            logging.error(f"[{self.name}] Error processing
data: {e}", exc_info=True)
            # Optionally, pass original data or a fallback
value
            for node in self.next_nodes:
                node.run(data)

# Test the DebugNode
debug_node = DebugNode("DebugNode")
debug_node.run("Test message")
debug_node.run(123)  # Should log an error due to wrong data
type
```

Explanation:

- **Logging Configuration:**
  The logging module is set to DEBUG level to capture detailed information.
- **Debugging Output:**
  The node logs the received data, processes it, logs the processed output, and handles exceptions gracefully.

B. Using Interactive Debuggers

Interactive debuggers, such as Python's built-in `pdb` or those integrated into IDEs (e.g., PyCharm, VS Code), allow you to set breakpoints, inspect variables, and step through your code.

Example: Using `pdb` to Debug a Node

```python
python

import pdb
from langgraph import Node

class DebugStepNode(Node):
    def run(self, data):
        pdb.set_trace()  # Set a breakpoint here
        processed_data = data[::-1]
        print(f"[{self.name}] Processed Data:
{processed_data}")
        for node in self.next_nodes:
            node.run(processed_data)

# Run the node to interactively debug
debug_step_node = DebugStepNode("DebugStepNode")
debug_step_node.run("Hello")
```

Explanation:

- **Setting a Breakpoint:**
  The `pdb.set_trace()` function pauses execution, allowing you to inspect variables and step through the code interactively.

---

3. FAQs

Q1: Why is my workflow not executing all nodes?
A:

- **Check Node Registration:**
  Ensure that all nodes are added to the Graph Manager using `add_node()`.
- **Verify Connections:**
  Confirm that nodes are properly connected using `connect()` or `add_next()`.

- **Data Propagation:**
  Ensure that each node's `run()` method iterates over `self.next_nodes` and passes the processed data forward.

Q2: How can I debug performance issues in my workflow?
A:

- **Profiling:**
  Use Python's `cProfile` or the `timeit` module to measure execution time for nodes or functions.
- **Caching:**
  Implement caching (e.g., using `functools.lru_cache`) to avoid redundant computations.
- **Parallel Processing:**
  Consider parallelizing CPU-bound tasks using the `multiprocessing` module or asynchronous programming with `asyncio`.

Q3: My custom node raises an exception. How do I handle it?
A:

- **Input Validation:**
  Implement input validation at the start of your `run()` method to ensure that the data is in the expected format.
- **Error Handling:**
  Wrap your processing logic in try-except blocks to catch exceptions and log meaningful error messages. Optionally, provide fallback logic to continue the workflow.

Q4: How do I secure API keys in my nodes?
A:

- **Environment Variables:**
  Store API keys in environment variables and retrieve them using `os.getenv()`.
- **Configuration Files:**
  Use configuration files that are excluded from version control (e.g., using `.gitignore`).
- **Secret Management Tools:**
  For enterprise applications, use secret management solutions like AWS Secrets Manager or HashiCorp Vault.

Q5: What should I do if I encounter unexpected behavior in data flow?
A:

- **Trace Data:**
  Insert logging or print statements to trace the data as it flows through each node.
- **Review Data Contracts:**
  Ensure that the output format of each node matches the expected input format of subsequent nodes.
- **Test Nodes in Isolation:**
  Run unit tests on individual nodes to verify their functionality before integrating them into the full workflow.

4.

Effective troubleshooting and a solid understanding of common issues are critical to the successful deployment and maintenance of LangGraph Python workflows. By leveraging robust error handling, comprehensive logging, interactive debugging tools, and automated tests, you can quickly identify and resolve problems. The FAQs provided in this appendix address common concerns and offer practical solutions, helping you to maintain high-quality, reliable applications.

Keep this appendix as a reference to streamline your troubleshooting process and ensure that your workflows continue to operate efficiently, even as your application evolves.

Index

Below is the comprehensive index for this book, designed to help you quickly locate topics, concepts, and practical examples related to LangGraph Python, graph theory, natural language processing (NLP), and advanced AI workflows. This index is organized alphabetically by key topics and includes references to chapters, sections, and specific code examples where applicable.

C

- **Chatbots and Conversational Agents**
  - Building Scalable Chatbot Systems: Chapter 10.1
  - Conversational Agent Workflow Design: Chapter 6.2
  - Dialogue Management and Response Generation: Chapters 6.2 and 10.1
- **CI/CD**
  - Continuous Integration/Continuous Deployment: Chapter 9.3; see also Section 9.3 Best Practices table
- **Code Examples**
  - Sample Code Repository and Project Templates: Appendix D
  - Troubleshooting Code Snippets: Appendix E
- **Configuration Management**
  - Secure API Key Management and Environment Variables: Appendix A; Chapter 8.1 and 8.4

D

- **Data Analysis Pipelines**
  - Dynamic Data Analysis Pipelines: Chapter 10.3
  - Data Flow and Dependency Management: Chapter 5.4; see also troubleshooting in Appendix E
- **Data Ingestion and Preprocessing**
  - Data Ingestion Nodes: Chapter 10.2 (Recommendation Engines)
  - Preprocessing Nodes for NLP and Graph Workflows: Chapters 3.1, 4.3, and 10.1
- **Deployment**
  - Deployment Best Practices: Chapter 9.2
  - Docker and Containerization: Appendix A; Chapter 9.2

E

- **Error Handling**
  - Robust Error Handling in Nodes: Chapter 7.4; Appendix E

P

- **Pipeline**
  - o Definition and Design of Data Pipelines: Chapter 5.1
  - o Dynamic Data Analysis Pipelines: Chapter 10.3
  - o CI/CD Pipelines for Automated Deployment: Chapters 9.3
- **Preprocessing**
  - o Data Cleaning and Tokenization: Chapters 3.1, 4.3, and 10.1
  - o Handling Data Quality in Dynamic Pipelines: Chapter 10.3

Q

- **Querying Graph Data**
  - o Techniques and Tools for Querying Graphs: Chapter 8.3
  - o Graph Databases and Graph Query Languages: Glossary in Appendix B

R

- **Recommendation Systems**
  - o Graph-Driven Recommendation Engines: Chapter 10.2
  - o Collaborative Filtering and Graph-Based Ranking: Chapter 10.2
- **Response Generation**
  - o Generating Responses in Chatbots: Chapter 6.2
  - o Using GPT-2 and Other Transformers: Chapters 6.2 and 10.1

S

- **Scalability**
  - o Strategies for Scaling AI Workflows: Chapter 9.2; Chapters 10.1 and 10.3
  - o Horizontal and Vertical Scaling, Container Orchestration: Chapter 9.2

W

- **Workflow**
  - ○ Graph-Based Workflow Design and Execution: Chapters 4.3, 5.1, 5.4
  - ○ Dynamic Adaptation and Conditional Branching: Chapters 7.2 and 10.3
- **Web3 and Blockchain**
  - ○ Integrating Blockchain with LangGraph: Chapter 11.3; see also API integration in Appendix E

X, Y, Z

- **X:**
  - ○ No major entries.
- **Y:**
  - ○ No major entries.
- **Z:**
  - ○ Zero-shot Classification: See NLP integration in Chapter 6.2; explained in Glossary (Appendix B).

This index is designed to be a comprehensive guide to the topics covered in this book. It should serve as a quick reference to help you navigate through the concepts, code examples, and best practices related to LangGraph Python, graph-based workflows, and advanced AI techniques. Use it to revisit key sections as you build, deploy, and optimize your applications.

Conclusion

As you reach the end of this journey through LangGraph Python, I hope you feel both empowered and inspired to transform the way you build, analyze, and deploy complex workflows. This book has taken you step-by-step through the fundamentals of graph theory, advanced techniques in natural language processing, and the cutting-edge intersection of AI and emerging technologies. From designing modular nodes and dynamic pipelines to integrating powerful external APIs and scaling your applications for production, every chapter has been crafted to give you a solid, practical foundation—and to spark your creativity.

The real magic of LangGraph Python lies in its versatility. Whether you're building a scalable chatbot system, a personalized recommendation engine, or a dynamic data analysis pipeline, you now have the tools, strategies, and best practices at your fingertips. Our exploration of error handling, security, and CI/CD practices ensures that your workflows aren't just innovative—they're robust, secure, and ready for real-world challenges.

I invite you to revisit this book, explore the detailed code examples, and experiment with the sample projects. Each reading can reveal new insights and inspire fresh ideas as you continue to refine your skills and develop even more sophisticated AI systems. Your journey doesn't end here; it's just the beginning of an exciting exploration into graph-based AI and NLP.

If you found value in this book, please consider leaving a review and sharing your thoughts with peers and colleagues. Your feedback not only helps us improve future editions but also guides fellow developers on their own journeys. Discuss the concepts, share your projects, and join the growing community that's shaping the future of AI workflows.

Thank you for embarking on this adventure with me. I look forward to hearing your success stories and innovative ideas inspired by LangGraph Python. Happy coding, and may your work continue to drive transformative insights and groundbreaking applications!